Also by Linda Porter

Royal Renegades:
The Children of Charles I and the English Civil Wars

Crown of Thistles:
The Fatal Inheritance of Mary Queen of Scots

Katherine the Queen:
The Remarkable Life of Katherine Parr

Mary Tudor:
The First Queen

LINDA PORTER

Mistresses

Sex and Scandal at the Court of Charles II

PICADOR

First published 2020 by Picador

This paperback edition first published 2021 by Picador
an imprint of Pan Macmillan
The Smithson, 6 Briset Street, London ECIM 5NR
EU representative: Macmillan Publishers Ireland Limited,
Mallard Lodge, Lansdowne Village, Dublin 4
Associated companies throughout the world
www.panmacmillan.com

ISBN 978-1-5098-7707-2

1 3 5 7 9 8 6 4 2

A CIP catalogue record for this book is available from the British Library.

Typeset by Palimpsest Book Production Ltd, Falkirk, Stirlingshire
Printed and bound by CPI Group (UK) Ltd, Croydon, CR0 4YY

Visit **www.picador.com** to read more about all our books
and to buy them. You will also find features, author interviews and
news of any author events, and you can sign up for e-newsletters
so that you're always first to hear about our new releases.

For George

Contents

Author's Note

IT WAS ONLY when I began work on this book that I fully appreciated how extraordinarily complicated were the politics of the reign of Charles II. This might seem of secondary importance in a work about his mistresses, but the controversy which surrounded his lifestyle seeped into the heart of British life for the twenty-five years of his reign – indeed, it had already begun to colour national and international reaction to him during the miserable years of his exile, during the latter years of the Civil Wars and throughout the period of the English republic that followed the execution of his father, Charles I. And, indeed, it matters far more that his mistresses were perceived as having influence at the time than whether they really did or not in hindsight. His tendency to shower money on them when he was frequently at loggerheads with Parliament over financial support and taxation made him reliant on other sources of income, notably from Louis XIV, the cousin who largely despised him. Though the king cheerfully took the money and fulfilled none of the promises he had secretly made in securing it (making him, at least on paper, a traitor to the country he ruled), this is scarcely an exoneration.

The mistresses themselves are a fascinating and flawed group of women. Only the actress Nell Gwyn is generally remembered today, but her predecessor Barbara Palmer, countess of Castlemaine, and Nell's rival, Louise de Kéroualle, duchess of Portsmouth, between them dominated the king in ways that Nell never could, the one through passion and the other through simpering guile. Frances Teresa Stuart, who arrived at the Restoration court from France in her mid-teens, hid a ruthless instinct for survival beneath a naive exterior and managed to stay out of the king's bed while having to submit to frequent public gropings that must have been excruciating.

Hortense Mancini, duchess Mazarin, had led such a colourful life before taking refuge in England that some of the other ladies seem almost tame in comparison. While the king's mistresses aimed at celebrity and wealth, only his rejected wife, Catherine of Braganza, seems ever to have truly loved him. I have tried to give a more positive picture of this Portuguese princess than is often the case. Recent research on her cultural interests and approach to queenship has revealed that there was much more to Catherine than the weepy, despairing foreigner retreating into religion than is often supposed. Nor should we underestimate one of her less obvious achievements, that of making the drinking of tea for pleasure, as opposed to a strange medicinal brew, so fashionable.

Charles II ruled a deeply divided country, where religious persecution, whether of Catholics or Protestant non-conformists, was rife. His reign saw the beginnings of the two-party system which still, for good or ill, underpins British politics to this day. He cared nothing for Scotland or Ireland and was happy to trade on a false reputation for bonhomie, of being the sort of man that other men like because of his penchant for women and his apparent approachability, which was, in reality, a sham. The fact that he is still viewed as the 'Merrie Monarch' and has been treated with indulgence by history (though not necessarily by historians) is something I find bewildering. Yet the contradictions remain. His private life makes Henry VIII look puritanical, but Charles II, despite the many and varied mistresses, could not be induced to divorce his wife, let alone execute her. His reign saw humiliation heaped on Britain from abroad and catastrophe overtake his capital in the mid-1660s, yet he somehow managed to survive and to dispense with Parliament in the closing years of his reign. The lasting impression of Charles II, when all the sordid glamour of his court and his mistresses is stripped away, is of a lazy, intelligent man, forever marked by the hardship of his formative years, a pleasure-loving cynic not quite redeemed by his death-bed conversion to Catholicism.

I should like to thank James Palmer at Dorney Court for letting me consult his archives on a very wet July day in 2017 and His

Grace the Duke of Richmond and Gordon for permission to use the Goodwood Manuscript at the West Sussex Record Office. Dr Sean Cunningham and Elisabeth Novitski at the National Archives gave advice on sources and private archives. Crispin Powell, archivist to His Grace the Duke of Buccleuch, gave enthusiastic support to a request to look at the Montagu Papers at Boughton House in Northamptonshire. The staff at the London Library, British Library, Bodleian Library and West Sussex Record Office were unfailingly helpful. Thanks, as ever, to my editor, Georgina Morley, to Laura Carr, Managing Editor at Pan Macmillan and to Penelope Price, my copy-editor. With much gratitude also to my agent of many years, Andrew Lownie, and husband of even more years, George Porter, to whom one of my books is, at last, dedicated.

July 2019

The Illegitimate Children of Charles II

By Lucy Walter: James Crofts (later Scott), duke of Monmouth and Buccleuch (1649–85)

By Elizabeth Killigrew: Charlotte Jemima Henrietta Maria Fitzroy, countess of Yarmouth (1651–84)

By Catherine Pegge: Charles Fitzcharles, first earl of Plymouth (1657–80)
    Catherine Fitzcharles, b.1658, died in infancy

By Barbara Palmer: Anne Fitzroy, countess of Sussex (1661–1722)
    Charles Fitzroy, duke of Southampton (1662–1730)
    Henry Fitzroy, duke of Grafton (1663–90)
    Charlotte Fitzroy, countess of Lichfield (1664–1718)
    George Fitzroy, duke of Northumberland (1665–1715)

By Nell Gwyn: Charles Beauclerk, duke of St Albans (1670–1726)
    James Beauclerk (1671–81)

By Louise de Kéroualle: Charles Lennox, duke of Richmond and Lennox (1672–1723)

By Mary (Moll) Davis: Mary Tudor, countess of Derwentwater (1673–1726)

Prologue

The Hague, United Provinces of the Netherlands, February 1649

IT HAD BEEN a subdued festive season at court, despite the host's attempts to lighten the atmosphere. Charles Stuart, Prince of Wales and heir to three kingdoms, had recently recovered from a bout of smallpox and, though restored to health without any of the disfiguring effects of a disease that often blighted the lives of those who survived, he was beset by concerns which could not be alleviated by the normal diversions of Christmas. In England, his father was kept a close prisoner with an uncertain fate. Here, in the United Provinces of the Netherlands, there was tension of a different sort. Charles was not blind to the failings of his sister Mary's husband or to the strains in their marriage. William of Orange seemed happier with drunken companions and whores than he did with his wife. Not that this was entirely surprising. Plucked from a secure childhood as Princess Royal of England, to be married at the age of nine to a fourteen-year-old whose father occupied an uncertain role in a struggling republic, Mary had never settled. Even the presence of an affectionate aunt and a bevy of cousins, all exiles themselves, had not entirely assuaged her heartache. Mary felt the marriage was beneath her, never bothering to learn Dutch, relying instead on the French that she had learned in the schoolroom at St James's Palace. Since her

arrival here seven years ago, she had grown apart from the handsome teenager she had married as an innocent child. Yet William,
keen on glory but low on funds, was still committed to helping
the beleaguered Stuarts. For that, Charles and his brother James
were grateful, especially as their mother, Queen Henrietta Maria,
had never succeeded in getting anything but fair words from her
relatives in France.

The anxieties that hung in the air that Christmas grew even
greater at the beginning of 1649. After two years enduring the
patronizing disdain of the French court – for it is always disquieting
to have close relations who seem to have lost their grip on power
– Charles was not sorry to be away from Paris and his mother's
ghastly matchmaking schemes. The queen's determination to arrange
a marriage for her tall, taciturn son, who conveniently forgot all his
French when forced to woo his incurably vain cousin, La Grande
Mademoiselle, did not make Charles eager to find a wife. In the
Netherlands, he was at least able to relax with Mary, of whom he
was very fond, and keep a careful eye on James, whose antics after
he had escaped from England nearly a year earlier had caused
Charles much dismay. His affection for James was always muted,
though he would remain true to him for the rest of his life.

For a family already reeling under the strain of a long civil war,
divided between three countries and with two children still effectively prisoners of the rebels in England, the year 1649 started
grimly. Word soon came across the North Sea that Charles I was
about to be put on trial for treason against his own subjects,
causing further consternation to the three oldest Stuart siblings.
The penalty for treason was death, but it was surely inconceivable
that such a fate would befall an anointed king.

When the news of the outcome of the trial reached the United
Provinces, nearly a week after Charles I's execution, no one knew
how to tell his eldest son. Though accounts vary, it seems likely
that he was gently taken out of a crowded room by his chaplain,
Dr Goffe, into a quieter, private place. The good doctor, uncomfortably aware of the gravity of what he was about to impart, was

unable to find the words to break such tidings. Instead, he knelt before the boy (Charles was still only eighteen years old) and addressed him, quite simply, as 'Your Majesty'.

Overwhelmed by the emotion of the moment, the new king burst into tears. But even as he tried to take in the enormity of what had happened, the weight of responsibility now thrust upon him and the loss of a father he had loved, he might, however briefly, have reflected on the fact that he was about to become a father himself.

Part One

Companions in Exile

LUCY WALTER

1630–58

CHAPTER ONE

'Mrs Barlow'

'A brown, beautiful, bold but insipid creature'
John Evelyn, on Lucy Walter

THESE WERE UNCERTAIN times. The Thirty Years War, the last great religious conflict in Europe, had just ended. The British Isles stayed largely aloof, before being consumed by their own woes. The Civil Wars that broke out in England in 1642 were preceded by serious revolts in Scotland and Ireland, fatally undermining the authority of Charles I. Families were divided and lives disrupted during the conflict. The loss of life was significant – a fifth of the population is estimated to have perished. Small wonder, then, that those who were determined to hold the king to account called him 'that man of blood'. For the royalist survivors of the wars, there were limited options. A significant number chose to stay and see if they could settle in the strange new world of an English republic. But some had decided to leave well before the axe fell on the monarch's bowed head on 30 January 1649. Clinging to the hope that there were opportunities in Europe, rather than the bitter bread of exile, they were willing to risk all. One of them was a girl, still in her teens, who believed that her prospects would be brighter across the North Sea. There, she might find, among the soldiers and cavaliers who had accompanied the Prince of Wales into exile, if not a husband, at least a protector. She had frequented the company of military men in London and knew how to make the most of her attractions. And those attractions were considerable.

Lucy Walter was the same age as Prince Charles when they met in the summer of 1648 at The Hague. Born in Pembrokeshire, in south-west Wales, Lucy came from a family with long links to the area. Her father, William Walter, was a local gentleman of moderate means whose lands included the medieval tower house known as Roch Castle, set high above the shoreline in Haverfordwest.[1] Socially, William Walter was a solid member of the gentry but his wife, Elizabeth, brought not only a substantial dowry but aristocratic connections; her uncle was the first earl of Carbery. Lucy did not, however, enjoy a happy childhood. Elizabeth Walter claimed that her husband was constantly unfaithful to her, and, worse, that he made her take in his bastard children by one of the family's maids. When she protested, he assaulted her.

Whatever the truth of this story, it is clear that the marriage had foundered by the time Lucy was eleven years old, because her mother, then living in London with her daughter and two sons, was granted financial support against her husband's estates in a case which eventually went all the way to the House of Lords. For six years, despite the ravages of civil war, Elizabeth Walter seems to have received enough of the settlement to live on but in 1647, with William Walter countering his wife's claims of abandonment and adultery by accusing her of the same conduct, the decision was reversed and Elizabeth was ordered to return her children to her husband's custody. Clearly, Lucy did not want to go back to rural Wales and a violent, unreliable father. She and her mother made the decision to leave England and cross to the Netherlands, where one of Mrs Walter's sisters lived. In order to avoid detection, they travelled under an assumed name, so that, when Lucy set foot on Dutch soil, she had been transformed into Mrs Lucy Barlow. The title did not denote married status; in the seventeenth century, all women who were not part of the aristocracy were known as 'Mrs'. To be referred to as 'Miss' was derogatory, since it indicated that you were someone's mistress rather than wife.

The time spent in London was a formative part of Lucy's chaotic upbringing. Though she probably received only the most basic education, she had acquired sufficient social polish to make her acceptable in polite society. This was coupled with very considerable beauty (even James II, who later had cause to belittle her and sully her reputation, acknowledged as much). She had learned how to look good on the arm of a young aristocratic soldier. The great republican thinker and brave Parliamentary army officer, Algernon Sidney, second son of the earl of Leicester, was said to have parted with fifty gold pieces in order to enjoy her company, according to the future James II: 'Algernon Sidney (though at that time a colonel in Cromwell's army of Saints) having got notice of her, entered into treaty about her and came to an agreement for fifty broad pieces (as he himself related this story to his RH). But being in the nick of time commanded hastily out of London to his regiment, he missed his bargain.'[2] The story cannot be corroborated, though Algernon Sidney's most recent biographer says that it should not automatically be discounted, even if it was put around subsequently as part of a concerted attempt to depict Lucy as a good-time girl and woman of easy virtue. She would, no doubt, have viewed such an arrangement as a reasonable business transaction. There were plenty of other young women in her situation doing exactly the same. Like them, Lucy knew that her physical attractions and a pleasant, flirtatious manner were her passport to security. She had every intention of deploying her weapons and using the connections she had made in London, once she got to Holland.

There, she attached herself to Algernon's younger brother, Robert Sidney, who was a royalist officer in the service of Prince Charles. Lucy was untroubled by the conflicting principles of the two brothers. Financial support and the prospect of enjoying herself were more pressing concerns for an eighteen-year-old whose mother soon returned to England, leaving her alone, much to the disapproval of Elizabeth Walter's Dutch in-laws. Ignoring their reaction to her lifestyle, Lucy enjoyed several months with Robert Sidney and was much admired by other young royalist officers who crowded around the Stuarts. It was a febrile community, united in equal parts by boredom and bravado, and Robert Sidney soon realized that it would be difficult to keep Lucy to himself. Certainly, he could not hope to compete with Prince Charles when the heir to the throne's eye lighted on Sidney's beguiling mistress. Humiliated by Lucy's abandonment of him, Sidney made disparaging comments about her sexual history, though the fact that she had long since lost her virginity could scarcely have come as a surprise to anyone.

We do not know how Lucy came to Charles's attention and contemporary sources are split as to who was the instigator of their affair. But some time in the summer of 1648 she left Robert Sidney for the Prince of Wales. She and Charles were the same age, both good-looking, dark haired and living for the moment, because, in truth, there was nothing else they could do. Their romance, if it can even be called that, was brief, perhaps no more than a few nights of passion. Lucy Walter was an amusing distraction while he waited for an opportunity to take decisive action that might help his father, then a prisoner on the Isle of Wight, triumph at last in the long struggle with his subjects. That chance came much sooner than he expected. A week or so after he bedded 'Mrs Barlow', Charles sailed away from the Netherlands at the head of a royalist fleet revitalized by the addition of turncoat Parliamentary captains and their mutinous crews.

This foray into naval warfare was unsuccessful. Prince Charles never managed to land in England and was back in the Netherlands by September 1648, where he passed the remainder of the year as a helpless spectator of the final act in the drama of Charles I's life. Yet if his sudden departure from Lucy had effectively ended their liaison almost as soon as it had begun, he could not quite brush it off altogether. For Lucy was pregnant and Charles acknowledged the child she was carrying as his own. Their affair

may have been short but its repercussions were long – for the
king, his brother, James, duke of York, and for the baby son who
became the first of Charles II's fourteen illegitimate children, the
ill-fated duke of Monmouth.

CHAPTER TWO

The Trouble with Lucy

'Before I take the liberty of writing to Your Majesty of Mrs
Barlow, I did sufficiently inform myself of the truth of what
I write, since I had the opportunity to save her from public
scandal . . .'

Daniel O'Neill to Charles II, February 1656

IN THE DECADE following her son's birth in April 1649, Lucy's
behaviour became increasingly reckless, leading to an irretrievable
breakdown in her relationship with Charles II. Even during her
pregnancy, the intention to keep her at arm's length was clear.
Charles may have been willing to acknowledge that he had fathered
her child but there was no question of Lucy giving birth at Princess
Mary's court at The Hague. Instead, the future duke of Monmouth
was born seventeen miles to the south, in the port city of
Rotterdam. The child was given into the care of an English wet
nurse and accommodated by a Dutch merchant who owned a
house just along the coast, in Schiedam. Lucy, after a suitable
period of recovery, was able to resume her life without inconvenience. She was young and healthy and would, no doubt, have hoped
to remain close to her royal lover. Her son was called James,
though we do not know who made the choice of name. Perhaps
it was a compliment to the king's brother, the duke of York. If so,
it was one that the duke would not find gratifying. Young James

was a healthy baby and grew into a strikingly handsome child. In his youthful portraits, we can see something of what his mother must have looked like, since no pictures of Lucy Walter, painted during her lifetime, survive.

Whatever Lucy's expectations that spring, her relationship with Charles was already on the wane. This was, in part, because circumstances made it difficult for him to remain in the Netherlands after the death of his father. Within weeks of his son's birth, he was on the move, returning to his mother in Paris. The United Provinces of the Netherlands was a republic and politicians there, remembering the prolonged and bloody struggle for independence against the Spanish monarchy, did not share the Prince of Orange's enthusiasm for monarchy. Charles was always rather good at realizing when he had outstayed his welcome. It has been speculated that he visited little James before his departure, though there is no firm evidence for this.[1] Lucy certainly travelled to Paris herself later in the summer but whether this was on her own initiative or at Charles's invitation is unknown. Given her subsequent behaviour, it is probable that Lucy was the instigator of this journey. The diarist John Evelyn, a royalist supporter, shared a coach with her on the way to Saint Germain, where Henrietta Maria and her sons were living on the grudging hospitality of the French court, and it was this enforced proximity that prompted his famous comments, quoted at the head of Chapter One, about her being both bold and insipid. He described her as the king's mistress, a quasi-official appellation of which Lucy would have been proud, but does not mention whether she had brought her son to France with her. At this point, obviously keen to remind the king of her charms and probably show off her son as well, Lucy had no particular reason to suppose that he would try to separate her from James. A year later, she knew differently.

What was Charles's attitude towards Lucy Walter and her offspring? It is unlikely that she was his first sexual adventure and the baby may not have been his first child. There were rumours of a liaison during his stay, in 1646, on the island of Jersey but he had never admitted to mistresses or paternity before. Yet his reluctance to keep Lucy with him on his travels is plain and, as she seems to have realized early on, absence, in the case of Charles II, did not always make the heart grow fonder. Given the nature of their encounter, Lucy's history and Charles's wandering eye (he would soon tell his cousin, Sophia, that she was more beautiful than Mrs Barlow), any expectation that the king would put their relationship on a more permanent footing was unrealistic. Perhaps she did dream of marriage, and Charles had his own parents' fidelity and happiness as an example, but his mother was a Bourbon princess, not a Welsh adventuress with an already murky past. Even as a '*maîtresse-en-titre*', as the other women in the lives of his French royal cousins were known, Lucy did not measure up. She was not an aristocrat. And besides, Charles well knew that his marriageability was a political asset, even for an impoverished exile. He was not likely to throw it away in a moment of romantic delusion. A more pragmatic woman than Lucy would have accepted that the best she could hope for was a regular source of income for herself and her son, and a measure of respect, if she conducted herself with decorum. Charles evidently did make some financial provision for James, though precise details are lacking and its regularity may have been dependent on his resources, which were always stretched. They would remain so until he could get his throne back. For the latter half of 1649 and the first months of 1650, he was preoccupied with the development of a strategy which would allow him to achieve this goal. Once his plans were made, Lucy Walter was effectively no longer part of his life.

The fall of Ireland to the forces of the English republic ended all hopes that it could be used as a springboard for a royalist invasion of England. Instead, in March 1650, Charles received a Scottish delegation at Breda and discussed with them the terms of an agreement by which he would use their support. The talks were difficult, for though Charles demonstrated all the charm for which he would become renowned, as well as his uncanny knack for spotting divisions and differences among his opponents, he

was unable, in the end, to exploit these to his benefit. It has been
said that he summoned Lucy Walter and his baby son to Breda
to show off his virility to the Scots but if this did happen it was
surely a miscalculation. A group of Scottish Calvinists were
unlikely to be impressed by the appearance of a bastard son of a
monarch whose freedom of action they intended to curtail. It
would merely have reinforced in their minds the need to keep
him away from unsuitable companions, of whom they were already
wary. Charles sailed for Scotland in June, leaving Lucy behind.
Though she did not know it at the time, he intended the parting
to mark a decisive end to their relationship. Nor did Lucy know
of his intentions for little James, though she would find out soon
enough.

*

THE FIRST ATTEMPT to kidnap the king's son might have
succeeded, since the plans for it seem to have been laid with care.
Soon after Charles II's departure for Scotland, the easily flattered
Mrs Barlow, who had always liked the attention of wealthy and,
preferably, titled men, was inveigled away to the Rotterdam Fair,
perhaps by the earl of Craven. Not that the earl really desired
Lucy's company. He was part of a plot masterminded by John
Eliot, one of Charles's longest-serving grooms of the bedchamber,
who had stayed behind in the Netherlands with instructions to
remove little James from his mother. The king wanted custody
but seems to have been unwilling, or, perhaps, unable to bring
this about openly, with Lucy's agreement. Evidently it had not
yet crossed her mind that an attempt might be made to remove
James forcibly and she was greatly distressed when, on her return
from Rotterdam, she found the child gone. 'She rent her apparel,
tore the hair from off her head and whole showers of tears bewailed
the greatness of her loss.' If this was the first, it would certainly
not be the last very public scene that Lucy would make in respect
of her son. Her theatrics, however, were soon replaced by a more
considered and organized response. She ordered horses and rode

through the night to the port of Maassluis, presuming that her son was about to be shipped off, back to England. How she came by such information is not clear but it was erroneous. Lucy made a great scene on the quayside, throwing gold coins at the local mayor and yelling that a royal child had been abducted. She certainly attracted a crowd but it was all to no avail, since her son was not there. Some ten days later, he was discovered in a village not far from The Hague, in the care of two of John Eliot's accomplices, unharmed and apparently unaware of the furore surrounding his disappearance. He was returned to his mother but only, according to one source, after a lawsuit. And if Lucy had at first thought that the king's enemies in England had ordered the abduction of her son, she now knew differently.[2]

Acceptance of reality was never one of Lucy's strong points and she seems to have clung to the hope, during all the time Charles II was away, that their affair could somehow be renewed. Even after the king's return from the crushing defeat of the royalist cause at the Battle of Worcester in 1651, she tried to rekindle their relationship by going, once again, to Paris. But it was abundantly evident that her status was nothing like it had been two years previously. As far as Charles was concerned, she was part of his past and he did not like the rumours about her conduct that were becoming more insistent. He would try his best, in these straitened times, to support their son, but he did not want anything more to do with Lucy herself. Yet whatever provision the king had made for her and James, it was clearly not sufficient from her perspective. She would need to leave Paris for good and find support elsewhere. Her choices were limited, so The Hague beckoned again.

There, she took up with Viscount Theobald Taaffe, an Irish peer in his fifties, who had for some time been a dubious influence on the king. Charles enjoyed Taaffe's company, conveniently overlooking his lax morals and military ineptitude because he was convivial and a good dancer. Taaffe was the ageing male equivalent of the good-time girl that Lucy, through inclination

and inevitability, had become. Their mutual attraction was predictable. Lucy, relieved to have found a new protector, enjoyed her
life with Taaffe. He treated her well and probably fathered her
second child, a daughter named Mary. As much as he could, he
tried to represent Lucy favourably to her former lover. There were
rumours of a possible marriage (Taaffe was a widower) but no
wedding took place. This was unfortunate for Lucy – and, indeed,
for Charles II – because marrying off a discarded mistress was
a time-honoured ploy for British royalty. Henry VIII had followed
this course with Bessie Blount, and Charles's Stuart ancestors,
James IV and James V of Scotland, had found husbands for the
mothers of their illegitimate children. We do not know why
the Taaffe marriage never materialized but it may be that even the
easy-going Taaffe was not in the end convinced that Lucy would
make a faithful wife. For, much to the king's unease, his erstwhile
mistress's reputation continued to go downhill.

*

BY THE MID-1650S, Lucy was becoming a serious embarrassment
to Charles II. The well-travelled king was far away from her at
that time, having tactfully removed himself and a small group of
followers from Paris to Germany. The invitation from the Imperial
Diet of Ratisbon at the end of 1653 allowed the king to leave
France without losing face, a move made all the more pressing by
the alliance of Cardinal Mazarin, chief minister to Charles's young
cousin, Louis XIV, with Oliver Cromwell, the undisputed leader
of the English republic. A seething Henrietta Maria stayed on in
Paris, despite the continued threat posed by the series of rebellions
known as the Fronde. In truth, she had little choice. For Charles,
the promise of a pension of £45,000 by the German states, and
an extra £23,000 from Emperor Ferdinand III, offered an honourable way out. He left in the summer of 1654 and spent an idyllic
few months with his sister, Mary, who had travelled from the
Netherlands to be with him, visiting the Shrine of Charlemagne
in Aachen, taking the waters at Spa and sailing down the Rhine.

We do not know whether they discussed the woman whom Mary referred to in letters to Charles as 'your wife'. Not too much should be read into this appellation; Mary was unlikely to refer to 'your mistress', though this reference has been used to bolster the claim that a marriage between Charles Stuart and Lucy Walter had taken place earlier.[3] But when the princess returned to The Hague, she would have been well aware of the continued problem Lucy posed, even if outwardly they remained on cordial terms.

The king did not need his sister to remind him of Lucy Walter. At first, he had accepted the advice that Lucy would behave herself if adequate funds for her upkeep and the needs of her son were forthcoming. Charles duly authorized an annuity of 5,000 French livres, a sum roughly equivalent to £650,000 today. His intentions may have been genuine but he simply did not have adequate funds to meet such a commitment. Lucy never received anything like the amount promised and since she was convinced that the only real prospect of finding a man wealthy enough to support the lifestyle she craved, as well as her two children, was from among the royalist exiles at Princess Mary's court, she was deaf to pleas that she should live quietly, away from public scrutiny. By May 1655, the king was imploring Taaffe to inform Lucy of his desire that 'she goes to some place more private than The Hague, for her stay there is very prejudicial to us both.'[4] Unfortunately for Charles, Lucy's behaviour was providing just the sort of ammunition that his enemies in the English republic could use against him. He stood to lose, in the short term, the support of more strait-laced rulers, such as Philip IV of Spain, who was viewed as a potential source of desperately needed money. Philip presided over a stuffy and very proper court and was hardly going to hand over money to an exile whose former mistress was renowned for her continuing life of sin. In the longer term, the Cromwellian propaganda machine would delight in using this apparently never-ending source of smut to scupper any hopes he might have of restoration.

When Taaffe failed to secure Lucy's cooperation, Daniel O'Neill, a groom of the bedchamber who was one of the most influential and loyal of Charles II's followers and effectively the king's spymaster, stepped in to try to bring a decisive end to the problem of Lucy Walter. O'Neill, an Irish Protestant, had spent the early years of exile on the move, dividing his time between Paris, The Hague and the Spanish Netherlands and was well regarded in all three places. The king's chief minister, Edward Hyde, nicknamed him 'Infallible Subtle'. It was an apt epithet. O'Neill's informers had been watching Lucy for some time and initially he had thought her little more than a nuisance who could be contained, paid off with a dribbling allowance. By 1656, he knew that this was not a viable option. Convinced that she posed a growing threat, O'Neill's tactics were ruthless. He was unswerving in his advice that Lucy must be negated as a threat to the reputation of Charles II. Nothing could be expected from Spain, he warned, if rumours concerning Lucy's wild behaviour continued to circulate. He had been told that 'one of the greatest exceptions the ministers of Spain had, was that there was nothing a secret in your court.'[5] In other words, Charles's private life must not be made public by the antics of his erstwhile mistress. Cutting Lucy off, both financially and morally, was an absolute necessity. It would also be necessary to gain permanent custody of young James, her son.

Deprived of what little money she had received from Charles II, Lucy followed what was, by now, a predictable path and found another lover. Thomas Howard, the younger brother of the earl of Suffolk, was Mary's master of the horse and had been at her court for some years. His wife, Walburga van der Kerckhoven, was governess to Mary's son, the future William III of England. He must have seemed an ideal beau, with his aristocratic connections and refined manners. Lucy was evidently smitten by Howard's attentions and his expensive presents. He was even willing to set her up in a house of her own outside Delft, at a tactful distance from The Hague. Howard was certainly a catch. Yet it may be that Lucy was the one who had been ensnared.

There is indirect evidence that Princess Mary had dangled

Thomas Howard in front of Lucy Walter deliberately, in a bid to free her brother of an increasingly troublesome woman, and that Howard knew very well what was expected of him.[6] Whether this was part of Daniel O'Neill's wider strategy for neutralizing Lucy is not clear. The cynicism of such a scheme is as distasteful as its crass immorality. Could Howard's wife, for example, really have been a party to such a plot, or was she as taken in by it as Lucy Walter? The idea was also inherently risky, as an unexpected development would soon show. Before Lucy could even move into her new house at Delft, she was heading back to republican England and the king's son was going with her. Unable, apparently, to dissuade her, Howard decided that he had better go along as well. Instead of enjoying the discreet and ladylike life offered by a mansion in the Dutch countryside, Lucy was about to be lodged in an altogether different venue: the Tower of London.

*

IF LIFE HAD taught Lucy anything, it was that opportunities for financial security should never be overlooked. So, when her brother, the soberly named Justus Walter, arrived from England to inform her that their mother had died in February 1656, leaving all of her estate to their aunt in the Netherlands, Lucy did not need much convincing to return to England with him to contest the will. The plans to contain her were suddenly thrown up in the air and the difficulties that might ensue with someone so unpredictable being let loose in Cromwellian England caused consternation. The level of anxiety may be gauged by the fact that Charles II, recently arrived in the Spanish Netherlands as a pensioner of Spain, had a brief meeting with Lucy on 22 May in Antwerp, shortly before she sailed. Since Antwerp was something of a detour from Flushing, the port Lucy was to depart from, this was not a chance meeting. We do not know who instigated it or what passed between them. Charles may have wanted an opportunity to see his son and perhaps to suggest that James remain with him while Lucy went in search of her inheritance. He could have ordered and

imposed such an outcome if met with resistance, but, mindful of
Lucy's talent for causing a scene, he would not have wished a
scandal to reach the ears of his new hosts within days of his
arrival. It was ironic that fate should have brought Lucy and
Charles together again when he had been trying to put as much
distance as possible between them. Both were now in their mid-
twenties, with difficult years behind them and uncertain futures
ahead. The summer of 1648 seemed a world away. Yet for all the
tension that hung in the air, neither could have known that this
brief encounter would be their last.

The Cromwellian England to which Lucy returned was by no
means the sterile military dictatorship depicted by the Lord
Protector's opponents. Literature and music flourished, private
performances kept the theatrical tradition alive and coffee houses
in London were thriving social hubs. Charles II and his threadbare
courtiers, roaming the smaller cities of Europe, could not hope to
match the English republic's standing in the eyes of the world.
No longer a small northern European country riven by civil war,
the republic was an international power. But it was a suspicious
city to which 'Mrs Barlow' returned, watchful of new arrivals,
especially those with royalist connections. Lucy was naive if she
thought that she and her little party could pass unremarked
through its streets. Within two weeks of her arrival in June 1656,
Lucy discovered that Thomas Howard could not protect her – or,
indeed, himself – from the well-oiled machinery of Cromwell's
spy network, controlled by Oliver's self-effacing but extremely
competent secretary, John Thurloe. Having watched her lodgings
in the Strand and followed her every movement, Thurloe's net
closed in. Lucy's group, including her children and maid, were
detained and taken to the Tower of London for questioning.

This frightening episode is glossed over in the hagiographic
biography of James, duke of Monmouth, which was published
thirty years later, when Lucy's son was desperately trying to mend
his relationship with his father. The grovelling author of this work
would have his readers believe that Lucy's time in London was a

triumph: '. . . the Cavaliers carried themselves towards her with a profound reverence and awful respect, treating her as a sacred person, serving her on the knee.'[7] Lucy's contacts in London before her arrest are unknown but her interrogation in the Tower was led by John Barkstead, a hard-line regicide not known for his gentle treatment of prisoners. He was more likely to have viewed Lucy as a royalist whore than a 'sacred person'. Under his initial questioning, Lucy claimed to be the widow of a Dutch sea-captain, explaining that she had returned to England to claim her mother's legacy. That part of the story was true but Barkstead knew that the rest was a pack of lies. Was she not, in fact, Charles Stuart's mistress, he asked, and the mother of his son? Cornered, Lucy did not deny that she had given birth to the king's child but claimed that he had died. The two children accompanying her now were the offspring of the conveniently dead Dutchman.

Barkstead was not fooled for one minute. From Lucy's blabbermouth maid, Anne Hill, the authorities had already learned all they needed to know. Howard was not a chance acquaintance encountered on the North Sea crossing but Lucy's lover and the boy was indeed the son of Charles Stuart. Their suspicions confirmed, the Lord Protector and his advisers now considered what to do with this unexpected opportunity. The conclusion they came to was that Lucy was not a royalist spy and that they would be better off deporting her. The damage she could continue to wreak on Charles Stuart's reputation was far greater if she was free than if she was detained in England. Accordingly, the order was given, signed by Cromwell himself: 'Lucy Barlow, prisoner in the Tower, to be sent back to Flanders with her child'.[8] The child, in this case, meant the seven-year-old James, there being apparently no interest in his young half-sister, Mary. The document describes Lucy and her son disparagingly, as 'Charles Stuart's lady of pleasure and the young heir.'[9] *Mercurius Politicus*, the official newspaper of the republican government, was quick to point out to the regime's royalist enemies that they were 'already furnished with an heir apparent.'[10] Lucy was lucky to escape from this ill-advised return to her native land without far more serious consequences. Her dreams of using her mother's money and Howard's continued largesse to buy a coach lined with red velvet had been met with a rude awakening, but much worse was to follow.

*

SCANDAL AND LUCY Walter were always close companions. A more placid woman might have been content with her fine house outside Delft but though she drew up plans for renovation with her brother, Justus, whose tastes for lavish living matched her own, Lucy's capacity for getting into trouble had not been contained by her sojourn in the Tower of London. She became embroiled in a dispute with a local wine merchant (the precise causes of which remain unclear) and ended up in jail. She was eventually released but ordered to leave Delft. No help was forthcoming from Thomas Howard, so Lucy, with the unexpected assistance in this extremity of Robert Sidney, decided to sell her splendid house with most of its contents and move to the Spanish Netherlands. If the affair with Thomas Howard was already cooling, it now descended into acrimony as Howard disputed Lucy's right to sell off the house's contents, most of which, he claimed, belonged to him. Deserted and wondering if she had been played for a fool all along, Lucy's thoughts turned to revenge. She would make Howard pay, and not just with money – for there seemed to be no more of that forthcoming – but with his life.

On 24 August 1657, a young cousin of Lucy's, Charles Bursfield, who had arrived from England to support her, attempted to assassinate Howard in Brussels. His earlier attempt to challenge Howard to a duel, a time-honoured way of defending a lady's honour, had been met with derision and so he resorted to a surprise attack with a stiletto dagger in an alleyway, not far, as it turned out, from where the king himself was lodging. The attack, like much else attempted by Lucy Walter, failed, though Howard suffered a severe arm wound. Charles II and Edward Hyde were left shaking their heads over this latest exploit involving Lucy

Walter. They were already plentifully supplied with other damaging titbits. For the past two years, Daniel O'Neill had been gathering more information about Lucy's unsavoury life. He learned of abortions, plots to murder a maid who talked too much; in short, he had a full portfolio of dirt on 'Mrs Barlow' to add to the escapade in Brussels.

Still, Charles hesitated. At his behest, Lucy had been lodged with Sir Arthur Slingsby, a royalist living in Brussels, who was supposed to keep an eye on her and suppress the possibility of further damaging behaviour. But Lucy had by no means exhausted her options and, having already sold letters Howard had written to her, revealing his activities as a royalist conspirator, she now announced her intention to 'post up' Charles's letters to her, in full public view, in the Grande Place in Brussels, unless her pension was increased. This threat prompted the king to arrange another attempt to kidnap his son. Slingsby was to remove him from his mother and take him to a secure place. The plan was put into action on a cold evening in early December 1657 but was, once again, thwarted by Lucy. She ran, screaming, into the street, causing a huge scene that naturally drew onlookers. The violence of Slingsby's attempts to restrain and quieten her brought the gathering crowd firmly on to her side. This bungled attempt proved a great embarrassment for Charles II. The Spanish ambassador to Charles's exiled court in Brussels, Don Alonso de Cárdenas, described Slingsby's behaviour as 'most barbarous, abominable and most unnatural'. He offered Lucy and her son his protection. The incident threatened to derail the relationship between Spain and the Stuarts, which had been so painstakingly established.[11]

The king, providentially away in Bruges when the kidnap attempt took place, could not afford to lose Spanish support. Equally, he could not let Lucy Walter continue to damage his international reputation by her shenanigans. He needed to tread carefully in his response to her latest aggravation and to get the Spanish on his side, not hers. Accordingly, he wrote a carefully worded letter of explanation to Cárdenas, explaining his side of the story. His concerns, he explained, had always been for the child, and, indeed, for Lucy herself. He needed Spanish help to prevent Lucy's 'mad disobedience to his pleasure' and settle matters once and for all. It would, he said, 'be a great charity to the child, and to the mother herself, if she shall now at length retire to such a way of life (that) may redeem in some measure the reproach of her past ways.'[12] The Spanish accepted this explanation and agreed to assist Charles in containing Lucy. She spent Christmas under the watchful eye of Cárdenas. Meanwhile, Daniel O'Neill told Slingsby to make sure that the potentially damaging letters that Lucy had so unwisely shouted about be removed from her possession as soon as possible and returned to the king. Like so much else connected with Lucy Walter and the written evidence of her relationship with Charles II, they conveniently disappeared.

It was now just a matter of time before she lost her last bargaining chip, her nine-year-old son. In April 1658, while his mother was in another part of the house, James was successfully removed from her custody by two of Charles's servants, by the simple expedient of distraction. For all her faults, Lucy was a stout-hearted woman and she immediately began to search for James. This time, however, she would not succeed. For months she tried, first in Brussels and then following James to Paris, where he eventually ended up in the care of William Crofts, a royalist politician who was on friendly terms with the king. But Lucy never saw James again. She was already ill when she arrived in Paris and now, in the autumn of 1658, she faded fast. The cause of her illness cannot be identified with any certainty. James, duke of York, subsequently claimed that she had contracted venereal disease because of the life she led but he had every reason to wish to blacken the reputation of a woman who was no longer able to defend herself. Whatever killed her, it is clear that, as she faced death, Lucy had regrets and expressed them in a confession made to John Cosin, the chaplain to the Protestant exiles in Paris, whom she had probably met on previous visits to the French capital. He, at least, did not judge her as her life ebbed away.

At the end, Lucy Walter was a lonely figure, attended to her grave in Paris (long since lost) by a spy from Charles II's exiled court. Nor has time been kind to her reputation. It might justifiably be argued that Lucy brought many of the difficulties that beset her on herself. She was ambitious, headstrong and overconfident, and relentlessly combative, mindful of her son's usefulness to her but completely neglectful of the education of someone who was a royal child. Crofts was astonished to discover that his new charge, though intelligent and willing to learn, could not read or count beyond twenty. But Charles II had never been able to make provision for a proper education for his son and probably would not have trusted Lucy Walter with the money while James remained with her. Her death, at the beginning of December 1658, relieved Charles of a thorn in his side. Very few people have spoken up for Lucy since and attempts to do so have been unconvincing.

There remains, of course, the intriguing question of whether Charles II, as a teenage prince in The Hague, did indeed go through some form of marriage ceremony with Lucy Walter. He denied it throughout his reign and his brother, challenged by Lucy's son for the succession, made sure that her memory was vilified. The papers which Lucy is said to have entrusted to John Cosin during her last days in Paris have never been found. Probably they were destroyed, if anything of any note ever actually existed. Cosin's extensive library and correspondence can now be consulted in the libraries of Durham University and Durham Cathedral and it may be that, among their pages, a surprised researcher could, one day, discover something that escaped the suppression of Lucy Walter's papers and will vindicate her brittle and sad life.

CHAPTER THREE

Marking Time

*'For I cannot choose but say she is the worthiest to be
loved of all the sex'*
Charles II reveals his admiration for Princess
Henrietta Catherine of Orange, 1658

THE EXILED KING had readily found a succession of ladies willing
to succumb to his considerable charms by the time Lucy Walter
met her cheerless end in Paris. Nor was young James Crofts his
only child, though it is unlikely that Lucy's son knew he had, by
1658, three half-siblings: two sisters and a brother. The first of
these, Charlotte Fitzroy, was born in 1651 to Elizabeth Killigrew.
Known as Betty, Elizabeth Killigrew was a member of Henrietta
Maria's household in Paris and the sister of playwright Thomas
Killigrew. The Killigrews were a well-connected royalist family
(Thomas acted as a diplomat for Charles II in northern Italy
during the 1650s) and Betty had been married to the Irishman
Francis Boyle, later made Viscount Shannon, since before the
outbreak of the Civil Wars. She was eight years older than Charles,
which has sometimes been taken as an indication of his weakness
for older women, though the king's very varied taste in women
does not really support this interpretation. Her marriage appears
to have survived this affair and her daughter was the first of
Charles's illegitimate children to be given the surname Fitzroy in

acknowledgement of her parentage. Charlotte was not, however, one of Charles's favourite children.[1] Her existence was kept quiet for almost twenty years.

Betty Killigrew was not Charles's only conquest in Paris. Eleanor Needham, the widowed Lady Byron, also shared the young king's bed. The 1664 portrait of her by Sir Peter Lely in the Royal Collection shows a dark-haired, good-looking woman, who was then in her late thirties but looks younger. There were no children of this liaison but Eleanor was, nevertheless, determined to get a pension out of the king in recognition for having slept with him. She doggedly pursued the collection of the considerable monies promised her but received very little.

During his time in Bruges, the king formed a relationship over several years with Catherine Pegge, the daughter of royalist exile Thomas Pegge of Yeldersley near Ashbourne in Derbyshire. She was said to be a great beauty but little is known of her beyond the fact that she bore Charles a son and a daughter, in 1657 and 1658. The son, Charles FitzCharles, was nicknamed Don Carlos, either because he was born in the Spanish Netherlands or because of his dark good looks. It took fourteen years for his father to acknowledge him formally and he had to wait until 1675 to be given a title, when he was made earl of Plymouth. His sister, named Catherine after her mother, died young. The complete opposite of Lucy Walter, Catherine Pegge obligingly stayed in the shadows. It is not clear what, if any, financial support Charles gave her. She was eventually married to Sir Edward Greene of Great Sampford in Essex, in 1667, and they had one daughter. It has been said that Catherine died a year after her marriage but her father's will, made in 1676, clearly shows that she was still alive then, as she and her sister are named as his main beneficiaries.[2]

Attempts to justify Charles II's sexual adventures during the period of his exile as being unremarkable for a young aristocrat in the mid-seventeenth century overlook the fact that his behaviour was in stark contrast to that of his own father, whose example he was clearly not inclined to follow. His lifestyle was also grist to the very productive mill of Cromwellian propaganda, playing into the hands of his enemies in England by allowing them to represent him as a sleazy playboy, unfit to rule. Edward Hyde and other advisers were seriously worried about the effect this would have on Charles's chances of regaining the throne. The king was certainly aware of how he was being represented in the English news-sheets. Referring to reports of his amours in England, Charles noted, with an air of wearied amusement, 'they have done me too much honour in assigning me so many fair ladies as if I were able to satisfy the half.'[3] But after Cromwell's death in 1658, he began to think seriously of the advantages that a marriage might bring. His choice fell on a girl he had known for some time. She had the right credentials of both birth and religion and he was also fond of her. The young lady in question was the twenty-one-year-old Princess Henrietta Catherine of Orange Nassau, sister-in-law of Mary Stuart, the Princess Royal.

Charles had got to know Henrietta Catherine during his time in the United Provinces and may have genuinely believed himself in love for a while. Letters exchanged between the king and the ever-obliging Viscount Taaffe refer to a young lady that Charles was keen to woo. They gave her the code name 'the infanta', and some historians believe that this mysterious but evidently desirable lady was, indeed, the Dutch princess.[4] At the beginning of 1658, Charles reported a meeting between himself and 'his friend, where he was very well satisfied and finds that absence hath wrought no ill effects, there passed many kind expressions between them, and I think I know him so well [Charles was here referring to himself in the third person] that I may say he loves her if it were possible every day more than any other and truly I find he has reason for I cannot choose but say she is the worthiest to be loved of the sex.'[5]

His enthusiasm is understandable. The Dutch princess was an attractive and spirited girl, who had raised eyebrows by refusing point-blank to marry the stolid Friesian cousin picked out for her in childhood, on the grounds that she found him physically repellent. At a time when the voicing of such attitudes by female aristocrats was almost unheard of, Henrietta Catherine was clearly not afraid to speak her mind. This combination of a pleasant appearance, independence of outlook, and suitability made Henrietta Catherine an appealing prospect as a bride. But whatever the couple's feelings for each other, the match was not to be. The ambassador of the English republic at The Hague, Sir George Downing, soon stepped in to inform the Dutch States-General that such a marriage would offend the regime in London. Nor was the formidable Amalia von Solms, Henrietta Catherine's German mother, convinced by the idea. Charles had earlier expressed an interest in another of her daughters and nothing had come of it. She did not believe that the alliance of Orange and Stuart had been of any benefit to her family. Having taken against the Princess Royal almost from the moment Mary had arrived at the Dutch court as a bewildered child bride in 1642, the relationship between the two as Mary grew to womanhood had become utterly poisonous. Amalia had no wish to cast one of her own daughters into the arms of a libidinous (and penniless) Stuart, a family that she despised. Whether the marriage, had it taken place, would have been a success, no one can say. Charles had already much too much of a wandering eye and could not change his essential nature. It seems unlikely that Henrietta Catherine would have accepted his serial infidelities. She would, though, have given him children; she had ten with the husband she married in 1659, the count of Anhalt-Dessau, seven of whom survived childhood. The restored Charles II would have given much to have such a fertile wife. For the present, his prospects looked as bleak as ever.

And then, as the year 1659 drew to a close, there came the first glimmer of hope in England. Richard Cromwell's protectorate had not survived its first year and his fall brought into the open the long-running differences between the army's leaders and republicans who favoured what they called the Good Old Cause and the supremacy of Parliament. Deprived of a strong leader, the republic looked unsteady. Hopes of a restoration of the Stuarts had been raised frequently during the 1650s but every ill-considered attempt at a royalist rising had been put down. When, on 1 January 1660, General George Monck, who commanded the army that effectively occupied Scotland, made the fateful gamble to march his men south, ostensibly to support Parliamentarians expelled by the army grandees, the course of history changed.

Monck was probably playing a longer game, even at this stage, than he dared acknowledge but he had always been an opportunist and he needed to wait before his true motives became apparent. While presenting himself as Parliament's saviour, he had been receiving letters from Charles II for some time, and his ultimate goal, if Parliament would go along with his call for new elections, was to restore the Stuarts. By the end of March 1660, it was apparent to the amazed and delighted Charles and his two brothers that they would, at last, be returning home. In the Declaration of Breda, issued on 4 April, Charles noted, 'If the general distraction and confusion, which is spread over the whole kingdom, doth not awaken all men to a desire and longing that those wounds which have so many years together been kept bleeding may be bound up, all we can say will be to no purpose.'[6] His hopes were never to be entirely realized during the twenty-five years of an increasingly fraught reign but, in the spring of 1660, they were easily understood and accepted by many, but not all. Charles's restoration was not greeted with the universal rejoicing that royalist sympathizers claimed.[7] But there was a general feeling of relief and widespread rejoicing. A new era of light-heartedness seemed to beckon.

Yet even with the rumours and scurrilous tales that had been spread by his enemies while he languished in exile, it is unlikely that England was prepared for the extent of debauchery that would all too soon come to characterize the court and the monarch. John Evelyn, the diarist, wrote after the king's death that he was 'addicted to women'. And by the time of his restoration, Charles was involved with one woman in particular who would dominate both him and his court for the first decade of his reign. She was Barbara Palmer, née Villiers, and her extraordinary boldness, extravagance and beauty made her one of the most famous – and reviled – royal mistresses of all time.

Part Two

The Lady

BARBARA VILLIERS

1640–1709

CHAPTER FOUR

'That blooming beauty'

*'The idea I have of your perfections is too glorious to be
shadowed either by absence or time'*
Philip, earl of Chesterfield
to Barbara Villiers, 1656

THE LADY WAS born into a powerful, if unpopular, family, still
regarded as upstarts by some members of the old nobility. George
Villiers, duke of Buckingham, favourite of both James I and
Charles I, was her grandfather's half-brother. When the infant
Barbara was baptized at St Margaret's, Westminster, on 27
November 1640, her mother, Mary Bayning, was only fifteen
years old, though her father, William Villiers, Viscount
Grandison, was in his mid-twenties. The viscount had fought a
duel for Mary's hand, in Hyde Park, with Mary's brother-in-law,
who seems to have suspected that this member of the Villiers
clan was more interested in the girl's money than inspired by
romantic love. And Mary's fortune was considerable. She came
from a mercantile family whose wealth had allowed them to
buy a title, and she was regarded as a great prize. No doubt
Mary's status as an heiress added to her attractions but there
does seem to have been a genuine affection between the couple.
But they had married at a time when the sense of dislocation
in England was palpable and the problems facing Charles I

were accelerating. Whatever happiness they knew was destined to be short-lived.

Grandison's behaviour might suggest a greedy and hot-blooded nature yet, though these and much worse criticisms were to be aimed at his daughter, he seems, in fact, to have been a serious young man, known for his piety and deep commitment to the royalist cause when the Civil Wars broke out. When Charles I left London after his disastrous foray into the House of Commons to arrest the five men he believed were the opposition ringleaders, Grandison accompanied him as he rode north to York. Serving the king was a duty and the viscount acknowledged the need to put personal consideration aside: 'If he had not understanding enough to know the uprightness of the cause, nor loyalty enough to inform him of the duty of a subject, yet the very obligations of gratitude to the king, on the behalf of his house, were such as his life was but a due sacrifice.'[1]

Whether his young wife was quite so enthusiastic about the possibility of losing her lord on matters of principle is doubtful. She came from a family who put business acumen above fine phrases but, sadly, her husband's words were to prove prophetic. He had been involved in various engagements in which he had acquitted himself honourably, and had risen to the rank of colonel when, in the summer of 1643, he left his wife and child at Oxford, the royalist headquarters, to join Prince Rupert's forces in the siege of Bristol. On 26 July, in a muddled assault on part of the city's defences that was typical of the ill discipline of royalist forces, Grandison was shot in the leg. He was taken back to Oxford, a considerable journey for a wounded man, where he lingered for a month before the gangrene that infected his wound killed him. At the age of just eighteen, Viscountess Grandison found herself facing an uncertain future with a three-year-old daughter. There was not even a male heir to carry on her husband's name and the title passed to his brother.

Barbara Villiers commemorated her father, many years later, by erecting a monument of marble over his grave in Christ Church,

Oxford. She had none of his self-effacement or sense of duty but perhaps she cherished, from the mists of her early childhood, fond memories of a gallant gentleman.

*

WE KNOW NOTHING of the next five years of Barbara's life. They were passed as the Civil Wars engulfed England and were times of some financial hardship. Lady Grandison's estates were in eastern England, an area firmly under Parliamentary control, and she could not recover the rents from them or the substantial loans her own father had made to the Crown. In 1648, she married again, to her late husband's first cousin, Charles Villiers, earl of Anglesey.

Evidently, she thought that a continued alliance with the family would be beneficial for herself and little Barbara, though it did not prove of much financial help, since the earl's property was also sequestrated by the king's opponents. However, the couple did not flee abroad after the execution of Charles I but stayed in London. It is unclear what part of the city they lived in or whether it was in a house owned or rented by Lord Anglesey. Their straitened circumstances made exile unappealing and they survived, as many other royalists did, in an uneasy acceptance of the republic that replaced the fallen king. Barbara's education must have continued during these years, though nothing is known of it beyond the fact that she was obviously literate, as would have been expected of all young ladies of her background. Emphasis on social graces and attainments, such as dancing, music and conversation, generally formed a more important part of a girl's upbringing than academic study. Barbara's letters are lively and well expressed, characterized by the archaic and inconsistent use of vocabulary typical of an age when there were no accepted conventions in spelling. She probably learned French, since foreign languages were considered an appropriate attainment for ladies, and many years later she would reside in Paris when life in England became uncomfortable. Her one recorded usage of French indicates that she could not spell in that language, either.

Scholarly shortcomings were of no real significance to the teenage Barbara Villiers, who soon learned how to enjoy life in Cromwellian London. Girls like Barbara, at the centre of royalist society, knew how to have fun, passing their days in a heady mixture of secret assignations and love affairs, cocking a snook at the Puritanism they despised. By the mid-1650s, Barbara was an established figure on the social scene, where her physical attractions and strong personality pushed her to the forefront of attention: 'Being left destitute of both a father and a fortune, when she first came to London she appeared in a very plain country dress; which being soon altered into the gaiety and mode of the town, added a new lustre to that blooming beauty, of which she had as great a share as any lady of her time. Thus furnished by bounteous nature and by art, she soon became the object of divers young gentlemen's affections.'[2] At the age of sixteen, Barbara had blossomed into a gorgeous, self-confident young woman, whose magnificent auburn hair, full figure and arresting dark-blue eyes made her impossible to ignore. All this attention went to her head but one admirer, in particular, won her heart. She fell madly in love with a man described as 'the greatest knave in England'. He was Philip Stanhope, second earl of Chesterfield, the first of many men of dubious morals and an air of disrepute who would share this uninhibited lady's bed.

Chesterfield had just the sort of colourful background, tinged with sadness, to attract women and his good looks merely added to his appeal. He was, at the age of twenty-three, already a widower. His wife, Lady Anne Percy, the daughter of the earl of Northumberland, guardian to the younger royal children during the Civil Wars, had died of smallpox after two years of marriage. The baby son she had given birth to shortly before her death only survived her by a few weeks. This double tragedy hit Chesterfield hard and he decided that he would leave England to travel in Europe, departing in the summer of 1655. Such a move seemed natural to him. He had been brought up and educated in the Netherlands as the result of his mother's second marriage to a Dutch nobleman, and spent time at the court of Princess Mary Stuart in The Hague, where his mother was the close confidante of Charles I's eldest daughter. He had also spent time at Henrietta Maria's exiled court in France and he knew Paris and Rome, as well as the other great cities of Italy, and had travelled in Germany. Chesterfield was just as much at ease on the continent as he was in England. This sophisticated background, his personal misfortune and a penchant for duelling made it hard for ladies to resist him and he was perfectly happy to bask in their adoration. Of course, he was looking for a new wife and one who could bring both money and connections. Few royalist ladies could offer these prospects and there was talk of him marrying the Protector's youngest daughter, Frances Cromwell, and also Mary Fairfax, the only child of Sir Thomas Fairfax, the lord-general of the Parliamentary army, who had retired from public life in 1650 and was a great landowner in Yorkshire. But while not wishing to fall out with the rulers of republican England, the earl's political sympathies lay with the royalists and when Barbara's cousin, George Villiers, second duke of Buckingham, stole the affections of the impressionable Mary Fairfax from under Chesterfield's nose, after the banns for their wedding had been read three times, the earl stepped aside. Mary Fairfax would come to regret her choice bitterly but, for the present, Chesterfield was content to pursue his hedonistic lifestyle as a single, highly desirable man.

Barbara was not his only mistress at the time and their affair had its ups and downs, but both were caught up in the passion of it, as can be seen from the frequent exchange of letters between them. Chesterfield strove to be the complete lover, in romantic prose – even, occasionally, in slightly awkward poetry – as well as in the bedchamber. The extent of Barbara's longing and her openness in acknowledging it can be sensed in her replies. The first letter in the sequence between the two lovers is from the gentleman and clearly follows a lovers' tiff that had caused both parties some distress:

> Madam, cruelty and absence have ever been thought the most infallible remedies for such a distemper as mine and yet I find both of them so ineffectual that they make me but the more incurable; seriously, Madam, you ought at least to afford some compassion to one in so desperate a condition, for only by wishing me more fortunate you will make me so. Is it not a strange magic in love, which gives so powerful a charm to the least of your cruel words, that they endanger to kill a man at a hundred miles distance; but why do I complain of so pleasant a death, or repine at those sufferings which I would not change for a diadem? No, Madam, the idea I have of your perfections is too glorious to be shadowed either by absence or time: and if I should never more see the sun, yet I should not cease from admiring his light; therefore do not seek to darken my weak sense by endeavouring to make me adore you less.

Warming to his theme, the earl finished off his epistle in verse:

> For if you decree that I must die,
> Falling is nobler than retiring,
> And in the glory of aspiring,
> It is brave to tumble from the sky.[3]

The letter was written from Chesterfield's house in Bretby, Derbyshire, probably in 1656. His tone is very much that of the wronged lover wishing to restore himself to his lady's favour but there is a playful undertone that gives the reader the impression he believes that, in the game of love, this type of high-flown sentiment is more to be expected than believed. He may also have been afflicted by the more prosaic inconveniences he referred to when writing to a friend at the end of the same year, when he complained of 'such a cold as I think is attended with a legion of devils; I mean head-ache, tooth-ache, cough and defluction [discharge] in my eyes; which makes me often wish that there was somebody now, as there was formerly, that could send them all into a herd of swine.'[4] In both cases, Chesterfield's wit and ability to express himself are readily apparent.

Barbara Villiers was well aware that she was not the only woman besotted with the earl. The earliest of her surviving letters to him begins with her regret that she had not seen him at church that morning but that she was not allowed (for reasons she does not give) to attend. Lady Anglesey was clearly not able to put a stop to the liaison but she may have resorted to other tactics to prevent her daughter behaving too obviously in public.[5] So a lovelorn and rather possessive Barbara stayed at home, writing to Chesterfield: 'I am never so well pleased as when I am with you, though I find you are better when you are with other ladies; for you were yesterday all the afternoon with the person I am most jealous of, and I know I have so little merit that I am suspicious you love all women better than myself.' She went on to say that she had written the previous day as well, hoping to convince him that she 'loved nothing besides yourself, no will I ever, though you should hate me; but if you should, I would never give you the trouble of telling you how much I loved you, but keep it to myself till it had broke my heart.' Other letters, in a similar vein, followed, telling him of her regret in not seeing him and suggesting assignations at his private lodgings in Lincoln's Inn Fields.

Barbara did have one friend with whom she was perfectly willing to share Chesterfield's attentions. This was Lady Anne Hamilton, the wayward and promiscuous daughter of the second duke of Hamilton. In the year that Oliver Cromwell was offered, and refused, the crown, Chesterfield was the recipient of a saucy letter, from both girls, suggesting an assignation: 'My friend and I are just now abed together contriving how to have your company this afternoon. If you deserve this favour, you will come and seek us at Ludgate Hill, about three o'clock, at Butler's shop, where we will expect you . . .'⁶ It is unlikely that the young ladies had coffee and cake in mind for their afternoon's entertainment, and this may be the earliest recorded invitation to a threesome in English history. Anne Hamilton went on to become the mistress of James, duke of York, while he was married to Anne Hyde, and was reported to have numerous other liaisons. During the first decade of the Restoration, she and Barbara continued their friendship and their rivalry in trying to outrage their husbands by their serial infidelity and brazen behaviour.

Chesterfield had never made any secret of the fact that he was, in his own words, 'making love to five or six at a time' and Barbara was not the foremost in his thoughts. Indeed, the earl's diary must have been rather complicated. By 1658, he had added Lady Elizabeth Howard to his conquests, though she assured him that she had never spoken lightly of their affair to her friends, 'being always careful of that for my own sake as well as yours'. Barbara does not appear to have exercised such caution, despite now having a serious suitor for her hand in marriage.

He was Roger Palmer, the second son of a respectable minor aristocrat, Sir James Palmer of Dorney Court, near Windsor. Sir James did not approve of his son's determination to marry a young woman of such dubious reputation who had no fortune of her own. The Palmers were a royalist family of probity and rectitude, and it is hardly surprising that their patriarch did not want his well-educated and serious son to ally himself with a girl who had nothing to recommend her beyond her undoubted beauty. It was true that she was a Villiers, but she came from a junior branch of the family. It has been said that Roger Palmer was seeking to marry above him but that was not really the case. He had been well educated, at Eton and Cambridge, and was a lawyer at the Inner Temple. Possessed of intelligence, a pleasant appearance, outstanding linguistic ability and a modest inheritance on the death of his father in 1658, Roger pressed his suit to the eighteen-year-old Barbara, who had seen rather less of Chesterfield since the earl, who loved duelling almost as much as women, had been temporarily confined to the Tower of London for wounding one Captain Whalley. Whether through the encouragement of her mother or her own calculation that it might be time for marriage, Barbara Villiers agreed to accept Roger Palmer. Their wedding took place at St Gregory's Church, near the Angleseys' home on Ludgate Hill, on 14 April 1659. It would bring intense unhappiness, humiliation and, eventually, self-imposed exile to a decent young man, who soon discovered that he had every cause to regret ignoring his father's advice, for the new Mrs Palmer had no intention of changing her lifestyle. Marriage vows meant nothing to Barbara.

The affair with Chesterfield went on regardless. If attempts were made at first to conceal it from Roger Palmer, his suspicions were not long in coming. In the same year that she was married, Barbara wrote a letter which combined disdain and desperation to her lover:

My Lord,

Since I saw you, I have been at home, and I find the *mounser* [monsieur] in a very ill humour, for he says that he is resolved never to bring me to town again, and that nobody should see me when I am in the country. I would not have you come today, for that would displease him more; but send me word presently what you would advise to do, for I am ready and willing to go all over the world with you, and I will obey your commands, that I am whilst I live, Yours[7]

Chesterfield did not call to see her when she caught the smallpox in London shortly afterwards. She was well enough to write in her habitually dramatic turn of phrase that the doctor believed her to be in a desperate condition and that only her fear of never seeing him again was keeping her alive. She would, she assured him, 'live and die loving you above all other things.' Ever the drama queen, Mrs Palmer not only survived, but her looks were unimpaired. And as the English republic teetered towards self-destruction, royalists like the Palmers and Chesterfield began to glimpse a very different future.

Royalist conspiracies in the late 1650s had foundered on disorganization, petty rivalries and betrayals. One of the leading lights of the royalist movement in England was Alan Brodrick, a distant cousin of Barbara's, who was always eager to recruit new agents for the cause and was delighted when Roger Palmer offered the king £1,000 at the beginning of 1660. He was equally pleased to have secret access to the deliberations of the Council of State via Roger's sister, Catherine, whose brother-in-law was principal clerk to the Council. How important this latter connection turned out to be in reality is debatable, since by this time General Monck's grip on power in London was tightening and he was already in communication with the exiled court of Charles II in Brussels. Brodrick was, though, keen to impress on Edward Hyde the absolute commitment of Roger Palmer and, indeed, the sacrifices that his family had made during the Civil Wars. To which he added the following shrewd analysis of Roger's overall situation: 'I must presume to whisper to your lordship his condition: a gay wife and great expense to a slender fortune in possession, the main of his estate being in lease for some years to come.'[8] The term 'gay', in the mid-seventeenth century, did not have modern connotations, but the inference that Barbara Palmer was both expensive and flighty would not have been lost on Hyde. He was yet to meet her but they grew to dislike one another intensely and she would play her part in his eventual fall from grace.

In the spring of 1660, Charles II was in Brussels and Roger Palmer was standing in the elections that were to be the death knell of republican England. Cautiously confident at last, the king wrote to Chesterfield that he hoped 'the time is at hand that will put an end to our calamities.' It has been speculated that Barbara Palmer was used as a messenger to the exiled court, but there is no evidence of this. We do not know her movements at this time, nor do we know when she first met the king, though it was subsequently asserted that she was already his mistress by the time he returned to England and that he spent his first night in London with her at Whitehall Palace. Even if they had not met before the Restoration itself, their affair started very shortly afterwards and soon became common knowledge. The diarist Samuel Pepys, whose lustful adoration of Barbara from a distance mirrors the celebrity worship of our own time, first refers to her connection with Charles II on 13 July 1660, saying that there had been 'a great doing of music at the next house . . . the king and the dukes there with Madam Palmer, a pretty woman that they have a fancy to make her husband a cuckold.' But the deed was already done, although another year passed before Pepys referred to her openly as the king's mistress.

By the autumn of 1660, Barbara Palmer knew she was pregnant. Whether she had any real idea who was the child's father is another matter. Her daughter, Anne, was born on 25 February 1661 and though acknowledged by Roger as his own, the king later acknowledged Anne as his child. Gossip at the time speculated that Chesterfield might even have been the father. The overactive earl accompanied Charles II back from Breda in the Netherlands, having been forced to flee England for some months at the start of 1660 when his penchant for duelling resulted in the death of the son of a London doctor. Chesterfield did not like being replaced in Barbara's affections by the king and apparently hoped his liaison with her might continue, although he himself took a second wife in September 1660. She was Lady Elizabeth Butler, daughter of the leading royalist exile, the duke of Ormond. This blue-eyed blonde, petite but with a good figure and, if the admittedly often colourful memoirs of Anthony Hamilton are to be believed, no great adherent of fidelity herself, was a good match for Chesterfield.

Barbara Palmer's star, however, was very much in the ascendant. As soon as she had recovered from her daughter's birth, she was back at the king's side, accompanying him to the theatre, to outings and dinners. Her hold over Charles II grew stronger and for much of the 1660s she was a powerfully disruptive force at the Restoration court, wrecking her own marriage and that of the king, while her greed and shrillness intensified. She was never a woman who set out to be liked, and in that respect her success would be complete.

CHAPTER FIVE

The Royal Whore

*'It was beyond the compass of art to give this lady her
due, as to her sweetness and exquisite beauty'*
Sir Peter Lely, portrait painter,
on Barbara Villiers

THE KING RODE into London with his two brothers, the duke
of York and the duke of Gloucester, on his thirtieth birthday, 29
May 1660. Huge crowds had greeted him along the way with a
mixture of cheerfulness and curiosity, since few had ever seen him
before and they knew little about him. Charles himself was wryly
amused by his reception, remarking that it must have been his
own fault he had stayed away so long, since he was evidently very
popular with the English people. A Kentish gentleman, Sir Edward
Dering, voiced the general delight of long-suffering royalists when
he claimed, 'there never was in any nation so much joy both
inwardly felt and outwardly expressed as was in this kingdom
from the day of his majesty's landing at Dover to his coming to
London.'[1] The earl of Leicester, disgruntled with both sides during
the Civil Wars, hurried from his Penshurst Place estate in Kent
to wait on the king, though he sounded a less effusive note than
Dering in his diary: 'The king, Charles II, made his entry into
London and passed to Whitehall, where the House of Peers and
House of Commons severally met and saluted his majesty and

welcomed him with orations by the Speakers . . . I saluted his
majesty among the rest and kissed his hand, but there was so
great disorder and confusion that the king scarce knew or took
particular notice of anybody.' The lack of organization and sheer
unfamiliarity with many of those present clearly distracted the
king. He wanted to be seen and his grasp of the importance of
public display was acute, but despite the aura of bonhomie that
he sought to exude as his reign progressed, he was never truly a
man of the people. The pushing and shoving of his first official
function in his capital was not forgotten. In the future, such events
would be handled in a way that preserved his majesty in a more
fitting manner.

Not everyone shared Sir Edward Dering's rosy view of the
king's restoration. 'There is none that love him but drunk whores
and whoremongers', claimed Margaret Dixon of Newcastle upon
Tyne. Margaret's outburst encompassed detrimental remarks about
Charles II's Scottish heritage as well as his morals. She demanded
to know whether there was 'not some Englishman more fit to
make a king than a Scot?' She did not think much of the Stuart
dynasty and feared that the new monarch would 'set on fire the
three kingdoms as his father before him has done.'² The Civil
Wars could not so easily be forgotten for Margaret or a considerable number of others, both Puritan and Catholic. They had, as
yet, nothing specific to fear, since the king's promises in the
Declaration of Breda, signed shortly before he left the Netherlands
for England, were so vague that no firm political or religious
direction could be read into them. It is hard to avoid the impression that, on his restoration, neither Charles II nor his country
had much idea what to expect of the other. His reputation, when
it came to women, preceded him. Pretty much everything else
was a blank canvas.

Though not obvious to his subjects, the experience of exile
had profoundly affected him. Charles left England as a handsome
boy in 1646, to be thrown on the mercy of quarrelsome courtiers
and an interfering mother. For the next fourteen years, he had

wandered around Europe, living on the grace and favour of other rulers, chronically short of money, clinging to the rites of kingship without the reality and keeping his views – if, indeed, he had any – very much to himself. The Restoration changed his physical circumstances but not his personality. He returned as a man no longer in the first flush of youth, swarthy but still impressive in appearance, full of superficial goodwill, relieved to have finally regained his throne. He was weary, cynical and apparently without an agenda, apart from enjoying the benefits of luxury and power. His pursuit of these related goals would define his reign, yet he could not escape their concomitants – the need for money, managing the competing ambitions of advisers in whom he actually had little confidence, the relationship between the Crown and Parliament, and the vexed questions of religion and the succession.

In the summer of 1660, he seemed generally well intentioned, though not towards the men who had been responsible for his father's execution, whom he was determined to pursue to the grisly end that the law meted out to traitors. Beyond that, he was giving little away. Marriage was, of course, an inevitability, but he could afford to wait to find the most advantageous bride, and why would he hurry, when there was such easy access between his Whitehall Palace and Mrs Palmer's house on King Street? It has been said that Charles II's approach to kingship was 'the politics of pleasure', that he deliberately set out to undermine conventional morals, to demonstrate his power and virility through the number of his mistresses and illegitimate children while presiding over a court famed for its debauchery.[3] He could, perhaps, have eventually justified his behaviour in this way, but as a deliberate policy it seems unconvincing. It would make him one of the most wayward, even anarchic monarchs in British history, a man who was trying to destroy the established order rather than restore it. Charles was certainly careless of his own and his country's reputation but time would show that he held fast to the idea of legitimate dynastic descent and that he concealed a deep-seated preference for the

Roman Catholic religion of his French predecessors and also of the brave men and women who helped him escape from England after the disastrous defeat at Worcester in 1651.

History has Charles II confidently treading his first steps on the primrose path of pleasure at the start of his reign, the ravishing Barbara Palmer on his arm. She may have offered sexual distraction but it was also a time of intense personal sorrow. The king lost his beloved younger brother, Henry, duke of Gloucester, and Mary, the Princess Royal, his nearest sibling and frequent companion in exile, to smallpox within three months of each other. Charles was not the sort of man to be told what to do by anyone but their influence was missed and he mourned them greatly. Their deaths may have strengthened Charles's need for Barbara because, though pregnant, she provided diversion at a difficult time. The king's relations with his surviving brother, James, duke of York, were never easy and were complicated in 1660 by the fact that James was obliged to marry Anne Hyde, daughter of the chancellor, who was carrying his child. The baby was a boy and the existence of what was, in effect, an alternative royal family, complete with male heir, was not lost on commentators at the time. Charles's other surviving sister, Princess Henrietta, had been brought up in France by her mother and was soon to marry Louis XIV's younger brother, the duke of Orléans. Barbara, always keen to the threat posed by rivals, must have soon realized that Minette, as Charles called his sister, was the woman he cared for most in all the world and that her influence on him was considerable. But she lived in Paris and only came to England twice during her brother's reign, so in all practical respects she was not to be feared.

What, then, was the nature of the relationship between Charles and Barbara? Politically and culturally, their affair was an important underlying element of the first decade of the Restoration and it took place against a backdrop of plague, fire, political upheaval and war. These were tempestuous times for Britain, and the character and behaviour of Barbara Palmer reflected them to perfection. From the teenage angst of being one among many of the earl of Chesterfield's lovers, she found herself, at the age of twenty, the mistress of an unmarried king. Untroubled by the fact that she herself had a husband, she saw clearly the advantages that could be derived from this situation. The world was at her feet. Money, jewels, titles were all things she could and did expect, as well as patronage, rewards for her wider family (the Villiers did not forget their own) and, above all else, fame. Barbara knew the importance of visibility and how it was fundamental to keeping her position. Other famous royal mistresses, from Rosamond de Clifford to Alice Perrers and Anne Boleyn, had all sought to exploit their success but Barbara Palmer made it an art – quite literally – through her love of public display and the portraits of herself she commissioned. Her desire for celebrity and defiant flouting of convention make her a recognizably modern woman. That she was heartily disliked by almost everyone who had dealings with her seems to have scarcely bothered her but even today's celebrities, accustomed to the viciousness of Twitter, might be shocked by the obscene verses and pamphlets aimed at Barbara. Few women can have had their genitals and sexual proclivities referred to quite so often in print and in such disgusting ways. A poem attributed to George Villiers, duke of Buckingham, the most highly born of her relatives but with whom she eventually fell out, reveals the level of contempt that male courtiers felt for the royal whore. She had been, according to him, a nymphomaniac while still in her mother's womb:

> She was so exquisite a whore
> That in the belly of her mother
> Her c—t she placed so right before,
> Her father f–cked them both together.
> Had she been male as female, without doubt
> She'd acted incest at her coming out,
> And least her Daddy shou'd not f–ck it home
> She frigged his pintle in her mother's womb[4]

For though women had found a voice and a role during the English Revolution, it was not necessarily one that Restoration society, still at root patriarchal, wanted to hear too loudly. Sexual liberation was viewed as acceptable for men but not for any respectable female. Barbara became, very quickly, the royal whore and a natural target for condemnation. Determined as she was to be her own woman, Barbara knew that her future depended on the king. She would need to get as much as she could from him because only then could she become self-reliant.

The affair was often stormy because Barbara was strong willed and passionate, prone to outbursts and threats. Clearly, she was not afraid of Charles and she knew her power over him. Others knew it, too. The historian and churchman, Gilbert Burnet, described Barbara as 'a woman of great beauty but most enormously vicious and ravenous; foolish but imperious, very uneasy to the king and always carrying on intrigues with other men, while yet she pretended she was jealous of him. His passion for her and her strange behaviour towards him did so disorder him that often he was not master of himself, nor capable of minding business, which at so critical a time required great application.'⁵ But knuckling down to governmental business was never going to be Charles II's strong point, though the rest of Burnet's characterization is almost that of an abusive relationship in which the king, and not his mistress, was the victim.

They were both naturally highly sexed and were drawn to each other by lust as much as love. Yet there must have been at least a degree of underlying affection. None of Barbara's letters from this period survive, but one written much later, in 1678, when Barbara's eldest child, Anne (then countess of Sussex), was causing her mother a great deal of trouble, does reveal a deep and long-lasting affection. Referring to the wayward Anne, Barbara wrote, 'Your majesty may be confident that as she is yours I shall always have some remains of that kindness I had formerly, for I can hate nothing that is yours.'⁶ In the early years, before their mutual infidelities and Barbara's moods began to undermine the relationship, the besotted king complied with most of his mistress's demands. At the end of 1661, she and her husband were granted the title of earl and countess of Castlemaine, in County Kerry, in Ireland. His ennoblement, and the knighting of his elder half-brother, Philip Palmer, brought the unhappy Roger little comfort. The warrant describing his title heaped humiliation on him, made out, as it was, 'for Mr Roger Palmer to be an Irish Earl, to him and the heirs of his body gotten on Barbara Palmer his now wife.' Pepys observed in his diary that everybody knew the reason that only Barbara's heirs were to be honoured. The reference to 'his now wife' was an unsubtle indication that the marriage was unlikely to last. Roger Palmer did not want this insulting ennoblement, the final proof, though he did not acknowledge it immediately, that his marriage was a disaster. He never took his seat in the Irish parliament but he found solace in conversion to Catholicism, the faith of his mother. His new religious zeal would, the following year, prove the final straw in his relationship with his wife.

Barbara's first son with the king was born at Roger's King Street house in June 1662, at a time when the court was celebrating the king's recent marriage and anyone of any significance was at Hampton Court with the royal party.[7] By this time, the brazen mistress was so confident of her position that she continued to attend the theatre until a few weeks before her delivery and Charles spent every night with her, though she was eight and a half months pregnant. Barbara even let it be known that she would give birth at Hampton Court, where the royal honeymoon was to take place. Whether her husband or her lover commanded otherwise is not clear but she did not leave London. The king attended an Anglican christening ceremony for the baby at St Margaret's, Westminster on 18 June, in which the question of the child's parentage was conveniently fudged and he was named Charles Palmer, Lord Limerick. What the king did not know, as he stood sponsor with Barbara's aunt, Lady Suffolk, for his bastard child, was that Roger Palmer, preserving the fiction that the baby was his, had already had him baptized into the Catholic faith.

When Barbara found out, a tremendous row ensued and she left their home to go to her uncle, Colonel Villiers, at Richmond Palace. Barbara was good at creating scenes and this one had been a long time coming. According to Pepys, 'she left her lord, carrying away everything in the house; so much as every dish and cloth and servant but the porter. He [Roger] is gone discontent into France, they say to enter a monastery.'[8] As a reversal of the time-honoured trope of an errant wife entering a nunnery, it was rich that the blameless Roger Palmer should be thought a candidate for the religious life. Barbara did return to her husband's house, but their marriage was over. Roger did, indeed, leave for Europe, where he travelled widely, honing his linguistic skills and deepening in his Catholic faith. In England he was pitied and laughed at but in Europe he could give full rein to his interests and abilities. He took service with the Venetian republic and sailed with the admiral of its fleet to the Middle East. Though the couple did not formally separate for another two years, Roger was prudent enough to ensure that he would no longer be held responsible for Barbara's excessive spending. Before he left England, his wife's uncle, the third Viscount Grandison, and her uncle by marriage, the earl of Suffolk, signed an indemnity which made them responsible for debts up to £10,000 contracted by Barbara. The pair remained in control of her financial affairs for many years.

Though she could no longer spend his money, Barbara continued to be an embarrassment to her husband. When he returned to England in 1664, he found that she had given birth to two more children using his surname – a son, Henry, and a daughter, Charlotte – though they were both fathered by the king. This impudence prompted Roger to seek a formal separation. For much of the rest of the decade of the 1660s, while his wife's star was firmly in the ascendant at Charles II's court, he continued to travel, going as far as Constantinople and Jerusalem. He also began a new career, as a writer and Catholic apologist, his lucid and elegant style earning him many admirers. His wife also converted to Catholicism in 1663, the result, it was said, of a brush with death rather than a close reading of the works of the man whose good character she had so flagrantly betrayed.

*

HER POSITION AS the king's mistress made Barbara an important public figure and she understood the need to enhance her visibility as much as possible. Her talents in this respect were outstanding. The hedonism of Charles II's court gave her a platform for display that she exploited to great effect. At court balls, in masques, in theatrical productions and in the royal box, seated between the king and the duke of York, Lady Castlemaine was an almost constant presence, her occasional absences caused only by the demands of childbirth, and from that she always seemed to make a swift recovery, her figure scarcely altered, still radiant and enchanting. Pepys spotted that she partnered the young duke of Monmouth (by now a fixture at court and high in his indulgent father's favour) at a ball on New Year's Eve, 1662, at which the king, very aptly, called for the dance 'Cuckolds All a Row'.[9] Naturally, Barbara had to dress the part for these appearances. When she acted in a performance of Corneille's *Horace* at Whitehall, the jewels she wore, which had been taken from the crown jewels in the Tower of London, were said by John Evelyn to be worth more than £40,000.[10] Some estimates put their value much higher and she was said to have far outshone the new queen, Catherine of Braganza, whom Charles had married in May 1662. This ostentatious dazzling was repeated later in the same year at the queen's birthday ball, where Barbara 'appeared so glorious in jewels that she was the wonder of all that saw her', in stones estimated to be worth £50,000.[11] Her dresses were equally admired and all of this was provided by the king to show her off to his courtiers and to satisfy her own determination that she would eclipse any other woman who might attract his attention. The admiration of the news reports was shared by other commentators. Pepys, somewhat creepily, was driven into raptures by the mere sight of her underwear hanging on a washing line: 'in the privy garden [of Whitehall] saw the finest smocks and linen petticoats of my Lady Castlemaine's, edged with rich lace at the bottoms, that I ever saw; and did me good to look upon them.'[12]

These high-profile appearances were very much of the moment but Barbara was determined that her beauty and social prominence should be celebrated for posterity. She was an important patron of the arts and particularly of Sir Peter Lely, the leading court painter of the Restoration. Lely, a Dutchman by birth, was official painter to the court, as his countryman Anthony van Dyck had been to that of the king's father, Charles I. Arriving in England at the start of the Civil Wars, he was favoured by grandees who supported Parliament, notably Algernon Percy, earl of Northumberland, who commissioned portraits of the younger royal children and the double portrait of Charles I with the duke of York. Despite Lely having painted Oliver Cromwell (the face probably based on a miniature by another artist, Samuel Cooper), the duke of York did not forget him, and York and his first wife, Anne Hyde, were Lely's chief patrons during the 1660s. Lady Castlemaine was not far behind. And while Anne Hyde was commissioning a series of portraits of the leading ladies of the court (Barbara was included but was only one of eleven sitters), known collectively as the Windsor Beauties,[13] the countess herself was keeping Lely and his studio busy with four portraits of herself, in classic and religious depictions. Barbara chose to have herself painted as Minerva, complete with elaborate feathered headdress, in a gold silk dress, staff in hand. As Minerva was the Roman goddess of wisdom and warfare, this was a bold statement. Barbara was undoubtedly intelligent and cunning but her intellect was not wide-ranging. The association with warfare, however, certainly sent a message that she was a lady whom rivals challenged at their peril.

It is the religious connotations of the other key Lely portraits that still have the power to shock. He painted Barbara as the saint for whom she was named, an early Christian martyr from the Middle East, supposedly executed by her own father and who may never have really existed. Untroubled by such questions of historical accuracy, Barbara was also painted as St Catherine, another popular female saint of the time. Most dramatically of all, she posed as St Mary Magdalene and as the Madonna. These two paintings have been described as audacious, scandalous and blasphemous. They still have the power to shock with their mixture of witty defiance of accepted standards and the mirror they hold up to how one woman personified a court glorifying in its own corruption. In the Magdalene portrait, a casually sexy Lady Castlemaine, her head tilted to one side, cheek resting on her right hand, hair loose and flowing, gazes sleepily at the viewer through those arresting come-to-bed eyes. The folds of her rich bronze dress hint at a trim but voluptuous figure, unchanged by pregnancy, while the stole carelessly draped around her shoulder is suggestively pulled across her groin, in a reminder that this is where her true power lies. It was probably painted around 1662, when she was an unstoppable force and her hold over the recently married king was absolute. It has been noted that 'what the symbolic portraiture also capitalizes on, outrageously, is the notion that the history of this whore and her royal lord might properly call to mind the story of Mary Magdalene and her Lord and Redeemer.'[14] Two years later, Barbara and Lely went one step further in mocking the idea of good taste when she posed with her son, Charles Fitzroy, the baby her angry husband had hastily christened as a Catholic, in the guise of Madonna and Child.[15]

Barbara sits in the classic Renaissance pose for this subject, on the edge of a chair, with her little son, notably more like a real child than in many other depictions, on her left, leaning towards her while perched on a wooden bench. His chubby, handsome little face and red lips give him the air of a cherub. But Barbara is looking ahead, not at him, though one hand is on his waist, more to balance him in an otherwise awkward position rather than in any great show of maternal love. Her gaze is not devoid of tenderness but there is calculation behind it and a hint of triumphalism. She is dressed in red and blue, the colours often

associated with Italian portraits of the Madonna and Child, her
hair caught up in a carefully draped veil, which sets off its dark
auburn colour. Nothing is left to chance in this picture and its
lack of spontaneity makes it look rather stilted. Yet it is easy to
tell that Barbara was very pleased with it. The heavy-lidded,
almond-shaped eyes and long nose so admired by Lely are prominent features and the mouth has just a hint of a smile. She does
not seem to have minded showing the world that she was already
putting on weight, as her face at this angle cannot hide the beginnings of a double chin. The Restoration favoured plump women
and it is unlikely that Barbara was concerned by a little broadening
of her figure. And she was also, at the same time, broadening her
interests. A woman as conscious of her status as Lady Castlemaine
was always bound to take a lively interest in politics and to use
her influence as effectively as she could.

*

THE POLITICIAN WHO suffered most from Barbara's relationship
with Charles II was the king's veteran councillor, Edward Hyde,
earl of Clarendon. The return of the king in 1660 vindicated all
that Hyde (who was made earl of Clarendon in 1662) had endured
and struggled for in the years of exile, and his position at first
seemed inviolable. Believing that the rule of law and justice within
a monarchical framework, together with the restoration of the
Church of England, were the keystones of the English constitution, Hyde received the office of lord chancellor almost as if he
was divinely ordained for it. His capacity for hard work, exceptional
powers of drafting and incisive legal mind gave him the edge over
potential rivals at the outset of Charles II's reign. His political
acumen, however, was less highly developed. Believing that dedication to office would raise him above court faction was a vain
hope and his experience of the squabbles of the royalists during
and after the Civil Wars should have better prepared him for what
might follow when the world had turned again. Yet he could be
excused for not anticipating the one development of 1660, affecting

his own family, which would complicate and even compromise his position within months of the Restoration. Hyde was almost the last to learn that his daughter, Anne, had become pregnant by the duke of York and was so appalled by the news that he initially opposed the idea that James should marry her and, in a notable display of paternal rejection, suggested she be put in the Tower of London and even executed. The elevation of Princess Mary Stuart's maid of honour to become a member of the royal family was genuinely not what her father desired. It laid him open, at a difficult time, to charges of seeking to enhance his role in an underhand way and even that he might be aiming, through Anne, to put his own descendants on the throne. Charles II was in good health but it would only take an accident or an unpredictable illness, such as the smallpox that had carried off Princess Mary and Prince Henry, for the duke of York to become king and his offspring with the new duchess to inherit in the future. Though the son born to Anne Hyde, given the title of duke of Cambridge, died as a child, her daughters, Mary and Anne, would both become queens regnant.

Clarendon's enemies, notably the Queen Mother, Henrietta Maria, and two of the duke of York's servants, Charles Berkeley and Henry Jermyn, cast aspersions on Anne's good name while James, who had married her secretly in September 1660, dithered over whether to repudiate her. His brother informed him that he must honour his commitments and so the chancellor's daughter entered into the highest echelons of the royal family, a role which she took to with aplomb, though her husband never entertained the idea of being faithful to her and seemed to wish to emulate Charles as much as he could in this respect. All of this the countess of Castlemaine, whose name would soon be linked with that of Henry Jermyn, watched with interest. She does not seem to have felt threatened in any way by Anne and later in the 1660s she would ally herself closely with the Yorks, but she soon became an enemy of Hyde's for other reasons.

The truth of the matter was that Clarendon and the earl of

Southampton, his chief ally on Charles II's council, disapproved of Barbara from the outset of her liaison with the king. He refused to let his wife visit her and certainly never tried to get her to influence Charles on his behalf. She reciprocated his hostility in the dramatic way that was so typical of her. In September 1662, it was reported to the duke of Ormond that she had publicly stated she hoped to see Clarendon's head on a stake outside Westminster.[16] Ill feeling between the pair inevitably seeped into the sphere of court appointments. Barbara, recognizing that the best way to remain prominent at court was to have an official role of her own, was well aware of the chancellor's reluctance to support her appointment as lady of the bedchamber to the queen in the same year.[17] Her obvious course was to continue to side with Clarendon's opponents, who included the rising politician Sir Henry Bennet, soon to be ennobled as the earl of Arlington, a supple operator who had ingratiated himself with Charles II during the royalist exile. Bennet was working with Berkeley to isolate Clarendon and remove the old advisers who had given so much to the king in the previous decade. Sir Kenelm Digby and Sir Edward Nicholas were both removed from office. Barbara did not always succeed in her political machinations. Her support of the earl of Bristol, who tried to get Clarendon impeached in 1663, nearly caused a rift between the countess and the king, who was also jealous of Bristol's frequent visits to Barbara's house. Undeterred, Barbara continued to let her home be used as a meeting place for the chancellor's opponents. The French ambassador believed that the 'debauches', as he called them, which took place there every evening, were part of a concerted plan to destroy Clarendon.[18] Whatever really happened at these rowdy dinners, frequented by the louche duke of Lauderdale, Charles II's enforcer in Scotland, and Anthony Ashley Cooper (later earl of Shaftesbury), we do not know, but dislike of Clarendon was common to those who attended.

The chancellor survived until 1667, when the king asked him to resign. Pepys wrote that his downfall 'was certainly designed in my lady Castlemaine's chamber.'[19] The king's surgeon told Pepys that 'when he went from the king . . . she was in bed (although about 12 o'clock) and ran out in her smock into her aviary looking into Whitehall garden, and thither her woman brought her night-gown and [she] stood joying herself at the old man's going away. And several of the gallants of Whitehall (of which there were many staying to see the Chancellor's return) did talk to her . . . telling her she was the Bird of Paradise.' Clarendon himself told the story rather differently. He recalled that, as he left Whitehall, he saw Barbara, Arlington and Baptist May, who had been appointed keeper of the privy purse at Barbara's suggestion, looking 'out of her open window with great gaiety and triumph, which all people observed.'[20] He did not add the observation, attributed to him by Nathaniel Crew, that, on looking up and seeing this leering trio, he said, 'O, Madam, is it you? Pray remember that if you live, you will grow old.'[21]

Clarendon intended, at first, to fight on and he had the support of the duke of York. Charles II, tired of his faithful supporter, easily swayed by the ill-intentioned clique with which he surrounded himself, wanted him gone. Impeachment proceedings were begun in Parliament, where an unexpected degree of support for this great servant of the Crown surprised his enemies and led to a procedural stand-off with the House of Lords, who brought in a charge of high treason. Deserted by the king, the fifty-eight-year-old Clarendon left England in November 1667. He hoped to return from his banishment in France but he never did, dying in Rouen in 1674, but not before he had written his *Life*, a more personal version of the *History of the Great Rebellion*, which he had begun on the Isles of Scilly in 1646. The *History* is the first great narrative history of its kind in the English language, still one of the major primary sources on the Civil Wars despite its inevitable partiality for the royalist side.

Barbara had seen off the most distinguished of her enemies but the unreliable Arlington soon deserted her for good. Nor would she recover the support of her cousin, Buckingham, with whom she had a volatile relationship throughout the 1660s.

*

BUCKINGHAM WAS ONE of the great wits of Charles II's court but his personality and beliefs made him a dangerous ally. He shared many personality traits with his Villiers cousin; they were both flamboyant, even outrageous, keen to be at the centre of power and not afraid to speak out. He believed that his birth warranted the highest office but was often at odds with other politicians, who were suspicious of his motives and uncomfortably aware of his powers of oratory as well as the effectiveness of his writings. Though the king laughed heartily at Buckingham's side-splitting mimicry – no figure in public life or at the court was safe from the duke's wicked ability to depict them, always to their disadvantage – Charles II never entirely trusted him and Buckingham had, in the past, been as contemptuous of him as he was of many others, remarking that, after the Battle of Worcester, the king was probably 'lying hid with some gent and lying with his wife more happy than if he were on his throne.'[22] His sneering may be partly explained by the king's refusal to appoint him as commander-in-chief of the royalist army in 1651. There were questions over his return to England in the 1650s, his connections with the Protectorate and his marriage to Mary Fairfax. Buckingham courted Mary with all the zeal of a Cavalier poet. If even Bishop Burnet found Buckingham 'a man of noble presence and that has an air that at first strikes all that see him; he has a flame in his wit that is inimitable',[23] it is hardly surprising that the rather plain Mary Fairfax, educated by Andrew Marvell and brought up in a pious Presbyterian household, was eager to give him her hand. The first years of their marriage, in which Buckingham was a dutiful son-in-law and affectionate husband, gave no indication of how his subsequent behaviour would break her heart.

The duke was a complex man. Naturally tolerant in religious matters, some people thought him a crypto-Catholic while others described him as being part of a 'Presbyterian gang'. He quelled a rising in Yorkshire, where he was lord-lieutenant of the West Riding, in 1662 with minimum retribution and he was always popular with his men. He believed it was his birthright to be at the centre of affairs and was active on the Privy Council, yet he wished to serve as a volunteer on the duke of York's flagship in the Dutch War of 1665 and was furious when he was given a ship of his own because York, perhaps anxious about the distraction Buckingham might cause, did not want him so close. His relations with the king's heir remained awkward thereafter. While Londoners died in their thousands from the worst ever outbreak of bubonic plague and the seamen Buckingham had disdained to join starved through lack of pay, the duke was keeping the king, Lady Castlemaine and the court (removed to Hampton Court, at a safe distance from the epidemic) in stitches with his impressions. 'His special talent,' wrote Anthony Hamilton, 'was for catching hold of and imitating in their presence anything that happened to be absurd in other people's behaviour or any peculiarity of speech they had, without letting them notice it. In short, he was apt at counterfeiting so many different parts, and with so much grace and humour, that when he wished to make himself agreeable, it was difficult to dispense with his company.'[24]

After the Great Fire of 1666, Buckingham turned on those he had consorted with at Hampton Court the previous summer. In Parliament, he spearheaded opposition to the government, criticizing its management of the recent Dutch War, which had led to the destruction of the English fleet in the Medway and national humiliation, attacking its handling of finance and supporting the introduction of a bill to ban the import of Irish cattle, which he believed would be detrimental to his tenants in the north of England. In so doing, he managed to insult the Irish so badly that the duke of Ormond's son, Lord Ossory, challenged him to a duel. Both men ended up spending time in the Tower of London. This episode caused a furious row between the king and Lady Castlemaine, who only the year previously had fallen out spectacularly with her cousin.

It was described as 'a mortal quarrel'. Yet better relations were swiftly established and Barbara pleaded Buckingham's cause so persistently that the king grew angry, calling her 'a whore and a jade'. He soon relented and was reconciled with Buckingham in Barbara's apartments.[25] But Buckingham's reconciliation with his kinswoman was to prove only temporary and his assessment of her depravity would make Charles II's outburst seem mild by comparison. Their alliance over Clarendon lasted only a few months. Buckingham did not necessarily view Barbara's hold over the king as wholly advantageous to his interests and was keen to encourage the king's enthusiasm for the theatre, and especially his monarch's growing fascination with the actresses Nell Gwyn and Moll Davis.[26] They were not the first alternatives to the monopoly of his cousin that he had sponsored, and his final judgement of her is made abundantly plain in the poem quoted earlier.

Soon Buckingham was involved in a scandal to match anything that Barbara had done. He began an affair in 1666 with Anna-Maria Brudenell, countess of Shrewsbury, a court beauty who had, like Barbara, made a career as a temptress and was perfectly accustomed to the adoration of men and their compulsion to fight over her favours. Her husband challenged Buckingham at the beginning of 1668 and, in the melee surrounding this winter duel, with three men fighting on each side, one person was killed and Shrewsbury himself seriously wounded. He later died of his injuries. Unabashed, the duke moved his mistress into his London residence, Wallingford House. When his wife objected that she could not live under the same roof as his mistress, Pepys reported that Buckingham replied, with casual cruelty, 'Why, Madam, I did think so, and therefore have ordered your coach to be ready, to carry you to your father's.'[27] The affair damaged Buckingham's standing and his decision to bury his illegitimate son by Anna-Maria in Westminster Abbey outraged public opinion. It would, in the end, contribute significantly to the collapse of his political hopes.

*

BY THE LATE 1660s, Barbara's relationship with the king was beginning to fade, though it was not yet completely over. She had seen off criticism from female courtiers such as Lady Gerard and Lady Harvey, both of whom had felt the king's keen displeasure at their temerity in attacking his *maîtresse-en-titre*. This unpleasantness was more than women's squabbles since both ladies, whatever their personal disapproval of Barbara, were the mouthpieces of political factions at odds with the king and court. And on occasion Barbara's opponents resorted to more sinister methods. Not long after giving birth to Charlotte Fitzroy, her second daughter with the king, Lady Castlemaine was returning one evening to her apartments in Whitehall through St James's Park, with only a maid and a page in attendance, when she was accosted by three masked noblemen who verbally abused her and threatened her with the same fate as Jane Shore, the unpopular mistress of Edward IV, whose body was said to have ended up on a dunghill. This was not the first such comparison, and it struck home. Normally so thick skinned, the countess was sufficiently shaken by the incident to pass out when she got back to her rooms and Charles II rushed to support her. His presence seems to have restored her equilibrium quickly, though the men who had menaced her were never caught, despite St James's Park being swiftly sealed off.[28]

By now, the future of her children was a prime consideration for Barbara. She was confident that her bastards with the king would be acknowledged and given titles and lands. Her maternal instincts in this respect were strong, though whether she was a loving mother is another matter. When Charles questioned the paternity of her last child with him while she was still pregnant, she threatened to dash the baby's brains out if he would not acknowledge it. Her other quarrels with Charles were about their mutual infidelities. Barbara's name had long been associated with that of Henry Jermyn and she took other lovers, including the acrobat Jacob Hall and the actor Charles Hart. The king, meanwhile, had casual liaisons with Jane Roberts and Winifred Wells, though neither was a threat to Barbara. He was also, throughout this period, pursuing Frances Teresa Stuart, another of his wife's ladies, and Barbara seems to have regarded her, at least initially, as a much more serious rival.[29] For most of the first decade of Charles II's reign, Barbara was dominant, using all her skills of networking (she did have female supporters, most notably her aunt, Lady Suffolk, and, towards the end of the decade, the duchess of York), sexual allure and self-promotion to maintain an unrivalled position at court. Her fame – or infamy, as others saw it – was hard won and came at a price, for the one court that Barbara never managed to capture was that of public opinion.

It could, of course, be argued that she cared nothing for what the population at large thought about her but the London crowd was a force that those in power ignored at their peril. The full extent of Barbara's unpopularity and the popular criticism of the court and its decadent lifestyle became apparent in March 1668, in the Bawdy House Riots, several days of unrest in London, when apprentices, fed up with their conditions, attacked the brothels whose prices they could not afford and held pitched battles with the city's militias who were trying to disperse them. There was a long history of riots on Shrove Tuesdays, with pros-titutes being a common target, but the level of disaffection in 1668 amounted to something more serious. At first, the authorities tried to make light of this mob violence. Pepys reported that 'the Duke of York and all with him this morning were full of the talk of the prentices . . . some blood hath been spilt but a great many houses pulled down . . . the Duke of York was mighty merry at that of Damaris Page's, the great bawd of the seamen.' The duke was less amused to have lost £15 a year in wine licences as the result of attacks on his property and Pepys himself sounded a more sombre note when he remarked, 'it was said here that these idle fellows have had the confidence to say that they did ill in contenting themselves in pulling down the little bawdy-houses and did not go and pull down the great bawdy-house at Whitehall . . . this doth make the courtiers ill at ease to see this spirit among

people . . . and then they do say that there are men of understanding among them, that have been of Cromwell's army . . .'[30]
This last comment is a telling indication of the insecurity of
England more than a decade after Cromwell's death as well as
reminding us that the enduring image of Charles II as a clever
and popular monarch, whose peccadilloes were viewed as endearing
by his subjects, is at considerable variance with reality.

The riots provided an opportunity for wider condemnation of
the court and a full-scale onslaught on Lady Castlemaine herself.
The Poor Whores Petition, addressed 'To the most splendid,
illustrious, serene and eminent lady of pleasure, the Countess of
Castlemaine' and purported to come from 'the undone company
of poor distressed whores, bawds, pimps and panders', is a satirical
libel written by an unknown author. It may well have been sponsored by the two most wealthy and important bawds in London,
Madam Cresswell and Damaris Page, but its underlying anti-
Catholicism is significant and suggests the involvement of one of
Cresswell's influential clients in the City of London. It is a short
document of just one page but effectively written. The petitioners
begin by noting that they have 'been for a long time connived at
and countenanced in the practice of our venereal pleasures (a trade
wherein your ladyship hath great experience and for your diligence
therein have arrived to a high and eminent advancement for these
last years.' Proceeding to note that the loss of their trade might
impede their ability to purchase medical help to recover from the
various sexually transmitted diseases that went with their trade (a
nasty hint that Castlemaine might suffer such inconveniences
herself), they issued a veiled threat to Barbara's safety, 'For should
your eminency but once fall into these rough hands, you may
expect no more favour than they have shown unto us poor infer-
ior whores.'[31]

However vexed Barbara might have been by the Poor Whores
Petition, she must have been even more aggrieved by the equally
satirical response, attributed to her, entitled 'The gracious answer
of the most illustrious lady of pleasure the Countess of Castel'.

The writer, who evidently knew the countess well, wreaked further damage on her reputation by depicting her as greedy, 'wonderfully decked with jewels and diamonds which the subjects of this kingdom have paid for', sexually promiscuous and nepotistic. Frequently using the royal 'we', the countess is made to acknowledge that 'we have always (without our husband) satisfied ourself with the delights of Venus; and in our husband's absence have had numerous offspring (who are bountifully and nobly provided for).' Moreover, and much more overtly than in the Poor Whores Petition, Lady Castlemaine's supposed reply viciously attacked the Protestant sects while promising to give full support to the Catholic Church, whose 'venereal pleasure, accompanied with looseness, debauchery and prophaneness are not such heinous crimes and crying sins'.[32] Finally, the writer urged the poor whores not to worry because the French would come and deal with the apprentices – a comment likely to feed xenophobia.

The king's response to this embarrassment was to buy a property for Barbara, Berkshire House, which backed on to St James's Park, and grant her a pension of £4,700 a year, paid out of post office funds and managed by her uncles, Viscount Grandison and Colonel Villiers. This looks like complete royal defiance of public opinion but it was also a way of drawing a line in their relationship. Their affair had cooled. Charles II understood very well his mistress's rapaciousness. If things were to end without tantrums and further public disaffection, he needed to let her down gently. He had one last gift to bestow.

CHAPTER SIX

The Duchess

'Paint Castlemaine in colours that will hold
(Her, not her picture, for she now grows old)'
Andrew Marvell,
'Last Instructions to a Painter', 1667

WHEN MARVELL WROTE these and the excoriating lines that follow, Barbara was, in fact, only twenty-seven years old and many thought her beauty undimmed. But she knew that she had never had a complete monopoly of the king's affections. She was well aware of the other women he pursued or who were dangled in front of him by courtiers jealous of her hold on the monarch. Expectations of exclusivity were not part of her calculations, nor, indeed, of his. The thing that bothered Charles II most about Barbara's behaviour was not her infidelity but her lack of discretion. 'Madam,' he told her, 'all I ask of you for your own sake is, live so for the future as to make the least noise you can, and I care not who you love.'¹ He could have put it more crudely (and perhaps did, in person), for Barbara had not really been in love since her affair with Chesterfield and that was more teenage infatuation than genuine devotion. What Barbara wanted from her royal lover, as the new decade of the 1670s approached, was assurance that her future outside his bed would be generously funded and that her status in society acknowledged by a title greater than that of a mere countess. She was rewarded in August 1670 by being made Duchess of Cleveland in her own right. In the same year, Barbara's financial situation was improved through the award of a series of grants, including the office of keeper of Hampton Court and the ownership of one of Henry VIII's favourite palaces, Nonsuch in Surrey. Though this did not completely mark the end of her influence, or her appearances at court, her physical relationship with the king had run its course.

As for Charles II himself, it is easy to think that sex was always his major preoccupation because this is how the 'Merrie Monarch' is remembered. The reality, as the king contemplated the second decade of his reign, was much more complicated. He had survived plague, fire, war, riots and the occasional uprising. By 1670, his stock abroad, which had plummeted, was recovering, and the scruffy duke of Lauderdale, his near-tyrannical lieutenant in Scotland, had reduced this troublesome kingdom to complete subjugation. Even relations between the king and the House of Commons were improving. Yet his finances remained inadequate, his politicians corrupt and quarrelsome, and his subjects, not to mention his own immediate family, divided over religion. His hopes of having a legitimate heir had disappeared and the issue of the succession would haunt him till his death. The ability to manage people was perhaps his greatest asset, while keeping his own counsel was, by now, second nature. His most recent biographer called him a gambling man and Charles certainly knew how to keep his cards close to his chest.[2] If he examined them closely, he must have realized that they were not very good ones. He would be obliged to improvise and, essentially, to make policy himself while encouraging his politicians to think that they were influential by playing them off against one another. But most of all he needed money. The Dutch Wars of the 1660s had bankrupted the exchequer and, since Parliament could never be relied upon to vote for taxation without attaching strings, the king had no scruples about obtaining it from other sources. Unlike his father, who had resurrected ancient laws to fund himself in the 1630s, Charles II decided to look elsewhere for financial backing.

France, home to his beloved sister, Henrietta, duchess of Orléans, and ruled by his cousin, Louis XIV, was rich and always in search of allies in its struggles with other European powers. It seemed the most promising source of funds and Louis had made the first approach. French support would, though, come at a price and that price would need to be kept secret from all but a very few trusted advisers at home. It might also bring him into conflict once more with the United Provinces of the Netherlands, where his nephew, William III of Orange, was recovering the power of the hereditary office of stadtholder in a carefully choreographed dance with his country's commitment to republicanism. Charles, mindful of his promise in 1660 to his dying sister, Mary, that he would look out for his nephew's interests, always tried to separate his policy towards the Dutch government from professions of personal regard for the young man. This convenient distinction was often lost on William, who increasingly saw himself as a figurehead for the Protestant cause against the might of Catholic France. He would have been even more disenchanted had he known of the secret treaty concluded between England and France on 22 May 1670, which committed the English to support France in a war against the Dutch, with the sole objective of destroying the republic. Given the fraught nature of Anglo-Dutch relations for much of the mid-seventeenth century and the Sun King's overweening ambition, this stipulation was predictable. England was also to provide 4,000 infantry and sixty ships to bolster the French military capacity.

Much more shocking was Charles's agreement that he would declare his conversion to Catholicism and return his country to the old religion. Though this undoubtedly pleased his brother, the duke of York, who was not immediately in the king's confidence about the preliminary negotiations for the treaty, and Charles's Catholic secretary, Sir Thomas Clifford, who played a major part in the discussions, it would have been political dynamite if even

a hint of it had slipped into the public domain.³ Neither realized
that it was a piece of breathtaking cynicism. Charles, whatever
his private inclinations, had no intention of ever making such a
claim, which would have endangered his hold on the throne.
Though he seems to have favoured greater toleration for both
Catholics and Protestant Nonconformists, he knew that any public
pronouncement of conversion to a form of worship abandoned
more than a century before would be at best unwise and at worst
catastrophic. It was not worth the risk. What he really wanted
was the subsidy Louis XIV offered him, his insurance that he
could continue to rule without a recalcitrant Parliament, should
the need arise. The subsidy amounted to £230,000 a year (about
£34 million today), plus an extra £160,000 (£24 million) when
Charles's change of faith was announced.

While Charles was sorting out his settlement with the new
duchess of Cleveland, the duchess of Orléans, or Madame, as
the second lady of France was officially known, arrived at Dover
for the signing of the treaty. There was to be a much more bland
official version but it was the secret one that had involved her
most. Brought up as a Catholic by Queen Henrietta Maria, in
defiance of her father's commands, Charles I's youngest child
was a committed Catholic who shared the desire of her brother-
in-law, Louis XIV, to see the Dutch state annihilated and France
triumphant in Europe. Though historical novelists and salacious
television series have characterized her as an empty-headed flirt,
Madame was an intelligent young woman, trapped in a ghastly
marriage, who found her métier in undertaking a difficult diplomatic mission in which she hoped to please both the brother
she had adored since she was a child and the French king, with
whom she was rumoured to have earlier enjoyed a passionate
affair. Louis was as fond of women as Charles, and the beauty
of some of his mistresses was legendary, but it is unlikely that
the reed-thin Minette was among them. Charles II could console
himself for the fading of his affair with Barbara Palmer in the
arms of actresses and other passing ladies but it was his sister

he really wanted to see in the summer of 1670. Their reunion was to prove bittersweet. Minette was never healthy and the stress of her marriage to Louis XIV's bisexual brother had been compounded by successive pregnancies that weakened her still further. She survived the journey back to France by barely a month, dying in agony, claiming that she had been poisoned, though an autopsy showed that an ulcer had perforated, leading to peritonitis. Charles was inconsolable. He and James were now the only two survivors of the six children that Charles I left behind when he was executed in 1649.

His grief did not, however, entirely overcome his baser urges. Minette had brought with her to Dover a lady-in-waiting who was the daughter of an impoverished family from the lower ranks of the nobility in Brittany. Though the duchess of Cleveland did not know it yet, this young woman, whose name was Louise de Kéroualle, would soon replace her as *maîtresse-en-titre*, and her greed, ambition and meddling in politics would far outweigh any kind of political influence Barbara had exercised.[4]

*

BARBARA'S OWN RELATIONS with French ambassadors had been cordial and she had received presents of money and finery, including an expensive pair of gloves. In order to keep in with Madame, she had sent the king's sister an expensive jewel, an action which seems as impertinent, given their difference in rank, as it was unnecessary, for Henrietta hardly had need of extra gems. It does, however, illustrate the quasi-regal status that Barbara had assumed during her affair with the king. But she had always been too volatile a person for the French to view her as being reliably on their side and, indeed, she seems not to have taken much interest in foreign policy. In the difficult last years of the 1670s, she stayed close to the duke and duchess of York, whose household offered something approaching an alternative court to that of the king's. It is easy to overlook the importance of the Yorks at this time, but their favour was eagerly sought and it was from their sphere that Barbara found a new lover soon after the king ended their affair.

John Churchill had been born in east Devon in 1650, the son of a royalist army officer who had lost everything in the service of the king during the Civil Wars. His father's situation began to improve after the Restoration and, by the middle of the 1660s, John had followed his elder sister, Arabella, into the household of the duke of York, as a page. Both of these appointments had been made with the help of Lady Castlemaine, who was a distant cousin, further evidence of Barbara's far-reaching networks and her desire to help her kin. Young Churchill's prospects in the Yorks' service were undoubtedly improved by the fact that Arabella had become the duke's mistress (James, like his brother, viewed his wife's ladies as extracurricular sport). Tall, ungainly and un-attractive, Arabella only came to the duke's attention when she fell off a horse and was discovered stunned and with her skirts up around her waist, revealing a pair of legs so beautiful that the duke was instantly smitten. It was not a temporary fixation as they went on to have five children together, much to the anguish of the duchess of York. Meanwhile, the duke was instrumental in starting John Churchill out on a military career that would see him become one of Britain's most famous military leaders and bring him and Britain great prestige in the early eighteenth century.

Barbara was also smitten by her relative, who was as handsome as his sister was plain. His future wife, Sarah Jennings, said he was 'as beautiful as an angel.' Contemporaries remembered in glowing terms his personal attractions and charm: 'Of all the men that I ever knew in my life (and I knew him extremely well),' wrote the earl of Chesterfield's grandson, 'the late duke of Marlborough possessed all the graces in the highest degree.'[5] The ten-year age gap between them was irrelevant to a woman of Barbara's confidence and sexuality. John Churchill was just what she needed after her affair with the king had cooled. Charles does not seem to have taken well to being replaced by a much younger man and he disapproved of the generous gifts of money that

Barbara lavished on her lover. Though Charles could not stop the affair, he did, for a time, block further military promotion for Churchill, which had been sought by the duke of York, and he opposed his brother's wish to appoint him as gentleman of the bedchamber. The court was alive with gossip and it was believed the liaison between Churchill and the duchess of Cleveland was the root of the king's displeasure but, as Charles always thought little of his brother's judgement, this may also have been a factor. When Barbara gave birth to her final child, a daughter to whom she gave her own name, in the summer of 1672, it was generally assumed that Churchill was the father. Barbara never claimed that the child was the king's but she did not publicly acknowledge who the father was and Churchill himself never came forward to accept responsibility for the infant. His critics at the time, of whom there were plenty, believed that he cared little for Barbara and less for their child, but that, cash-strapped as he always seemed to be at this time, his primary interest was in the duchess of Cleveland's money.

Churchill must also have been aware that he did not have a monopoly of the duchess's affections. Within months of giving birth to Barbara, she began an affair with the handsome and witty playwright William Wycherley, who dedicated his first play, *Love in a Wood*, to her. The duchess enjoyed verbal sparring, often of a very coarse kind, and Wycherley was a good match for her in this. He was also renowned for his sexual prowess. He benefited from her patronage and she from the spice he added to her life. It may also have been her way of demonstrating to the king that he was not the only one who had an interest in the stage. Charles had been consorting with actresses for several years.

The arrival of her new daughter and the fact that Nell Gwyn, an actress who became the king's mistress in 1669, had recently given birth to a son, spurred Barbara into taking action. She determined to ensure the future of her own children with Charles. They must make advantageous marriages and this would require the king's support. The idea of arranging marriages for children under twelve is offensive to modern sensibilities but it was seen as an essential aspect of parental responsibility among the upper classes in those days. Although Charles II did not acknowledge Barbara's second son, Henry, as his until the summer of 1672 (a busy time for the duchess), he made up for his lingering doubts about the boy's paternity by giving him the title of earl of Euston and the surname Fitzroy, which became the surname of all Barbara's children by the king. Shortly afterwards, the nine-year-old Henry was married to five-year-old Isabella Bennet, daughter of Charles II's leading minister, the earl of Arlington. Arlington was said to be exceedingly fond of his daughter and concerned for her future, but not sufficiently to wonder if marrying her at the age of five might be an outrage. Thus the duchess of Cleveland tied her son's future to a man whose political influence she thought would last. It did not, but, however shocking the age of the children concerned in this transaction of self-interest might seem, Henry and Isabella stayed married, became the duke and duchess of Grafton and eventually produced a family.

Henry had married before his elder brother, Charles, because Arlington was less precious about child marriage than the father of Mary Wood, the rich heiress chosen by Barbara for her eldest son by the king. The contract, signed shortly before the death of Mary Wood's father, stipulated that the marriage would not actually take place until Mary was sixteen. She went to live with her aunt, Lady Chester, but was removed by the duchess of Cleveland in what amounted to an abduction. Barbara wanted the girl brought up with her own daughters and dismissed Lady Chester's protests with all the venom that her detractors associated with her: 'The duchess,' she announced, grandly referring to herself in the third person, 'hath her and will keep her and the duchess wonders that so inconsiderable person as the Lady Chester will contend with a person of her quality.'[6]

Nor were her daughters forgotten. The eldest, Anne, was married at the age of thirteen to yet another distant relative, Thomas Lennard, who became earl of Sussex. But, unlike her brothers,

Anne's marriage was not happy. She became infatuated with the king's final mistress, Hortense Mancini, and was removed to France by her mother, where further, even more serious problems arose. There was much less difficulty with Charlotte Fitzroy, the king's outright favourite among his illegitimate children. Renowned for possessing her mother's beauty but not her nature or proclivities, Charlotte was married in 1674 to Edward Lee, created earl of Lichfield on the occasion of his marriage. Shrewdly balancing her political bets, Barbara favoured Lee because of his connection to Thomas Osborne, earl of Danby, the Lord Treasurer. Danby was originally a client of the duke of Buckingham's but was now seeking to become the king's chief minister in his own right, at the expense of Arlington, who survived impeachment proceedings brought against him in Parliament in the year of Anne Fitzroy's marriage.

*

No ONE KNEW better than the duchess of Cleveland that times were changing. She owed her gradual, well-managed eclipse to recognition of the mutability of influence and power. But by 1676 she also had to accept that, however impressive her pensions might sound in theory, collecting them in full remained a challenge and she had consistently lived beyond her means. It would be necessary to economize and consider her options. At the end of 1672, as a result of the restrictions on Catholics holding office that would form part of the Test Acts, Barbara lost her place as lady of the bedchamber to the queen. A period of time abroad, in a more congenial religious and social environment, beckoned. Never one to brood, the duchess of Cleveland packed up her household and left for France with her eldest and youngest daughters, to take up residence in Paris.

Scandal followed Barbara wherever she went. Her daughters were to be educated at the English convent of the Order of the Immaculate Conception of our Blessed Lady, on the Rue de Charenton in the Faubourg St Antoine. Barbara donated £1,000 to the convent, eager to demonstrate both her commitment to the Catholic religion and her generosity. This action does not seem to have made her any more acceptable to the ladies of Parisian society, whose reluctance to visit her she was reported to find aggravating. Barbara did not like being snubbed. Reservations about the duchess's colourful reputation were not, however, shared by gentlemen in the French capital. Soon there were rumours of an affair with the archbishop of Paris, François de Harlay de Champvallon, duc de Saint Cloud, whose own private life was certainly not beyond reproach. The celebrated French lady of letters, Madame de Sévigné, would remark, in connection with the funeral oration delivered at his funeral, that there were only two trifles that made it difficult – his life and his death. Barbara also had an affair with the marquis de Châtillon, a gentleman of the bedchamber to Louis XIV, who sent her a number of love letters. If this relationship had the underlying intention of gaining access to useful information about the Sun King himself, it backfired spectacularly when some of the letters were intercepted by the English ambassador in Paris, Ralph Montagu, and sent back to Charles II in an attempt to discredit the duchess.[7] Nor were the ambassador's motives entirely patriotic, for he had been Barbara's lover himself.

Ralph Montagu was typical of the ambitious, self-serving men of the period. The reign of Charles II is littered with politicians like Ralph, who saw in the hollowness of politics, the moral vacuum at the very centre of the regime, a means to self-advancement. He was, even so, a larger-than-life figure. Montagu came from a family whose loyalties were bitterly divided during the Civil Wars but the Restoration brought him office, first with the duchess of York and then as master of the horse to the queen. He had undertaken a mission to France early in Charles II's reign and was gratified to receive the much more important posting of ambassador in 1669. His official entry to Paris was said to have been the most impressive by any diplomat but his first period of residence there ended after three years. Although he got wind of the negotiations surrounding the Secret Treaty of Dover, the king did not trust him to have any hand in them and Ralph was soon angling for higher office back at home. Ensuring that he had a wife whose fortune would underpin his longer-term goals, he married in 1673 Elizabeth Wriothesley, the widowed countess of Northumberland. This lady's own hopes of a more glorious future as the second wife of James, duke of York, following the death of Anne Hyde, were dashed by the duke's marriage to the Italian Catholic noblewoman, Mary of Modena. Ralph and Elizabeth's union was uneasy and its early months saw Ralph briefly confined to the Tower of London for challenging the duke of Buckingham to a duel when Buckingham shoved him in the queen's presence chamber. But though made a privy councillor and finding the funds to purchase the office of master of the great wardrobe, Montagu was sent back to Paris the same year that the duchess of Cleveland took up residence. It is not clear how well she knew Montagu before they both found themselves in what they saw as a kind of exile in France but it would have been natural for them to socialize. Both were philanderers by nature and so their mutual attraction is understandable.

Ralph Montagu's reputation as a ladies' man preceded him to Paris though it is far from obvious in his portrait. A thickset, heavy-jowled man under the fashionable enormous wig of the times, he looks more like a satiated judge than a nimble lover. And though quick of wit, mentally agile and an indefatigable correspondent, being gossipy and often full of inconsequential information, he certainly realized the importance of representing Louis XIV to Charles II as full of vanity and unloved by his subjects. Though never entirely satisfied with his lot, and still hoping for a position as secretary of state in England, he might have survived politically if he had not fallen foul of the duchess of Cleveland. For Ralph was to find that the old adage that hell hath no fury like a woman scorned was epitomized in the attitude of a formidable woman whom, it turned out, he had badly misjudged.

When Barbara returned briefly to England in the spring of 1678, she discovered that some of the love letters between herself and Châtillon had ended up in the possession of Charles II. It is not clear whether they were intercepted or opened and copies made, which were then sent across the English Channel. Either way, Barbara thought she knew who had betrayed her and her suspicions were correct. Ralph Montagu was responsible. His motives remain mysterious. Was he jealous or merely trying to be mischievous, hoping that he could curry favour with the king? Perhaps he had taken it upon himself to keep an eye on a woman known for her promiscuity and lack of discretion, in which case he might have been able to justify sleeping with her himself, in order to find out more about her life in Paris. It is much more likely, however, that he had another motive and it was one that Barbara found out about while in England. Never one to hang around, Ralph had taken advantage of her absence by starting an affair with her daughter, Anne.

The revelation left Barbara cold with fury and, while not confirming or denying the affair with Châtillon to Charles II while still in England, she determined to have her revenge on Ralph Montagu as soon as she returned to France. It was not merely that she had been replaced in the arms of the ambassador by her own eldest child but that he had so evidently played on Anne's insecurities and unhappiness. Originally placed by her mother in a convent outside Paris, the wayward Anne had moved back into the centre of the French capital, ostensibly to a convent in Saint Germain. Most of her time was in fact spent with Montagu, 'he being always with her till five o'clock in the morning, they two shut up together alone', as Barbara informed the king in the first of two lengthy letters. She found the relationship between the ambassador and her daughter the talk of the town. 'I am so much afflicted that I can hardly write this for crying, to see that a child that I doted on as I did on her, should make so ill a return and join with the worst of men to ruin me.' And why had this happened? Because, she told Charles, she had spurned

Ralph Montagu's advances. She pleaded with her former lover not to let her be ruined by this 'most abominable man.' Deciding that it was time to confess, at least a little, she owned up to the fact 'that I did write a foolish letter to the Chevalier de Chatillon', which she excused on the grounds that love could make one do silly things.

Now that she had justified herself, Barbara went on an all-out attack on Montagu. She was determined to ruin him. 'Nor will you, I hope, follow the advice of this ill man, who in his heart I know hates you, and were it for his interest would ruin you too if he could. For he has neither conscience nor honour and has several times told me that in his heart he despised you and your brother; and that for his part, he wished with all his heart that the parliament would send you both to travel, for you were a dull governable fool, and the duke a willful fool.'[8] Even worse than Ralph's unguarded comments about the king was the duchess's assertion that he had found an astrologer through whom he hoped to influence Charles II, a reminder that the king, despite his interest in science, was still believed to be susceptible to more primitive forces. Ralph cheerfully acknowledged that his underlying aim in all this was to become Lord Treasurer. Then he could control the purse strings, supply the king with all the money and women that he wanted, and lead him, in Ralph's own words, by the nose.

Aware that his career was on the line, though he seems to have felt that Thomas Osborne, earl of Danby, was the main enemy, Ralph returned without permission to London, to plead his case personally with Charles. He did not get far into his explanation when the king interrupted him, demanding to know what could be so important that he had deserted his post. For Ralph, it was too late; he had been trumped by Barbara. He was removed from the ambassadorship in France, where he was replaced by the earl of Sunderland, and lost his place on the Privy Council. His political career, however, was far from over; he was elected as a member of Parliament and the French ambassador, Barrillon, soon recruited him as a source of information in return for a pension.

The affair was Barbara's last foray into court politics. She had brought Montagu low, but the problem with Anne, her daughter, was not so conveniently solved. Anne seems, not unnaturally, to have resented her mother, and though she did go on to have children with her husband, to whom she returned, the marriage was never a success and the earl of Sussex and his wife separated in 1688. Though the king had acknowledged her, Roger Palmer still regarded her as his daughter and her relationship with him was better than that with her mother.

Roger's life remained unpredictable. While abroad he had to deal not just with the difficulties of a self-imposed exile but also the constant importuning of his half-brother, Philip Palmer, and Philip's equally desperate wife. To their frequent requests for monetary help, Roger responded with frigid politeness, saying, 'I confess no letters can be more ungrateful to me than those that press me beyond my power; I thought your ladyship had known that I had disposed of my estate and consequently that it lay not now as much in my power to serve you as formerly, for though my brother is near to me yet I have those that are in blood nearer.'[9] Barbara's husband returned to England in 1677 and, as an active writer and Catholic apologist, found himself caught up in the Popish Plot. James II's accession in 1685 saw him recognized for his loyalty to the Catholic religion and his diplomatic skills. He was despatched to Rome with considerable pomp as the new king's ambassador extraordinary. James's downfall meant that Roger was once again on the wrong side and he found himself in the Tower of London on suspicion of Jacobite sympathies, which he undoubtedly had. His quiet death in the Welsh Marches in 1705 finally released Barbara from her marriage of forty years. It was not quite the end of her story, as we shall see.

Barbara was a remarkable woman. Self-possessed and confident, she saw clearly how to derive the maximum advantage for herself and her children. It was not in her nature to be embarrassed, indeed she gloried in her role as the king's mistress, determined that the telling combination of her beauty, connections and business sense would triumph over anyone who stood in her path. Her unabashed sexuality was unusual, even at a court renowned for its lack of any conventional morality. She had a mind that was both daring and calculating. Several ladies of the court, including Montagu's sister, Lady Harvey, who challenged her behaviour and criticized her openly, came off worse in their struggle with the woman who had risen from the fringes of the aristocracy and genteel poverty to become a duchess in her own right. But the woman she wronged most, and whose life was forever changed by Barbara's very existence, was the Portuguese princess whom Charles II married with notable lack of enthusiasm in 1662.

Charles II in the early years of his reign.

Charles II, *c.*1680. The elaborate clothes and shoes cannot hide the ravages of time.

Princess Mary Stuart, Charles II's sister, and her husband,
William II of Orange. The picture is charming but
the marriage was unhappy.

This miniature of Lucy Walter, Charles II's
first mistress, was painted after her death.
No contemporary likenesses of Lucy survive.

James, duke of Monmouth,
Charles II's son by Lucy
Walter, as a child.

Eleanor Needham, Lady Byron, one of Charles II's mistresses in exile.

Barbara Palmer, née Villiers, countess of Castlemaine and duchess of Cleveland, painted as Mary Magdalene by Sir Peter Lely.

Barbara Palmer as the Madonna with her eldest son. This voluptuous, almost sacrilegious painting aptly illustrates Barbara's disdain for conventionality.

Philip Stanhope, second earl of Chesterfield. An inveterate ladies' man, he was one of Barbara Palmer's earliest lovers. He later became a loyal adviser to Catherine of Braganza.

Roger Palmer, earl of Castlemaine, with his secretary. A Catholic royalist whose early infatuation with his wife soon turned sour, her behaviour forced him to live abroad.

Catherine of Braganza, Charles II's Portuguese queen consort. Adrift in the moral vacuum of her husband's court, the shy queen eventually forged an independent life for herself.

Queen Catherine shortly after her arrival in England, wearing the Portuguese fashions and hairstyle derided by the king and court.

Left John IV of Portugal, Catherine of Braganza's father, who came reluctantly to the throne in 1640 following a coup against Spanish rule led by the Portuguese nobility.

Right Luisa de Guzmán, Catherine of Braganza's Spanish mother. The capable queen ruled as regent for her disabled son after John IV's death in 1656.

Left Catherine of Braganza's arrival at Portsmouth and the king and queen leaving Hampton Court by river for Whitehall, in two contemporary German prints.

Frances Teresa Stuart. The daughter of Scottish royalists in the service of Queen Henrietta Maria, she was brought up in the French court. She evaded Charles II's advances and secretly married the duke of Richmond.

Charles Stuart, duke of
Richmond and Lennox.
Frances' husband was disliked
by his cousin, Charles II.
He died while serving as
ambassador to Denmark, in
a bizarre boating accident.

Cobham Hall in Kent, one of the homes of Frances and her husband,
in a nineteenth-century painting.

Part Three

The Queen

CATHERINE OF BRAGANZA

1638–1705

CHAPTER SEVEN

A Wealthy Wife

*'I have often been put in mind by my friends that it was
high time to marry'*
The king's speech to Parliament, 8 May 1661

CHARLES II'S RESTORATION had made him the most eligible
bachelor in Europe. Yet he did not marry for another two years.
There had been other, more pressing concerns: the shape of government, the settlement of the Church of England, suppression of
discontent and pursuit of the regicides. His coronation at
Westminster Abbey took place on 23 April 1661, nearly a year
after his return, the hiatus caused not just by the demands of his
new situation but the absence of the regalia needed for the ceremony, which had been melted down or sold by the republican
regime. A new crown, based on the one supposedly worn by
Edward the Confessor, was made. It was extremely heavy at over
two kilograms and encrusted with jewels. Charles can be seen
wearing it in his coronation portrait, in which the dandified
glamour of his doublet and hose contrast uncomfortably with his
almost threatening expression. He was thirty-one when the portrait
was painted but looks older. He enjoyed being the centre of
attention without the distraction of a consort but he was now
under pressure to find a bride, though he would claim that he
had 'thought so myself ever since I came into England.' The delay,

he said, had been caused by the difficulty of finding a suitable wife but he had concluded that it would be impossible 'to make such a choice, against which there could be no foresight of any inconvenience that may ensue', without so much loss of time that the lords and gentlemen assembled 'would live to see me an old bachelor.' He went on to announce in his speech to Parliament in May 1661 that he had resolved to marry 'the daughter of Portugal.'[1] It may seem strange that this lady was not even referred to by name but such were the formalities of the time.

The future queen consort was born Catarina Henriqueta de Bragança in the Palace of Vila Viçosa, in the Alentejo region of Portugal, east of Lisbon, in 1638. At the time of her birth, Catherine of Braganza, as she would be known in England, was a duke's daughter. Her father, John of Braganza, came from a noble line, descended from an illegitimate son of John I of Portugal, who had reigned in the late fourteenth and early fifteenth century. Luisa de Guzmán, Catherine's mother, came from an equally venerable Spanish family, the Medina Sidonias. Catherine was high-born, but not yet a king's daughter.

Portugal had a long and often fractious relationship with its neighbouring kingdoms in the Iberian peninsula, centuries before the birth of a united Spain. It had survived Roman, Visigoth and Moorish occupation before breaking away from the kingdom of León Castile in the twelfth century. The height of its power and influence had come during the period from the mid-1490s to the 1540s, when its explorers discovered new lands as far apart as Brazil, Africa and the islands of south-east Asia. Trade brought the burgeoning Portuguese empire enormous wealth, a cultured society grew up and the daughters of Portuguese kings married into the Spanish Habsburgs. But a series of personal tragedies and premature deaths depleted the Portuguese royal family and the advent of the Inquisition sucked the lifeblood out of society. The crisis came in 1580, when Philip II of Spain, whose mother was a Portuguese princess, claimed the throne following the death of the childless King Henrique. To his vast domains in South

America, Philip now added the entirety of Portugal's empire, making him perhaps the first and only truly global monarch. England's paltry gains on the world stage under Elizabeth I pale in comparison. In his person, Philip united the crowns of Portugal and Spain, rather as James I would, just two decades later, for England and Scotland – though in his case, with much less immediate impact on the world. In one respect, however, there was a strong similarity. Portugal, though retaining its autonomy, was very much the junior partner in this new arrangement, as Scotland was to England in 1603. For a while, Philip considered moving his court to Lisbon, but it remained in Madrid. The Portuguese had lost their nation but not their sense of identity. In 1640, they would regain it again, with a new king, John IV – Catherine's father.

In the sixty years of Habsburg domination of Portugal, unrest had grown. Popular uprisings were put down and, while some of the senior Portuguese nobility were content to mingle with their counterparts in the Castilian court, other, younger men grew progressively discontented. In December 1640, a group of lesser nobility led what was, in effect, a coup d'état against Spanish rule, spurred on by the convenient distraction of a revolt in Catalonia, another disaffected Iberian region. They murdered the secretary of the Council of State in Lisbon and proclaimed the duke of Braganza king, as John IV, summoning him from Vila Viçosa to Lisbon to begin his reign. He acted swiftly in calling the Cortes, Portugal's representative body, but he had not sought the throne and he accepted it with some reluctance. He knew the dangers that threatened the restored dynasty of Braganza, and his own limitations: 'His background was that of a country gentleman who before his elevation to the throne had never left Portugal.'[2] This of course made him more acceptable to the junior aristocrats who wanted him as their king. John had not bent the knee to the Habsburg kings in Madrid and could be represented as a true patriot. But the early years of his rule were uneasy, as he sought to promote himself and his country in Europe. Spain tried to frustrate him at every turn, using its greater power and diplomatic experience, and even France, Spain's traditional enemy, was slow to recognize an independent Portugal, pointedly refusing the offer of Catherine as a bride for Louis XIV, despite the promise of a very generous dowry. The only country that was willing to negotiate with him and offer him protection was Oliver Cromwell's republican England. A treaty was signed in 1654 but not ratified for another two years, and its commercial terms were highly favourable to England. When John IV died in 1656, the Portuguese empire was under threat in both Brazil and south-east Asia and Portugal's survival as an independent country was once more menaced by Spain after the 1659 Treaty of the Pyrenees ended a century and a half of conflict between France and Spain. Philip IV's daughter, Maria Teresa, married Louis XIV, while Catherine of Braganza remained unwed in Lisbon.

She was – as her mother, the very capable Queen Regent Luisa, recognized – a natural choice of bride for the newly restored Charles II and, feeling let down by the French, Luisa pursued the idea with determination. She was ruling on behalf of her son, Afonso VI, who had been badly affected both mentally and physically as a child by meningitis. The years since her husband's death had been a challenge but the marriage negotiations, led by the experienced Francisco de Mello, Portuguese ambassador to London, eventually bore fruit. Ratified in the Treaty of London of 1661, Portugal's future seemed much more secure. But it had been bought at a very high price, not just for Portugal but for the twenty-three-year-old Catherine of Braganza herself.

The bargaining had taken longer than Charles and Edward Hyde, who played a major part in the negotiations, let on in Charles's speech to Parliament, though many of the king's leading politicians had known something of what was going on, for the simple reason that Mello, armed with a very sizeable fund to back up the Portuguese case, had bought off most of them. Though Charles had begun his reign with a desire to restore good relations with Spain after Cromwell's regime had sided with the French and vilified the Spanish as the fount of all evil, he swiftly discovered that Spain wanted concessions he could not give. Turning to Portugal, with its long history of alliance with England going back to the fourteenth century, seemed a natural alternative as well as a very attractive one financially. For Charles and his advisers, including his brother, the offer was too good to miss. The Spanish ambassador, though dangling the promise of impressive dowries for various minor princesses in different Habsburg lands, in a desperate attempt to match the Portuguese, was outmanoeuvred by Mello's bribes and hamstrung by the not unreasonable scepticism of the English that Philip IV simply could not find the money he was promising. In addition, the French, despite their newly discovered friendship with Spain, were more than happy to support the Anglo-Portuguese match, hoping that it might prove an annoyance and preoccupation for the Spanish government.

In return for supplying Portugal with 10,000 men to back up its still inadequate army, Charles received the most generous marriage settlement of any English monarch. He was given the ports of Bombay and Tangier, privileged access for English merchants throughout the Portuguese empire and a lump sum cash payment of about £330,000 (worth over £11 billion today), as well, of course, as a royal bride. This was an exceptional windfall and the king's reference to his marriage in his speech to Parliament seems almost casual in comparison with the reality of what he was getting. The Portuguese, now much more secure in their place in Europe, had gained much as well, for, though Bombay and Tangier seemed powerful inducements, the Portuguese were, in reality, in danger of losing both of them as the Dutch challenged them in the east and the Spanish in North Africa. Catherine was to be guaranteed a personal income of £30,000 (nearly £4 million today) per year and she was permitted to practise her Catholic religion, as Charles II's mother had been when she married his father in 1625. In retrospect, Catherine thought these concessions were a small price for England to pay. She would remark, years later, after Charles's death: 'There were reasons for my coming to this kingdom, solely for the advantage of Portugal, and for this cause and for the interests of our house, I was sacrificed.'³ It was a bitter comment, born of the long years of humiliation and unhappiness she endured, though this could not have been foreseen when she eventually set sail from Lisbon on 23 April 1662.

Princesses had always been diplomatic fodder but Catherine, unlike the more spirited Dutch princess, Henrietta, who might have been Charles's wife, had no say in the matter. In truth, little was known about her because there was little to know. The English consul in Lisbon reported that she had been 'bred hugely retired. She hath hardly been ten times out of the palace in her life.'⁴ There is no evidence, however, as earlier writers claimed, that Catherine was brought up in a convent. Her early life seems to reflect that of her father, no traveller himself. As the only surviving daughter of King John and Queen Luisa, the royal couple knew that her marriageability was an important asset but they do not seem to have given much thought to preparing her for a future that would inevitably be outside Portugal itself. She was brought up to be devout, ladylike and respectful. Catherine could speak Spanish (or at least understand it well enough to communicate with Charles II until she learned sufficient English) and her subsequent interests as queen indicate that she had an appreciation of music and art. In dress and hairstyle, she favoured the stiff and, by other European standards, conservative fashions of her country. These looked heavy on Catherine, who was short and slim. Her eyes were acknowledged to be very attractive, though her portraits suggest that she might have been short-sighted. In days when few people had good teeth into their adult years, Catherine's were her worst feature. They protruded badly (none of her portraits show this, as smiling with your mouth wide open, such a feature of celebrity in our time, would have been considered unseemly), but observers did not fail to remark on it when she came to England. Queen Luisa praised her daughter as gentle, virtuous and prudent. Charles II pronounced himself eager for her arrival, telling Catherine in July 1661, 'I am going to make a short progress into some of my provinces . . . seeking in vain tranquillity in my rest-lessness, hoping to see the beloved person of Your Majesty in these kingdoms, already your own, and that with the same anxiety with which, after my long banishment, I desired to see myself in them.'⁵ He had a good way with words. However, there was little public comment in England and certainly no great rejoicing when the match was announced. In September 1661, Sir Richard Fanshawe was despatched as ambassador to Lisbon to hasten the signing of the treaty by the Portuguese. Charles sent a diamond-framed miniature of himself and a wardrobe of silk dresses for Catherine. It seems, in retrospect, rather a cheap gesture for what he was getting. Catherine's reaction to this limited largesse is unknown.

The Portuguese, however, were determined that their princess's marriage would be an occasion of great display, a public demon-stration of the clout of the Braganza dynasty. Nor were they in any hurry to send Catherine to England until they had fully milked this opportunity. Their willingness to spend money on public celebrations to mark Catherine's betrothal and the signing of the treaty was remarkable for a small country still struggling to establish itself. The Portuguese empire may have been extensive but wars with the Spanish and the Dutch had weakened the exchequer. Visitors to Lisbon were not impressed: 'it is a very poor dirty place – I mean the City and the Court of Lisbone', wrote Pepys in his diary. He had dined with an English sea-captain, recently returned from Portugal, who reported that the young king was 'a very rude and simple fellow'. He went on to add that fine dining was a rarity at the Portuguese court. The king, he had been told, 'hath his meat sent up by a dozen of lazy guards . . . and sometimes nothing but fruits and now and then half a hen.' Catherine's enhanced status meant that she got the pick of the rather meagre diet of the royal family: 'she is come to have a whole hen or goose to her table – which is not ordinary.' It certainly was not and, in an apparent effort to broaden their future queen's culinary experiences, English diplomats in Lisbon had requested 'neats (beef) tongues, bacon, oil anchovies, pickled oysters, Cheshire cheese and butter' be sent over.[6]

The celebrations in the autumn of 1661 may have lacked sophisticated fare but in every other way the Portuguese Crown stepped up to the occasion. Over an entire week, there were marvellous spectacles. Fireworks, bullfights, pageants and processions announced Catherine's marriage to the populace. Proceedings were chronicled by an anonymous writer, thought to be António de Sousa Macedo, the Portuguese secretary of state, who had represented the country in London during the reign of Charles I. He told his readers that the occasion 'much exceeded the Coliseum of Rome.' Conspicuous at the bullfights, among the assorted members of the aristocracy and Church, as well as professional dancers and musicians, was 'Her British Majesty', Catherine herself. Her upbringing may not have prepared her for such occasions but by the time she left Portugal the following spring, she would have fully understood the importance of her marriage to her own country.

Edward Montagu, earl of Sandwich, arrived with a fleet to bring Charles II's wife to England on 1 March 1662, having secured the new English possession of Tangier. His stay in Lisbon was more fraught and protracted than he had hoped, though his dealings with the Portuguese royal family the previous autumn had alerted him to their talent for prevarication. Montagu's background as a staunch supporter of both Oliver and Richard Cromwell while in joint command of the English fleet under the republic had turned to pragmatic acceptance of the likelihood of a Stuart restoration in the first months of 1660. He was a competent naval commander and diplomat, who, unlike his cousin, Ralph Montagu, in France, was able to avoid getting into serious difficulties. In the spring of 1662, he faced considerable challenges in getting both Queen Catherine and her dowry back to England.

Sandwich started by making sure that he observed all the proprieties. 'I came with my whole fleet,' he recalled, 'and rode above the palace (on the river Tagus), which I saluted with 41 guns and my flag struck.' The next day, he went ashore 'to wait upon the Queen of England to see whether she had any commands for me and to present the compliments of my Lord Chancellor (Clarendon) and my Lord Treasurer (the earl of Southampton) unto Her Majesty.' Catherine received these good wishes graciously and, apparently mindful that there was an important financial dimension to all of this, 'she did very earnestly recommend into my care the schedule of the portion delivered me the day before by the Conde da Ponte.' She went on to tell the earl that she had 'overcome almost all impossibilities to hasten her voyage and that I must put myself to mastering some difficulties also; and that I should consider the poverty of the Portuguese nation caused by the oppression of their enemies.'[7] The new queen of England was also concerned to impress on Sandwich that he would need to reinforce Portugal's naval defences because, as soon as he left, the Spanish would be waiting to invade at the mouth of the Tagus. Catherine was no doubt briefed on what to say by her mother and other political advisers but she clearly handled this interview with firmness and an understanding of the awkward underlying issues that remained between Portugal and England where her marriage was concerned. She does not come across as the clueless ingénue that the English would soon be depicting.

Sandwich gave reassurances about reinforcing the fleet and, on the other matters, of the payment of the dowry and Portuguese obligations under the terms of the Treaty of London, he proceeded with a mixture of tact and rigour. 'Concerning the schedule of the portion (the dowry), I gave Her Majesty a paper, to avoid uncertainties of interpretation.' This was a polite way of saying that he did not trust the Portuguese government to pay in full – and, indeed, they never did. Nor was it the only disappointment that he faced. The Portuguese were dragging their feet on loading the sugar that formed part of the treaty. He urged Ponte 'to put merchandise aboard and not bills of exchange. He told me it was both unreasonable and impossible for all Portugal to do it.'[8] Although irritated, Sandwich forbore from pointing out that Portugal seemed to be reneging on key parts of the alliance.

By mid-April, he was relieved to be able to set sail finally with the new queen of England on the *Royal Charles*, the ship that had brought Charles II and his brothers from Breda two years earlier. Catherine was given an appropriately regal send-off by her family, going aboard with her brothers, King Afonso and Dom Pedro, after she had taken an affectionate but restrained farewell of her mother outside the royal palace. She knew that it was unlikely that she would ever see any of them again. Her last gesture to the country of her birth was heavily symbolic. 'As I passed by the Castles,' Sandwich wrote in his diary, 'the Queen commanded me to loose the Standard, which was done.' But very soon human frailty overcame regal bearing. Once they were out on the open sea, Catherine and her ladies were all violently seasick.[9]

The voyage to England was stormy and Sandwich's fleet of fourteen ships, five ketches and three accompanying merchantmen only sighted Land's End on 4 May. A week later, off Torbay, James, duke of York, came aboard with the duke of Ormond to greet Catherine, and did so every day until she reached Portsmouth. She landed from his yacht, the *Anne*, on 14 May, and almost immediately took to her bed to recover from the journey and a heavy cold. The king, who had been in Barbara Palmer's bed until just before he set off for Portsmouth, was in no hurry to meet his bride.

*

CATHERINE HAD LEFT her native land in a blaze of fireworks, serenaded on her last night by sweet music below her cabin. She was to find a much colder, quieter reception in England. Surrounded by her Portuguese ladies-in-waiting, she was no longer a proud Iberian princess but a virgin queen, waiting to have sex with a stranger. What she felt about her husband's dilatory attitude to welcoming her we do not know but it cannot have been an easy time. Charles I had been so keen to meet Henrietta Maria in 1625 that he had made an early-morning dash from Canterbury to Dover and arrived before she was ready to receive him. His son's attitude was in stark contrast. Charles justified his tardiness by claiming he needed to be in London for an important parliamentary session at which the Act of Uniformity, settling the shape of the restored Church of England, was passed. His presence did not, in the end, assure the passage of any of the amendments to the legislation that he wanted. He found consolation elsewhere. Pepys reported that 'the King dined at my Lady Castlemaine's and supped every day and night the last week. And that the night that the bonfires were made for the joy of the Queen's arrival, the King was there.'[10] There were joys of another sort to be found in the arms of the heavily pregnant Barbara.

Apart from bonfires, the greatest celebrations of Catherine's arrival were left to the writers of ballads, often in the most appalling verse. One such was 'A Votive Song for Her Sacred Majesty's Happy Arrival', composed, if that is the right word, by Edmund Gaiton, a captain in the duke of York's regiment at Oxford. In its triumphal tone, it captures both the national and international implications of the Portuguese marriage:

> What general joy is here in our glad land
> All parties will agree, join hand in hand,
> Contented loyalists do patient stay
> And swear, if ever, now they're like t'have pay.
> Come then and quickly land, thy Charles doth fear
> No winds blow fast enough till thou art here.
>
> 'Tis not your fragrant oranges are wanting
> Of China breed, but better by transplanting.
> Nor your rare bacon, fed from chestnut-trees,
> (which brings Westphalia hams upon their knees)
> Nor Brasil sugar nor your Indian gold.
> Thou art the purchase, which thy Charles will hold.[11]

At breakfast time on the morning of 21 May, the king wrote to Clarendon with details of his first meeting with Catherine. He had found her in bed, 'by reason of a little cough and some inclination to a fever, which was caused, *as we physicians say*, by having certain things stopped at sea which ought to have carried away those humours. But now all is in their due course and I believe she will find herself very well in the morning as soon as she wakes.' He was somewhat relieved to find that 'I was not put to the consummation of the marriage last night; for I was so sleepy by having slept but two hours in my journey as I was afraid that matters would have gone very sleepily.'[12] The king's frankness about his postponed wedding night was amplified in a letter written two days later to his sister, Minette, in France: 'I was married the day before yesterday but the fortune that follows our family is fallen upon me, *car Monr. Le Cardinal m'a ferme la porte au nez*, and though I am not so furious as Monsieur [Minette's husband, the duke of Orléans] was, but am content to let those pass over before I go to bed with my wife, yet I hope I shall entertain her at least better the first night than he did you . . .'[13] Poor Catherine. Already her menstrual cycle was becoming the subject of international comment.

Charles did not reveal much about his wife and her appearance to Minette, saying that Lord St Albans, his mother's right-hand man, would do so, though he added, 'I must tell you I think myself very happy.' To his mother-in-law, Queen Luisa of Portugal, he managed a more flowery response, saying how much he was enjoying, 'in this springtime, the company of my dearest wife.' He was the happiest man in the world, 'and the most enamoured, seeing close at hand the loveliness of her person and her virtues . . .' All these reminded him of his obligations to Portugal itself but it was Catherine who was his chief delight: 'I wish to say of my wife that I cannot sufficiently either look at her or talk to her.'[14] Perhaps the canny Queen Luisa, who had apparently heard the tales of Charles II's fondness for women and the fact that he had a mistress, was comforted, if not entirely convinced, by these professions of devotion. If so, she would have been right. The king was an accomplished liar.

To Clarendon, he was much less effusive in his description of his bride:

> Her face is not so exact as to be called a beauty, though her eyes are excellent good, and not anything in her face that in the least degree can shock one. On the contrary, she has as much agreeableness in her looks altogether, as ever I saw: and if I have any skill in physiognomy, which I think I have, she must be as good a woman as ever was born. Her conversation, as much as I can perceive, is very good; for she has wit enough and a most agreeable voice. You would much wonder to see how well we are acquainted already. In a word, I think myself very happy; but am confident our two humours will agree very well together.[15]

Much of this was damning with faint praise and Charles was later reported to have reacted to Catherine's unusual hairstyle by saying that he thought they had brought him a bat rather than a queen. The diarist John Evelyn was also struck by Catherine's hair, which he described as, 'her foretop long and turned aside very strangely.'[16]

Unaware that she and her ladies were being viewed as deeply unfashionable, olive-skinned oddities by the English, Catherine was soon entranced by her husband, who was dark himself. She seems to have fallen deeply in love very quickly and her affection for him never diminished. He was always her Prince Charming, despite his behaviour towards her. The marriage ceremonies – one Anglican, the other Catholic (despite Charles having been explicitly warned by Clarendon that he could not be married by 'a Roman priest') – took place on 21 May 1662. Whether deliberately or through carelessness, Charles was playing a dangerous game, potentially undermining his position as head of the Church of England by marrying in a secret Catholic ceremony. The officiating

priest was Ludovic Stuart, Lord d'Aubigny, a member of a distinguished Scottish Catholic family whose links with France went
back into the Middle Ages. He was Henrietta Maria's almoner
and would serve Catherine in the same capacity. This marriage
ceremony, which took place in Catherine's bedchamber, actually
preceded the Anglican ceremony in the Governor's House in
Portsmouth, which was conducted by the bishop of London,
Gilbert Sheldon.

Charles did not use the marriage as an occasion for prolonged
public celebrations or spectacle. The idea that he was a man of the
people, eager for his subjects to have access to him, is false. Like his
father, he wanted display to be controlled. There was symbolism in
the royal couple's arrival at Hampton Court on 29 May, his birthday
and the date of the Stuart dynasty's restoration, but there was little
possibility of crowds flocking to see their new queen, since the
royal party did not arrive till late in the evening, as it was growing
dark. There were spectators, as there had been along the route from
Portsmouth, but they were kept well away from the king and his
bride. The Scottish Stewarts had gone out among the people and
their accessibility and visibility were key to the dynasty's success.
The English Stuarts lived in different times and had different
priorities. There was still considerable discontent in England in
1662 and security could not be guaranteed at large gatherings. But
it is possible to make too much of Charles II's failure to put on
lavish celebrations in connection with his marriage. The last major
royal wedding had been that of Princess Elizabeth, daughter of
James I, to the elector palatine nearly fifty years earlier. There was
not much of a tradition in England of royal weddings being public
events or opportunities for the monarchy to enhance its standing
– a contrast with such occasions nowadays. The opportunity for
merchandising was not, however, lost. Commemorative plates and
embroidered boxes of carved wood, decorated with silk, linen and
metal threads, showing Charles and Catherine in central panels,
were produced. It has been said that this was the first time a royal
marriage was marketed for public consumption.[17]

The newlyweds did not make their official entry into London as king and queen for another three months. This may seem dilatory but was probably dictated by a number of factors, not the least of which was that the court always avoided London in the plague months of the summer. London was also prone to rioting and its sizeable population of Protestant dissenters was often at odds with the Crown on religious matters. When, at very short notice, the City of London was asked to put on a pageant to celebrate the king and queen's arrival in the capital, it responded with an aquatic display that featured the livery guilds rather than the royal couple. Pepys wrote that he could not even make out which barge the king and queen were sitting in, though Evelyn, better positioned, gave a detailed description: 'His Majesty and the Queen came in an antique-shaped open vessel, covered with a state or canopy of cloth of gold, made in a form of a cupola, supported with high Corinthian pillars wreathed with flowers, festoons and garlands.'[18] The themes of the pageant were a mixture of chivalry and Roman values, with echoes of the kinds of entertainments so loved by the young Henry VIII. Almost overlooked, it was reported that Catherine appeared uncomfortable, 'like a prisoner at a Roman triumph.'[19] Certainly the speeches made by the sea deities reinforced the idea of an England cut off from the European continent but still powerful enough for its name alone to strike fear into its enemies' hearts. There was also praise for the Anglo-Portuguese alliance, albeit in terms harking back to the past rather than the present.

Adrift on the Thames, surrounded by a gaggle of little bobbing boats, Charles took his wife to Whitehall. After the formalities of her departure from Portugal, this was probably not the stately entry into London that Catherine might have envisaged. Yet in its gaudy shallowness it was a metaphor for the Restoration court. It would be an exaggeration to claim that, during the three months they had spent together at Hampton Court, Charles had grown tired of his wife because, despite saying all the right things to his mother-in-law, the king's lack of enthusiasm for his bride was always hard to disguise. He had signed himself, in his first letter to Catherine in 1661, as 'the very faithful husband of Your Majesty'. The queen was soon to discover how very empty those words were. Charles did not actively dislike Catherine but his passion for Lady Castlemaine was unabated. The little Portuguese princess could not compete with Barbara or any of Charles's subsequent mistresses. She would learn, eventually, to accept this reality and forge a life for herself, but only after much humiliation had been heaped upon her.

CHAPTER EIGHT

'Full of sweetness and goodness'

*'As for the queen . . . you may credit her being a very
extraordinary woman'*
Philip Stanhope, earl of Chesterfield,
lord chamberlain to Queen Catherine

HISTORIANS HAVE LARGELY been dismissive of Catherine of
Braganza, writing her off as an unsophisticated Iberian princess,
out of her depth in Charles II's dazzling court, prone to hysteria
and retreating into religiosity as her only defence against the
entirely unfamiliar, unkind world in which she now found herself.
In this interpretation, Catherine retreats to her chapels and apartments, surrounded by Catholic priests and the Portuguese ladies
whose age and appearance so appalled English commentators, an
overlooked irrelevance in Charles II's hedonistic lifestyle. The
truth, as is so often the case, is rather different. For, as Chesterfield's
views suggest, there was much more to the new queen than the
enduring popular image of a wronged, neglected wife.

She was, of course, both, but over time she learned to deal with
humiliation and sorrow and to forge a separate identity for herself.
Her good qualities were immediately apparent to all who saw her.
Chesterfield went on to describe them in more detail and they
echo those of Charles II in their depiction of her piety, discretion
and intelligence. The earl noted that she was very fond of her

husband and was 'exactly shaped, and has lovely hands, excellent eyes, a good countenance, a pleasing voice, fine hair, and, in a word, is what an understanding man would wish a wife.' Yet one detects a note of caution in this last phrase and he went on to make his reservations clearer, without naming names: 'I fear all this will hardly make things run in the right channel; but, if it should, I suppose our court will require a new modelling . . .'[1] Chesterfield was an accomplished letter-writer. He could charm mistresses, wives, even his mother-in-law with his pen, but he was also a fair judge of what was going on around him. He was gratified with the roles he and his second wife, Lady Elizabeth Butler, had been given in Catherine's household but he had no illusions as to the main – and perhaps insuperable – problem that the royal marriage would face. There was no escaping Charles II's passion for the recently ennobled Lady Castlemaine. She had been Chesterfield's own mistress just a few years ago and he knew her all too well.

Catherine was still at Hampton Court when she was introduced to the woman who would ruin her brief happiness. Speedily recovered from giving birth to her first son by the king, Barbara was living close by, at her uncle's house, in Richmond. In an age in which many women still died in childbirth and infant mortality remained high, Barbara and her offspring were remarkably robust. Many of Charles's biographers, as well as the writer of the only major life in English of Catherine of Braganza, have been at pains to excuse him for what is often passed off as an unfortunate, if understandable, lapse of judgement in thrusting his mistress in the face of his wife and then proceeding, with a determination that bordered on calculated cruelty, to insist that Barbara become one of the ladies of the queen's bedchamber. One wonders if Charles and his mistress had discussed their strategy beforehand, while Catherine was lying in bed with a cold and a heavy period at Portsmouth. Certainly, whatever his protestations at the time of his marriage, Charles never seems to have had the slightest intention of giving up the countess of Castlemaine or of adopting a course of action which might, at least, have allowed his wife and mistress to be kept apart. Catherine was presented with a fait accompli. The difficulty arose in her inability to curb a highly emotional reaction and assert herself effectively and consistently thereafter. But for this she can hardly be blamed, and Charles and Barbara gave her no quarter.

The queen was no innocent in the matter of her husband's mistress. She already knew about Barbara and had, according to Clarendon, made up her mind that she would never, ever, allow this rival to be in the same room as her, subsequently telling those closest to her that 'her mother had enjoined her so to do.' Charles had other ideas about how his wife should conduct herself. 'The king thought that he had so well prepared her to give her [Barbara] a civil reception, that within a day or two of her majesty's being there, himself led her into her chamber, and presented her to the queen.' As Barbara did not give birth to her son until 18 June, her first meeting with Catherine cannot have been within a few days of the queen's arrival at Hampton Court and was probably not before mid-July. Catherine had met many English courtiers by this time. In the heat of what was an unusually warm summer, she had sat on public display, her make-up sometimes sliding off her face, striving to keep up with English formalities and the press of people who wanted to be presented to her. At first, this new arrival seemed no different than many other ladies of the court. Catherine was still struggling with English names and titles and either did not hear, or did not understand, at first, the identity of this handsome woman. She nevertheless responded graciously and held out her hand to be kissed. Some sources say that the queen's chief Portuguese lady-in-waiting, the countess of Penalva, standing behind her chair, hissed in Catherine's ear that this was the countess of Castlemaine. Clarendon describes it somewhat differently, saying that recognition dawned on the queen almost instantly. Everyone there saw her anguished reaction: 'her colour changed and tears gushed out of her eyes and her nose bled and she fainted; so that she was forthwith removed to another room.'

The king, far from being concerned about his wife's evident distress, took this very public embarrassment as a personal affront. He looked on it 'with wonderful indignation and as an earnest of defiance for the decision of supremacy and who should govern, upon which point he was the most jealous and most resolute of any man; and the answer he received from the queen, which kept up the obstinacy, displeased him more.'² So the brief honeymoon period of the marriage came to an abrupt end. There would be no more sightings of the royal couple eating cherries together in the window seats of Hampton Court.³ Both parties dug in their heels. But there would only be one winner.

Like other queens consort before her, Catherine discovered that she had little real influence over the personnel of her household as a new wife. Charles I and Henrietta Maria had quarrelled about the same subject and that also led to a public spat. Henrietta Maria had also been compelled to accept the existence of someone her husband valued far more dearly than herself – in this case, his male favourite, George Villiers, duke of Buckingham, Barbara's kinsman. After several years, an assassin conveniently removed the queen's rival. Catherine was not so fortunate. Perhaps if she had remonstrated with the king privately and less emotionally she could have retained more dignity but he would still not have given way. Charles knew that Barbara had her enemies at court and perceived that a faction might form around the queen, encouraging further defiance. He was determined to regain control of the situation quickly and, since Barbara made it abundantly clear to him that she expected to be appointed as a lady of the bedchamber, he would brook no opposition. Clarendon was ordered to state the case for accepting Barbara as one of her ladies to the queen. It was not a task he undertook with any enthusiasm, given his own dislike of 'The Lady', but he had no option. The king told him that anyone who tried to thwart his determination to make the appointment, 'I will be his enemy to the last moment of my life.' He continued in the same vein:

You know how true a friend I have been to you. If you will oblige me eternally, make this business as easy as you can, of what opinion soever you are of, for I am resolved to go through with this matter, let what will come on it; which again I solemnly swear before Almighty God. Therefore, if you desire to have the continuance of my friendship, meddle no more with this busi- ness . . . and whosoever I find to be my Lady Castlemaine's enemy in this matter, I do promise, upon my word, to be his enemy as long as I live.

This letter, remarkable for its repetition and cold vindictiveness, shows just how little Charles II thought of his wife. He had been nice enough to her for a few weeks but if she opposed him, espe- cially when it came to Barbara, he would have as little to do with her as possible. Clarendon saw the queen several times and attempted on each occasion to make her accept the reality of the situation, while yet flattering her that she must not have such a low opinion of her own attractions to feel threatened by another woman. As a wife, she must expect her husband to recommend servants and submit to his commands in this respect. Wisely, he advised her to give in with as much good grace as she could. Catherine, adrift from her homeland, struggling with a new language and new customs, insulted and distressed, could not comply. Each meeting with Clarendon had led to floods of tears. She tried desperately to have the last word: 'the king might do what he pleased, but that she would not consent to it.'[4]

The king retaliated by dismissing most of Catherine's Portuguese servants and allowing Barbara to take up residence in Hampton Court. He brought his mistress into Catherine's presence every day, conversing with her freely and pointedly ignoring his wife. Catherine was excluded from court entertainments and treated disrespectfully by some of her English servants, who believed that her influence was negligible and likely to remain that way. The final straw for the unhappy queen was the arrival from France of the queen mother, Henrietta Maria, a fellow Catholic, who might have been expected to support her. Instead, the queen mother appears to have played a part in persuading Catherine that what could not be prevented must be endured. She did little to help her new daughter-in-law and actually acknowledged the countess of Castlemaine in public. By the time the royal couple arrived at Whitehall at the end of August 1662, Catherine was reported as declaring that 'she had no other will but his Majesty's.'[5]

It was subsequently claimed that Catherine's capitulation was so complete that she changed her stance and became friendly towards Barbara, laughing and chatting with her, and that Charles viewed his wife with even more contempt as a result. The evidence, however, points to a rather different interpretation of relations between the two women and suggests that the queen only ever accepted Barbara as one of her ladies under sufferance. Barbara was determined to be seen to fulfil her duties publicly, even attending the queen at mass before her own conversion to Catholicism became known. But there was a delay in making further appointments to Catherine's bedchamber until the spring of 1663, much to the irritation of the earl of Chesterfield, and the ladies were not actually sworn in, on the king's warrants, until June of that year. This was probably because of continued friction about appointments between the king and queen. There is no evidence that Catherine herself ever authorized a warrant for the countess of Castlemaine. She had been forced to put up with much but submitting to her husband's will and having this woman, with whom he spent all his nights, flaunting herself in Catherine's bedchamber by day did not mean that Catherine agreed to pleasant socialization with her. Despite her anguish, Catherine always knew that she was a queen and that Barbara was a servant. She derived from this what little comfort she could.

*

CATHERINE'S HOPE, AS she was compelled to endure the presence of this rival, was that she would bear the king a son. Though it is highly unlikely that the arrival of a legitimate heir would miraculously have cured Charles II's priapism, Catherine's position would have been enhanced and she could have directed much of what was undoubtedly a loving nature towards her children. But in this, as in so much else in that miserable first eight years of her marriage, she was to be disappointed. The king himself had first alluded to the gynaecological problem that seems to have been at the root of Catherine's inability to give the king a child. She suffered from abnormal uterine bleeding, which results in frequent, heavy periods and a tendency towards miscarriage. The causes of this condition are still not fully understood but modern techniques of imaging and management with drugs can produce more positive outcomes for patients than were available to women in the seventeenth century. Aside from the discomfort and disruption to the normal marital relations Catherine would have liked to have established with the husband she adored, she had to put up with the embarrassment that knowledge of her condition was widespread. Even foreign visitors like the Italian Lorenzo Magalotti commented on 'the extraordinary frequency and abundance of her menses', while Sir John Reresby, a client of the duke of Buckingham who wrote extensive memoirs for his descendants, noted that she had 'a constant flux upon her.'[6] Since, in the twenty-first century, we are only just beginning to talk openly about women's periods and their associated problems, it may seem extraordinary that there should be such references 350 years ago, but the reproductive aspects of a queen's body were bound to be of interest when one of the key arguments for the monarchical system was the idea of legitimate descent. Queens were reproductive machines. There was essentially no difference, despite the passage of a century and a half, between the plight of Catherine of Aragon and that of Catherine of Braganza, except that Henry VIII's first wife had more pregnancies than her Portuguese namesake and did eventually manage to produce one child, Mary I, who survived into adulthood.

Charles II's wife was denied even this comfort, though the king, like Henry VIII, wanted sons rather than daughters. At the outset of his marriage, he would have settled for any sign of pregnancy. None came. By the end of 1662, rumours began that Catherine could not conceive and the first of many whisperings that Charles might legitimate his eldest son, the duke of Monmouth, fluttered round the court. Monmouth was now high in his father's favour. He was thirteen years old when he arrived back in England in August 1662, accompanied by his grandmother, Henrietta Maria, and was soon established at court, where Charles II suddenly discovered a fondness for the boy that had been hard to discern in the years following his abduction from Lucy Walter and removal to Paris. James Crofts, as he had been known up till then, was showered with favours and titles and found a suitably rich bride in the eleven-year-old Anna Scott, countess of Buccleuch. This young Scottish aristocrat was summoned to London to acquire the polish which would be required of someone about to become a duchess. Her mother, being a canny woman, took steps to ensure that most of Anna's inheritance was entailed outside the teenage bridegroom's grasp. Her caution proved especially prescient where James was concerned, though her daughter would prove to be equally extravagant. When James married Anna in the summer of 1663, he was given the title of duke of Monmouth. Neither he nor his father could then have had any real idea of the trouble he would cause.

Eventually, Monmouth's role in English history would endanger even Catherine of Braganza but initially he and his stepmother got on well. He spent considerable amounts of time with her, playing cards with her maids of honour and establishing his place as a member of the royal family. Yet already he was upstaging Catherine. When Pepys attended an audience with Henrietta Maria in Somerset House, her daughter-in-law sat beside her. But most people present only had eyes for 'Mr Crofts, the king's bastard.'[7] James was the living proof of Charles II's youthful virility and the queen had yet to prove that she was even fertile. As the countess of Castlemaine, never slow to see an opportunity, ingratiated herself with the king's impressionable son, Catherine was packed off to Tunbridge Wells and Bath to take the waters, hoping, like others before her, that they would help her conceive. Still there was no sign of pregnancy, and then, in the autumn of 1663, Catherine fell seriously ill.

For several days, as a high fever raged, the queen's survival was thought to hang in the balance. Charles spent most of the daytime at her bedside, which seems to have calmed her, though she might have been less tranquil had she known that he left her most evenings to sup with Lady Castlemaine. In her delirium, Catherine revealed just how deeply she was affected by the overriding need to bear children. She believed that she had already given birth. She talked to Charles of a son and then to her doctor of three babies, asking him, 'How do the children?'[8] Gradually, the fever left her and, by 2 November 1663, the king was able to tell his sister that 'my wife is now out of all danger, though very weak, and it was a very strange fever, for she talked idly four or five days after the fever had left her, but now that is likewise past, and desires me to make her compliments to you and Monsieur, which she will do herself as soon as she gets strength.'[9] In his next letter to Minette, he asked her to send 'some images to put in prayer books' as a gift for Catherine, who attended religious services three times a day.[10] He sounded almost wistful about his wife's piety and ended with the information that he was just off to the theatre to see a new play. The contrast between this apparent frivolity and Catherine's earnest religious devotions may or may not have been intentional. Minette, after all, knew her brother very well. Charles does seem to have been genuinely concerned about his wife's illness. Catherine was touched by his tenderness but if she thought it marked a change in his essential nature, she was deceiving herself.

Nevertheless, between 1666 and 1669, Catherine did conceive three times. Each pregnancy ended in early miscarriage. The first, in Oxford at the beginning 1666, seems to have happened when the king was away and took him so much by surprise that he doubted that his wife had actually been pregnant. When the queen lost a second baby, more than two years later, Charles told his sister that he had feared for a long time that Catherine could not conceive at all. After a third miscarriage, in June 1669, the royal couple abandoned any real hope that Catherine would produce children. There had already been talk of divorce and this reached new heights when the divorce of Lord Roos came before Parliament. Irritated by her husband's interest in the case (he seems to have enjoyed it as theatre as much as a reflection on his own situation), Catherine apparently said that she would be perfectly content to retire to a convent. Despite a great deal of encouragement, much of it from the duke of Buckingham, Charles stood by his queen. She also had the support of the duke and duchess of York, who were well advanced on their own journey towards Catholicism and whose prospects would have been diminished by a new, fertile queen.

The talk of divorce died down and Catherine's rival, Lady Castlemaine, lost her hold on Charles II's affections. The death of Minette in 1670 also removed the greatest female influence over her husband. There were other passions, not always requited, and other mistresses by then, but the queen had learned acceptance – and something more. She was beginning to see how she could use these women to her advantage when it suited, allowing her to play a subtle role in court politics. The realization that she would never have children but that her position was safe, at least for the foreseeable future, allowed Catherine of Braganza to move on. She could now forge her own identity as queen. It was something she did with considerable aplomb.

*

IN CREATING A life for herself, Catherine drew on the rich cultural heritage of the Portuguese empire. She is often credited with introducing that most British of activities, tea drinking, to her adopted country. This is not true, as tea was already known in the British Isles, but, at the time of the Restoration, it had only a small following in comparison with the huge success of coffee.

Coffee houses had flourished under Cromwell and those who frequented them were often suspected of harbouring radical ideas. Charles II closed them down temporarily in 1675 – though, by the turn of the eighteenth century, contemporaries believed there were over 3,000 such establishments in London. It was not so much that tea was thought to be somehow less political as a beverage but that it had not caught on in the same way. Catherine's arrival began a slow change that would come to define the British character. Instead of viewing tea as a medicinal brew, Catherine introduced the ladies of her household to the drinking of tea 'solely for pleasure.'[11] It was one of a number of ways in which Catherine influenced the cosmopolitan nature of Charles II's court, steering it away from being merely a cut-down version of the magnificence of Louis XIV's court at Versailles. Charles II was impressed by all things French (unsurprisingly, given that he was half French himself and had spent a considerable number of his formative years in exile in Paris) but he always viewed his pint-sized cousin as a rival. He was happy to be able to display his own version of luxury and good taste.

Queen Catherine's contribution to British life went beyond the merely financial. She brought with her an entirely new sensibility in matters of interior design and furnishings. Her rooms were hung with colourful cotton calicoes from India, the same bright designs and materials used for clothes and bedcovers. Furnishings of cane, intricately detailed lacquer cabinets and exquisite porcelain adorned the queen's apartments. Entranced, many courtiers hastened to copy her. In 1673, John Evelyn visited Lady Mary Tuke, one of Catherine's dressers, at Goring House, her London home, where 'she carried us up into her new dressing room . . . where was a bed, two glasses, silver jars and vases, cabinets and other so rich furniture, as I had seldom seen the like.'[12] Evelyn did not have much taste for what he clearly regarded as pretty fripperies but Lady Tuke was very happy to show off her style.

Catherine also used her patronage to support the arts and music in ways that were distinctly her own. Her Catholic chapel (first at St James's Palace and, after 1671, at Somerset House) was at the heart of her interest in music and its importance has only been fully appreciated since the beginning of the twenty-first century, when detailed research revealed its composition and influence. 'Her chapel employed a diverse team of musicians, many of whom were skilled virtuosos trained in leading European musical institutions.'[13] Shortly before Catherine's arrival, extensive work was undertaken on the organ loft at St James's, part of a wider refurbishment of the original chapel designed in 1623 by Inigo Jones. The ability of the queen to worship freely was a key part of her marriage contract and the work being undertaken at St James's was intended to meet this obligation, gratifying Catholics such as Henry Howard, duke of Norfolk and the half dozen English Benedictines appointed by Charles II as part of the clerical bureaucracy of the queen's chapel. Charles was eternally grateful to Father Huddlestone, an English Benedictine who had helped him escape after the Battle of Worcester in 1651.

Less impressed were the Protestant commentators who heard the first performances of Catherine of Braganza's Portuguese musicians. Portuguese music was very different from what was then admired in Britain and it attracted almost as much derogatory comment as the hairstyles and fashions of the queen and her ladies. The ubiquitous Evelyn and Pepys, of course, had their say. At Hampton Court on 9 June, Evelyn heard a Portuguese ensemble of 'pipes, harps and very ill voices.' The following month, the Venetian ambassador noted that, while the queen did not like the English and French musicians of Charles II's court, the king and his courtiers were disgusted by the 'discordant' concerts of the Portuguese. This pronounced difference of opinion seems to have been caused by English unfamiliarity with the prevalence of woodwinds in Portuguese music and distaste at the use of castratos – or 'eunuchs', as they referred to them – as singers. Pepys wrote his own critique of Portuguese music in September 1662 and it was as unflattering as Evelyn's: 'I heard their music too, which may be good, but it did not appear so to me, neither as to their manner of singing, nor was it good concord to my ears, whatever the matter was.'[14]

Dismayed by this early setback, a number of Catherine's musicians may have left with some of her other servants later in 1662, but the majority remained. By 1666, they were becoming more accepted and their prestige was enhanced by the arrival of a group of Italian musicians who were employed by the queen. The Albrici brothers had previously sung for Queen Christina of Sweden and had entertained in the German courts. Pepys approved of the new sound coming from the queen's chapel, saying in 1668 that its music 'was beyond anything of ours'. Catherine had succeeded in making an effective amalgam of Portuguese and other European musical styles and brought round doubters in Britain. It was all the more gratifying that there was no French involvement.

In art as well as music, the queen soon moved to establish her own identity and to patronize Italian and Catholic Flemish painters. She was painted by Peter Lely in the 1660s but never tried to compete with his adoration of Lady Castlemaine. Instead, she chose a different image in her portraits by Jacob Huysmans and Benedetto Gennari. She would not be the nearly blasphemous Madonna of the countess of Castlemaine but she could be much more than the virginal princess in Portuguese dress, painted by Dirk Stoop. Lely's portrait, which hangs today in the Throne Room of the Palace of Holyroodhouse in Edinburgh, shows Catherine in the style of the Windsor Beauties, complete with the hairstyle of the period and the pearl necklace that adorned the throats of so many of the ladies in Lely's portraits. The queen wears a pretty dress of silver satin embroidered with pearls but the painting lacks the sensuality of Lely's portraits of Barbara. Huysmans decided to present the queen in a very different way, as a shepherdess (Barbara had also been painted in this fashion) but one whose very low neckline and stunning satin costume belied the pastoral context. Huysmans' Catherine is mature and confident, her expression a far cry from the slightly hesitant smile on the lips of Lely's queen. There was also opportunity to play on her name by painting her as St Catherine, a saint who had converted pagans to the true religion and was oppressed by a Roman emperor. The painting was engraved so that it could be circulated more widely, thus ensuring that its image and underlying message of a pure and devoted woman could reach a large audience. The contrast with the king's mistresses and the implied reproach to his treatment of his wife was hard to avoid.[15]

Catherine's determination and success in establishing her own image seems to have pleased Charles II. Though he never loved Catherine, he did develop a gentle affection towards her and she may, as their marriage continued, have had more political influence than is sometimes thought, even if only indirectly. It is probable that she knew about the Secret Treaty of Dover; her private secretary, Sir Richard Bellings, was one of only four men who signed the secret document. This, especially after Minette's death, gave her something of a hold over her husband that went beyond Charles II's appreciation of her cultural interests. Talk of divorce never entirely went away in the 1670s and Catherine was horrified to be accused of being involved in plans to murder the king during the furore of the Popish Plot in 1678, but Charles stood by her. She could never, though, escape the humiliation of having to endure her husband's constant infidelities, the knowledge that most of these women, from actresses to aristocrats, had produced children. Her greatest failure was constantly brought home to her and, after 1671, she had to compete with another *maîtresse-en-titre*, this time a French one, Louise de Kéroualle. Small wonder that she still occasionally lost control of herself and wept with frustration in public. He may have liked the style of Catherine's apartments but Charles seldom used them for socializing. Politicians and ambassadors wanting access to him did not see the queen as a conduit for their ambitions.

Accepting what she could not change with as much dignity as possible, Catherine was at last in control of her own bedchamber and staff appointments. She abolished the post of lady of the bedchamber, giving the role, unofficially, to the countess of Penalva, one of the few Portuguese ladies who remained with her, and reducing the salary of the countess of Castlemaine's aunt, Lady Suffolk, who was retained as lady of the robes. A mother of the maids was appointed to supervise her maids of honour, who were usually the aspiring young daughters of courtiers, and protect them from the king's wandering eye. Catherine also now exercised control of her council, appointing Lord Cornbury, Clarendon's son, as her lord chamberlain in 1667, to replace the earl of Chesterfield. Wherever she could, she sought to balance the influence of the king's mistresses. On a personal level, she got on well with the duke of York and his first wife, Anne Hyde, and also with his second duchess, the Italian, Mary of Modena, who was a further counterbalance to French influence.

In 1685, as her husband lay dying, Catherine visited him twice but was so appalled at his suffering that she could not remain. It was Father Huddlestone, then one of the priests of her household, who gave Charles II the last rites as a Catholic. Catherine would no doubt have seen this as her greatest triumph.

Part Four

'His Coy Mistress'

FRANCES TERESA STUART

1647–1702

CHAPTER NINE

La Belle Stuart

'She is the rising sun'
The French ambassador, Honoré de Courtin, on
Frances Teresa Stuart, July 1665

SHORTLY AFTER NEW Year in 1662, Minette wrote in glowing terms to her brother about a young lady who was about to leave her service to join the English court. 'I would not lose this opportunity of writing to you by Mrs Stuart, who is taking over her daughter to become one of your wife's future maids. If this were not the reason for her departure, I should be very unwilling to let her go, for she is the prettiest girl in the world and one of the best fitted of any I know to adorn your Court.'[1] It is not clear how this appointment, before any official announcement of the queen's household was made public, had come about. One might also question Minette's motives for dangling in front of Charles II such a delicious prospect, since she knew his proclivities very well. Perhaps she hoped that a fresh-faced innocent would act as an antidote to the all-powerful countess of Castlemaine and actually improve the prospects of a successful marriage for her brother. If so, she was to be disappointed, but not for the reasons that she might have anticipated. The young lady in question would, for a number of years, be pursued, pawed and adored by a hopelessly infatuated Charles II without ever becoming his mistress. This in itself was quite a feat. But she could not dislodge Barbara Palmer and was a source of further anxiety for the queen, even if she did not intend to be.

Frances Teresa Stuart was known to contemporaries as 'La Belle Stuart'. She was the daughter of a royalist Scot, Walter Stuart, third son of Lord Blantyre, and his wife, born Sophia Carew, a member of a West Country family, who was a widow with one son when she remarried at the end of the first Civil War. It has been said that Walter Stuart was a doctor but there is no evidence to support this. He had, however, been a member of Parliament for Monmouth. As a younger son of minor aristocrats, Walter Stuart had few prospects after the execution of Charles I and he and his wife, like many other royalists, decided to leave for France, where they joined the throng of disgruntled exiles at Henrietta Maria's court. As a very distant and loyal relation to the ruling Stuarts, Walter had perhaps a better claim than some to the queen dowager's support and his wife was undoubtedly an asset. Renowned for her style and accomplishments as a dancer, Sophia Stuart became one of Henrietta Maria's ladies-in-waiting and adapted well to life in France, though the French thought her cunning as well as courtly.

Her three children with Walter Stuart were brought up as Catholics in France. The family was originally Protestant and Sophia's son by her first marriage, George Nevill, remained resolute in that religion in England. Clearly the Stuarts felt that their family's prospects would be improved by observing their hosts' Catholicism. Nothing is known of Frances' education but she was thoroughly prepared for a role in which she would hope to be noticed in the service of royalty. The favour of Henrietta Maria, coupled with warm approval from Minette, who had known Frances since they were children, was more than sufficient to secure her a place with Catherine of Braganza. Louis XIV may have begun to ogle Frances himself but her mother did not see her future in France. Instead, she manoeuvred to have her sent from one libertine court to another. The novelty of this young

Anglo-Scottish girl with her French polish was instantly felt in London.

Frances was to be one of the queen's maids of honour, a role intended for younger girls of good family, who were part of the consort's entourage but did not have the more onerous duties of a lady-in-waiting. A maid of honour would expect to learn more about the courtier's craft while hoping for a good marriage and advancement to one of the principal roles in the royal household in due course. In return, they were required to be decorative, socially adroit and to behave with discretion and propriety. It was something like a finishing school for well-connected girls but it was not without its dangers. The maids, though generally chaperoned by an older lady, were the objects of keen attention from male courtiers, not to mention the king and the duke of York. The loss of their virtue, if they succumbed to the charms of a persuasive and influential man, could have a devastating effect on their future. It was this exciting world, full of rivalries and pitfalls, that the fifteen-year-old Frances Teresa Stuart was now about to negotiate. In her case, its passage would be made all the more difficult by the inescapable fact that her chief admirer was the monarch himself.

What was it about Frances that attracted such attention and made her one of the most admired ladies at court? The answer is not immediately obvious from her portraits, at least not to a twenty-first-century eye. She is certainly pleasant enough in appearance, with light auburn hair and a good figure, but she lacks the commanding presence of Barbara Palmer. Most of the accounts of her personality come from the so-called memoirs of the count of Gramont, an unreliable source but one whose judgement on Frances has been widely accepted. He describes a rather silly, shallow young woman, who passed her time playing childish games like blind man's buff and building castles of playing cards with the duke of Buckingham. She was easily amused and laughed at everything. 'It is hardly possible,' Gramont concluded, 'for a woman to have less wit or more beauty.' So why on earth should this

vacuous and potentially irritating teenager have become the darling
of the corrupt Restoration court? Her only biographer, writing in
the inimitable and now wholly politically incorrect style of upper-
class male authors of the 1920s, describes, in a passage worthy of
Barbara Cartland, why Charles II found this giggly girl so irresistible:

> While Frances Stuart's gaiety and charm made her enchanting
> to the king as a companion, his senses were held in thrall by
> her peerless beauty. Golden-brown hair in which red lights
> glinted here and there crowned the small head poised on a neck
> that had the smoothness and clarity of alabaster. She possessed
> a bewitching nose, eyes like harebells and an exquisite mouth,
> the upper lip rivalling the curve of the bow which Lely has
> placed in her hand in his most famous portrait of her, the lower
> rather full, a little petulant and perilously fascinating.[2]

It is true that Charles II had tastes in women that might char-
itably be described as catholic and that intellect was not necessarily
high on his list of priorities but, as time would show, there was
more to Frances Teresa Stuart than this fulsome description
suggests. She was soon established as a celebrity in an age which,
much like ours, was constantly on the lookout for instant sparkle.
Novelty may have been a powerful weapon in Frances' armoury,
since she had come from a far more luxurious court, where style
was everything. Anne Boleyn had a similar impact, on her return
from France, in Henry VIII's reign. Both women would find that
being the object of royal desire had dangerous consequences,
though in Frances' case there was a much happier outcome.
Whether her initial flirtation with the king was a result of inex-
perience and perhaps some nervousness on her part, rather than
deliberate calculation, is impossible to say, but Frances was not
an innocent child. She soon understood the power of her attractions. Even though her upbringing had largely been within the
confines of Henrietta Maria's exiled court, the queen mother's

household was not impervious to rumours of scandals and the more colourful behaviour of Louis XIV and his brother, Minette's husband. Her mother, though careful to keep in the background, was also an influence and undoubtedly had ambitions for Frances and her other daughter, Sophia.

Contemporaries certainly shared the king's approval of this new arrival. Pepys could scarcely contain his admiration: 'But above all, Mrs Steward . . . with her hat cocked and a red plume, with her sweet eye, little Roman nose, and excellent *Taille* [figure], is now the greatest beauty I ever saw, I think, in my life; and if ever woman can, doth exceed my Lady Castlemaine; at least in this dress. Nor do I wonder if the king changes, which I verily believe is the reason of his coldness to my Lady Castlemaine.'[3] In these musings, Pepys had touched on an interesting point – namely, the relationship between Barbara and Frances and how it would develop.

Acutely aware of the king's wandering eye, Barbara had swiftly discounted Catherine of Braganza as a rival. She was much less confident about the pretty, disarming Frances Teresa Stuart. Her strategy was to make an ostentatious display of killing the newcomer with kindness. She would become this little girl's best friend, making sure they spent a great deal of time together. And if Frances liked games, Barbara could play them as well as anyone. One evening after dinner she arranged a mock marriage between the two of them, with Frances as the blushing bride and Barbara as her husband. This unseemly diversion soon became the talk of the court: 'Lady Castlemaine a few days since, had Mrs Stuart to an entertainment and at night they began a frolique that they two must be married – and married they were, with ring and all other ceremonies of church-service, and ribands and a sack posset in bed, and flinging the stocking.' This was all very silly but it had a more troubling aspect: 'but in the close it is said that my Lady Castlemaine, who was the bridegroom, rose, and the king came and took her place with pretty Mrs Stuart.'[4]

The court lapped up this sort of gossip and often much worse.

In the same diary entry, Pepys noted reports that at a recent ball, 'a child was dropped by one of the ladies in dancing; but nobody knew who, it being taken up by somebody in their handkerchief.' This sounds like the description of a very public miscarriage. In order to protect the identity of the young lady concerned, all the maids of honour had appeared the next morning as if nothing had happened but it was noted that one of them, Winifred Wells, had fallen sick in the afternoon and then disappeared from court. Winifred's name had been connected with the king before and Charles II was believed to be the father of the child she had lost. There was an even more distasteful rumour that the king, whose interest in science was well known, had subsequently dissected the foetus in his laboratory. While none of this may actually be true, the fact that such lurid stories circulated widely reveals the moral bankruptcy of the Restoration court.

A young woman like Frances Teresa Stuart had to tread very carefully in such surroundings. She evidently liked being the centre of attention and did nothing to discourage Charles II, who petted and caressed her in public. After his marriage, with Frances in regular attendance on Catherine of Braganza, it was said that the queen dreaded going out from her bedchamber into her dressing room in the morning for fear that she would find her husband canoodling with Frances. But though the king would have liked to have showered Frances with expensive presents she seems to have refused anything that was not appropriate to her role as the queen's servant and she consistently refused to sleep with him. Nor did she exhibit the slightest interest in playing a part in factional politics. Buckingham thought she might be of use in furthering his own ambitions and balancing the influence of Lady Castlemaine but soon realized that Frances had nothing to offer him in that respect. Henry Bennet also tried to gain her good offices and fared even worse. It was said that during their discussion she had been reminded of how effectively Buckingham had mimicked him behind his back and was unable to suppress her laughter.

In a court full of self-serving, untrustworthy political operators, no one had realized that Frances Teresa Stuart was more than able to match them when it came to manipulation. Even the duke of York was said to have fallen for her and during Catherine of Braganza's illness the word went around that the king was intent on marrying Frances if his wife died. Frances had held Charles II in thrall for so long precisely because she would not give him what he desired most – a fully sexual relationship. Yet what she herself wanted has never been easy to comprehend. It may have been nothing more than attention and fame, gratification that her beauty was an achievement in itself and that its purity was not for sale. She had played a dangerous game with remarkable consistency and much more intelligence than anyone realized. By 1667, after five years as the darling of the court, she knew that she could not keep it up for very much longer.

CHAPTER TEN

The One Who Got Away

'The court in Farthing yet itself does please
And female Stuart there, Rules the four Seas'
Andrew Marvell, 'Last Instructions
to a Painter', 1667

MARVELL'S BITTER, BRILLIANT poem demonstrated the disdain he felt for the English Crown, court and politicians at the end of the First Dutch War. Underneath the brittle hedonism of the first decade of the reign, there was a palpable sense of fury and despair. What was a man who had tutored Mary Fairfax, the unhappy wife of the duke of Buckingham, written a stirring ode to Oliver Cromwell on his return from Ireland, and yet still entertained hopes for the Restoration, to make of the humiliating end of a conflict that had seen Dutch warships destroy the English fleet at anchor on the River Medway? To the Great Plague of 1665, followed swiftly by the Great Fire of 1666, was added the loss of Surinam and Nova Scotia to a more effective enemy, while any hope of compensation for English merchants was abandoned. Though the profligacy and immorality of Charles II's court rubbed salt into wounded national pride, there was a deeper, inescapable reality that at least absolved the king of dallying with his mistresses at the expense of national interest: 'As during the previous hundred years, the English monarchy was simply priced out of the market of sustained European warfare.'¹ Lack of funds was a powerful restrictive force on Charles II, as it had been on the Tudors. The country Charles ruled was still a marginal player in the seventeenth-century world. Small wonder, then, that he looked elsewhere for financial support, since squeezing it out of his Parliament was such a thankless task. And while his mind ran over the consequences of defeat at the hands of another small country – ruled, nominally, by his own nephew – he was still hopelessly in love with a girl regarded by most of those who thought they knew her as an empty-headed flibbertigibbet, who continued to refuse his advances despite the temptations of titles and property. The general feeling was that the king would give Frances Teresa Stuart anything she wanted so long as she agreed, at last, to sleep with him.

While she still resisted, Frances was set to be remembered for something more than being the eternal object of the monarch's desire. At the height of her fame at court, she sat as the model for Britannia on the new coinage. If Charles could not yet possess the young lady's body, he could have her face immortalized and she would become, in effect, public property. In 1667, Frances was the model for the Flemish-born artist John Roettiers, who was chief engraver at the Royal Mint. Unlike Marvell, Pepys and Evelyn both applauded the choice of Frances as Britannia. At a difficult time, her depiction represented a positive hope for the future, an antidote to cynicism and the loss of Britain's reputation in the world. Pepys noted that, while visiting his goldsmith, '[I] did observe the king's new medal where in little there is Mrs Stewart's face, as well done as ever I saw anything in my whole life I think . . . and a pretty thing it is that he should choose her face to represent Britannia by.'² Writing later, Evelyn complimented Roettiers on how well he had caught Frances' expression: 'Monsieur Roti . . . so accurately expressed the countenance of the Duchess of R – in the head of Britannia, in the reverse of some of our coin . . . as one may easily and almost at first sight know it to be her Grace. And though in the smallest copper . . . such as may justly stand in competition with the ancient Masters.'³ So, indeed, she remained, her image surviving on British coinage until decimalization. But the reference to Frances as duchess of Richmond rather than Mrs Stewart is revealing. For, by March 1667, at the age of twenty, even as she sat for Roettiers, Frances had realized that she could not fend off Charles II for much longer. She desperately needed a husband, preferably of high birth, with a title and wealth, who could protect her and keep her in the manner to which she had become accustomed. Luckily for Frances, one such gentleman had just lost his second wife at the beginning of the year.

*

CHARLES STUART, SIXTH duke of Lennox and third duke of Richmond, was one of the most prominent, if not necessarily the most popular or influential, members of the aristocracy at Charles II's court. He was of noble descent on both sides, his father, George Stuart, being a member of the Franco-Scottish d'Aubigny branch of the Stuarts and his mother, Katherine Howard, the daughter of the second earl of Suffolk. Despite this illustrious pedigree and the possession of extensive lands in England and Scotland, the course of his life had not always been easy. His parents' marriage had been a love match, undertaken in secret despite the disapproval of her family and Charles I, the guardian of the children of this junior branch of his dynasty. Katherine Howard (in itself a name with unfortunate associations) was a considerable beauty, as can be seen in Van Dyck's portrait of the young couple, which bears the motto, 'Love Conquers All'. It could not, alas, ensure safety against the perils about to convulse the nation. In 1642, when he was only three years old, Charles Stuart's father had been mortally wounded at Edgehill, the first battle of the English Civil Wars. His mother moved to join the royalist court at Oxford the following year but was imprisoned in the Tower because of her involvement with the Waller plot, an attempt to rouse support for the king in London. She later remarried but remained true to her royalist past, joining the exiles at The Hague and dying there in 1654.[4]

Wardship of the fifteen-year-old Charles Stuart now passed to his second cousin, the Parliamentary general Charles Fleetwood, who was Oliver Cromwell's son-in-law. Hopes were entertained by senior politicians of the English republic that the young man might fit well into the new Cromwellian elite but Charles's sympathies, like his appearance, were those of his mother. By 1658 he was in Paris, living with his uncle, Ludovic Stuart, the man who would later officiate at the Catholic marriage ceremony of Charles II and Catherine of Braganza. France suited Charles but he had inherited his mother's penchant for conspiracy and, when he took part in the unsuccessful royalist uprising of Sir George Booth in August 1659, the Council of State sequestered his goods and lands. The fall of the English republic changed his fortunes once again and not long after he accompanied Charles II on his triumphal entry into London, the unexpected death of his young cousin, Esmé Stuart, brought him the dukedoms of Richmond and Lennox. This confirmed him as a significant power in Scottish politics and a leading courtier in Whitehall.

The duke was already a keen, though often unsuccessful, gambler and this was a hand he did not play at all well. Scotland had been neglected by the Stuart monarchy since James I came south in 1603 and to thrive in its politics took far greater cunning, ruthlessness and intelligence than Richmond possessed. Though a member of the Scottish Privy Council, he rarely attended meetings, preferring instead to exercise his hereditary rights as lord of Dumbarton Castle and fit out privateers, a particular interest of his. A clumsy attempt to strike at Charles II's powerful lieutenant in Scotland, the earl of Lauderdale, by reforming the Edinburgh parliament failed badly. Charles II had never shown much personal warmth towards his cousin and now he actively disliked and distrusted him. This did not stop Richmond from fighting duels or amassing further titles in England. He had not actively courted royal displeasure but he was to feel its full fury when he secretly married Frances Teresa Stuart at the end of March 1667.

Richmond's second wife, Margaret, had died just three months earlier but a remarriage within this time frame was not necessarily thought unseemly in those days. It was not the brevity of his widowerhood but the identity of his new spouse that mattered, and, in particular, the way they had gone about tying the knot. Charles II seems not to have suspected that Frances had any interest in Richmond until the nervous couple approached him for permission to marry. Evidently stung, and perhaps hoping that he could still win Frances by stalling, the king agreed to the match, with the proviso that Richmond must make an appropriate financial settlement on Frances. In theory, this would not have been difficult, but Richmond's extravagant lifestyle was already well known and making provisions that would have met with royal approval might have been time-consuming. Frances feared that the king would not, ultimately, give his consent. She left London secretly and travelled by coach with Richmond to his mansion, Cobham Hall, in Kent. They were probably married on Saturday, 30 March 1667.

The circumstances of Frances' departure are open to speculation. Gramont has a characteristically entertaining story that the elopement (for that is what it amounted to) was triggered by the jealous Lady Castlemaine, who, wishing to cause trouble between the king and her rival, suggested that Mrs Stuart's excuses that she must leave the royal presence one evening because of fatigue had an altogether different cause. The king, so accustomed to cuckolding other men, did not take kindly to the idea that the duke of Richmond might be enjoying a lady who had resisted him for five years. Marching angrily into Frances' apartments at Whitehall, he found her lying in her bed with the duke seated beside her at her pillow, talking to her. This scene was sufficiently compromising to enrage him even further: 'The King, who of all men was one of the most mild and gentle, testified his resentment to the Duke of Richmond in such terms as he had never before used. The Duke was speechless and almost petrified . . . he made a profound bow and retired, without replying a single word to the vast torrent of threats and menaces that were poured upon him.' He left immediately. Frances was said to have responded with some spirit, saying that she considered herself a slave in a free country and that 'she knew of no engagement that could prevent her from disposing of her hand as she thought proper.' She claimed that the duke's intentions were honourable though she could offer no other justification for his being in her bedchamber at midnight.[5] Whatever the truth of this tale, Frances and Richmond were clearly not inclined to wait around any longer.

Despite the drama surrounding the beginning of their married life together, Frances and Richmond do seem to have been genuinely in love. Like many other men at the Restoration court, he was evidently smitten by her beauty but seems also to have trusted and valued her judgement. After the early death of his first wife and a far from happy relationship with his second, he was looking for a woman who would not just enhance his status, since that was high already, but of whom he was genuinely fond. Richmond was not greatly admired by contemporaries, some of whom dismissed him as a spendthrift and drunken sot with a weakness for gambling, but it is unlikely that Frances would have married him on the basis of that reputation, no matter how imperative it had become to escape the clutches of Charles II. Both Richmond and his new wife seem to have seen in one another something that commentators at the time did not discern – a desire to live comfortably and companionably and an ambition to succeed on their own terms. They had behaved with some daring, a quality not until then associated with either of them, and it was widely thought that they would pay the price. Pepys reported on 3 April that 'the king hath said that he will never see her more'.[6]

They were certainly testing the waters when they arrived back in London on the same day as Pepys's diary entry, staying with Mrs Sophia Stuart in her lodgings at Somerset House. When it was made clear to them that they would not yet be welcome back at court, they retired again to Cobham Hall. Their return coincided with the fall of Clarendon and rumours circulated that he had encouraged Richmond to marry Frances to prevent the king from divorcing Catherine of Braganza and marrying Frances himself. Given his consistency in rejecting the idea of divorce, it is unlikely that Charles ever realistically harboured the idea of making Frances Stuart his queen. She was not of appropriate rank and though he had lusted after her for years any remarriage would surely have been for political rather than personal reasons.

While the court may have missed Frances and her warmth and spontaneity, the new duchess of Richmond was enjoying the first months of married life at Cobham Hall, a house that captured her heart and where she was to spend increasing amounts of time. By June, news that she was pregnant reached Richmond's tenants in Scotland. His agent wrote of the enthusiastic response that had come from far and wide: 'I am afraid the news of her Grace's being with child will make all your Grace's vassals mad; some of them have come to me almost 100 miles only to be informed of the certainty. It is looked upon here as no small miracle to hear so great brutes as they be so heartily zealous for both your Graces and the young Lord Darnley . . .' This suggests that, as well as displaying their loyalty, Richmond's tenants were relieved that, at last, they might have assurance for their own futures. They were, however, to be disappointed. If Frances was pregnant, she must have miscarried, for there was to be no heir then or in the subsequent five years of her marriage.

Frances and her husband hoped for a reconciliation with the king but it was so slow in coming that they appear to have seriously considered moving to France to take up residence on the duke of Richmond's estates there. The marquis de Ruvigny wrote to Louis XIV in late October 1667, saying that, 'the duchess of Richmond, formerly Miss Stuart, is preparing to go to France soon to request your majesty to place her husband in possession of the estate of Aubigny.' It was believed that Frances would join Henrietta Maria's household once again, taking the place of the countess of Guildford, who had recently died. Ruvigny went on to add that, 'she despairs of a reconciliation [with Charles II] and she is right.' But he was, in fact, wrong, though it took a dangerous illness for the past to be suddenly forgotten and forgiven. In March 1668, almost exactly a year after her marriage to Richmond, Frances contracted smallpox.

Though very ill, Frances was expected to recover. No one believed, however, that her famous beauty would survive unscathed. Smallpox could permanently disfigure the most handsome of men and women. In the previous century, Lady Mary Sidney nursed Elizabeth I through smallpox, only to succumb herself to the disease, with heartbreaking results for her appearance. Her husband, away on royal business, recorded: 'I left her a full fair lady, in mine eye, at least, the fairest, and when I returned I found her as foul a lady as the smallpox could make her.'[7] This was the future that many believed now awaited the duchess of Richmond, and the king himself, immediately forgiving Frances for her behaviour, was only too well aware of the dangers: 'I cannot tell whether the duchess of Richmond will be much marked with the smallpox,' he wrote to Minette, 'she has many and I fear they will at least do her no good.' The damage to Frances' much-admired beauty was less than feared, but did affect one of her eyes, which was left with a permanent slight droop. Noting that he had not seen Frances in over a year, Charles II was able to reassure his sister that Frances was 'not much marked with the smallpox . . . and I hope she will not be much changed, as soon as her eye is well, for she has a very great defluction in it and even some danger of having a blemish in it.'[8] Frances' illness had, he said, 'made me pardon all that is past.' Her rejection and betrayal, as the king saw it, was now put to one side, if never entirely forgotten. He had experienced the bitter taste of the kind of humiliation he consistently wreaked on his wife, though it would not suddenly turn him into a faithful husband. Nothing could change his essential nature. The duchess of Richmond, meanwhile, was relieved to have survived her illness and to be able to enjoy royal favour once more. She returned to court as a lady of the bedchamber to Catherine of Braganza, who seems always to have liked her regardless of Charles II's infatuation, and remained resolutely loyal to the queen when Louise de Kéroualle became the king's mistress.

Her marriage continued to be happy, though the duke of Richmond was frequently absent, visiting his estates or fulfilling military duties. He was undertaking extensive building work at Cobham Hall and left Frances in charge of its management. The woman once regarded as little more than an empty-headed decoration at court proved herself both capable and businesslike in handling Richmond's affairs and he clearly trusted her judgement. His financial position remained precarious but he evidently considered that a man of his status could not be expected to economize or cut back on costs. He was accustomed to spending freely. His accounts show that, in 1662–3, he owed his London goldsmith more than £450 for 'twelve dishes and thirty-six trencher plates of silver', more than £57,000 today.[9] His estates did not produce an income commensurate with such spending. Their upkeep and improvement were a constant drain and his gambling and love of horse racing only added to the difficulties he faced. In 1669, he spent six months in France following his recognition by the French government as the eleventh seigneur d'Aubigny. His uncle Ludovic Stuart had actually died four years earlier but Richmond now felt it necessary to make good his claim. During his absence, Frances worked hard to get him an English pension of £1,000 a year, as reparation for losses during the Civil Wars, but she was unwilling to apply directly to Charles II and grew embarrassed at having to importune friends. Her husband, though not a popular figure in the king's immediate circle, was not without friends. Sir Anthony Ashley Cooper, later earl of Shaftesbury, was a prominent politician who took up Richmond's cause, lobbying for the duke to be sent as ambassador to Poland. He did not succeed because, though chancellor of the exchequer, he was not close to the king and he was still recovering from a serious illness, which had nearly cost him his life the previous year when a cyst on his liver ruptured. Besides, the duke of Richmond had further compromised his already awkward relationship with Charles II by doing homage to Louis XIV in return for confirmation of his rights to the Aubigny lands. Nor did he help his overall image by becoming involved, in 1671, with the dukes of Monmouth and Albemarle in a fracas in Whetstone Park in London, which resulted in the death of a local constable who was only trying to keep the peace. The king was obliged to intervene personally to save his son and two of the country's leading noblemen from being brought to trial for murder.

The incident seems to have caused Charles II and his advisers to reconsider Richmond's request for a diplomatic posting, perhaps on the basis that he would be less of an embarrassment abroad than he was at home. Accordingly, he was appointed as ambassador to Denmark in February 1672. There never seems to have been any suggestion that Frances would accompany him, though it was certainly not uncommon for wives of ambassadors to do so. The couple decided that there were greater advantages if she remained in England. She continued to reside in their apartments at Bowling Green in the Whitehall Palace complex and to enjoy court life in the service of the queen. Her husband left her in charge of managing all his financial affairs, a complex, time-consuming task but one which Frances carried out with single-mindedness and aplomb. Richmond's confidence in her was absolute: 'I cannot so well leave money in any hands as yours,' he told her.[10]

The duke found Denmark a major disappointment. He took with him a large entourage of servants decked out in new livery and two new coaches, one lined in crimson velvet, but he soon felt lonely and trapped under the leaden skies of the north. He had arrived in a rainy spring but even summer and its lighter days could not lift his mood: 'Never man was so weary of a place as I am of this,' he wrote of Copenhagen, 'it being I think the least diverting of any place I ever came in.'[11] He and Frances exchanged letters frequently, but the post was unreliable and she thought that his correspondence had often been opened before it got to her. But while there may have been little to do, Richmond, true to form, alleviated the boredom by amassing considerable debts and drinking too much. As a senior aristocrat representing the interests of his king to the Danish monarchy, the duke was not going to skimp on appearances. The goal of his mission was to encourage the Danes to join the Anglo-French alliance against the Dutch and, while he may have been unenthusiastic about his surroundings, he undertook meetings with Danish politicians in a committed and serious manner, without making any major diplomatic breakthrough. Danish foreign policy was directed by the chief minister of state, Count Peder Griffenfeld, who did not want to annoy either his powerful neighbour, Sweden, or France, but who was stymied by opposition at home.

Richmond's mission ended in tragedy. Less than two weeks before Christmas 1672, wrapped up in the furs he had brought with him to keep out the cold of the Scandinavian winters, the duke had himself rowed out into the sound, off the coast of Elsinore, to go aboard an English frigate that was at anchor there. Ignoring advice that such an action might be interpreted as an insult by the Danish government, he decided to brave the heavy snow and freezing temperatures for the sake of a change to a wearisome routine and the prospect of some good company. Accompanied by Sir John Paul, the English consul in Elsinore, Richmond was entertained by Captain Taylor, in command of the ship, and it was, according to Paul's perhaps rather tactful report, a very enjoyable occasion: 'several healths were drunk but I cannot say to any great hight of drinking as I have seen his Grace at other times do . . . it's true his Grace was a little merry but not to say much concerned.'[12] The duke had, in fact, drunk at least a couple of bottles of wine but this might have been of less relevance were it not for the extreme cold. When he came to leave, disaster struck. Missing his footing, he 'fell betwixt the ship and the boat and sank straight . . .' The sailors managed to fish him out alive but a combination of shock and hypothermia were too much for a system already weakened by years of overindulgence. In the coach taking him back to Elsinore, he suffered violent convulsions and died in his lodgings that evening.

Richmond's passing was a great blow to Frances and left her with problems that would take years to resolve. The duke's extravagant lifestyle and the expenses of running so many properties in England, Scotland and France meant that his debts were huge. Even repatriating his body proved difficult and it was over a year before his remains were returned to England and his final resting place, in Henry VII's chapel in Westminster Abbey. If this was not distressing enough, his widow faced an uncertain future. Her childlessness was itself a problem. In such circumstances, the titles and estates of Lennox and Richmond reverted to the Crown. Charles II, his resentment of Frances and her behaviour towards him now firmly in the past, allowed her the use of the Lennox estate for the rest of her lifetime. The situation in England was not so straightforward.

The duke had made a will before he left for Denmark. He hoped that his lands and possessions, 'a great personal estate consisting in money, jewels, plate, debts, leases, rich hangings, furniture, household stuff, cattle and several shares in several ships . . . a great part of which remained at Cobham, in Denmark, at Whitehall, at Duke's Yard and at his house in St Martin's Lane and divers places in England and other rents in Scotland and France', would be 'sufficient to pay his debts with an overplus.'[13] But he was never very good with money and his executors found that, while the will might sound impressive, reality was something quite different. Frances was left £2,000 a year and the right to remain in Cobham Hall for life, provided she remained unmarried. On her death, it was to revert to his sister, Lady Catherine O'Brien.

Problems arose when Lady Catherine, who had never been on the best of terms with Frances, contested the terms of the will. She filed a lawsuit claiming that Frances should not have been given possession of Cobham Hall nor allowed to keep any of the jewels and personal gifts from the duke until all the debts had been paid. This would, in practice, have left Frances in straitened personal circumstances – not penniless, because she had her income from her position as lady of the bedchamber to Queen Catherine and she was still allowed to keep apartments at Whitehall, but she would hardly have been able to live as befits a duchess. The legal wrangling dragged on for five years. Frances, with characteristic tenacity, filed a counter-suit against her sister-in-law, claiming that Catherine was intent on depriving her of her legacies. The dispute was finally settled in 1677, when Frances agreed to sell her life interest in Cobham Hall to Lady Catherine. In the same year, she resigned her interest in her husband's French estates to the king in return for a pension of £1,000 a year, about £150,000 today. He would pass both the French and English titles that had belonged to Frances' husband to his youngest illegitimate son, the product of his long-term affair with Louise de Kéroualle. Frances could not stand Louise but she needed the financial security that came from giving up the Aubigny estates. Her income was supplemented by collecting the aulnage (a duty on cloth) that had formed part of Richmond's estate.

Frances lived on into the beginning of the reign of Charles's niece, Anne, attending the new queen's coronation in April 1702, six months before her death. Though a Catholic, she did not join James II and Mary of Modena in exile and was buried next to her husband in Westminster Abbey. Most of her estate was left in trust, the money to be used to purchase the Scottish estate of the Maitlands, where the house was to be named Lennoxlove and settled on the Blantyres, her father's family. Today her portrait adorns the walls of Lennoxlove House, one of the finest homes in southern Scotland, a testament to an extremely clever woman who had kept the amorous king dangling on a string for years and eventually got away from him with her honour intact.

Part Five

❧

The Stage and the Throne

NELL GWYN

1651(?)–87

CHAPTER ELEVEN

From Bawdy House to the King's Bed

'... saw pretty Nelly standing at her lodgings door in Drury
Lane in her smock-sleeves and bodice ... she seemed a mighty
pretty creature'

Diary of Samuel Pepys, 1 May 1667

CHARLES II WAS enthralled by the theatre. It was in his blood,
on both the Stuart and Bourbon sides of his heritage. Six weeks
after the king's return from exile, Sir William Davenant drafted
a document for Charles's signature which would give himself and
fellow royalist Thomas Killigrew control of the public theatre in
London. Davenant had been knighted by Charles I for his 'loyalty
and poetry', and his career during the 1630s and the Civil Wars
demonstrated both in abundance. As Prince of Wales, Charles II
had watched his parents perform in the masques written by
Davenant; poignantly, the only one they ever acted in together, in
1640, was the last written by Davenant before the troubles that
engulfed the monarchy. Like Tom Killigrew, Davenant carried
messages between Charles I and Henrietta Maria when the wars
separated them. Both men were seasoned courtiers with a love
for writing and experience in the production and management of
plays and opera. Charles II had every reason to trust and support

them, not just for their talents and unswerving loyalty, but because they were also a link with his past, being of his parents' generation.

Davenant's draft of the royal warrant, dated 19 July 1660, announced that it was 'our will and pleasure . . . that you prepare a Bill for our signature to pass our Great Seal of England, containing a grant unto our trusty and well-beloved Thomas Killigrew Esquire, one of the Grooms of our Bedchamber and Sir William Davenant, Knight, to give them full power and authority to erect two companies of players consisting respectively of such persons as they shall choose and appoint; and to purchase or build and erect at their charges as they shall think fit two Houses or Theatres.'[1] Thus Restoration theatre was born, a shared monopoly between two men, whose managerial capabilities would prove very different, with Davenant's Duke's Company eventually absorbing Killigrew's King's Company in 1682, when financial difficulties overwhelmed the latter. Davenant was dead well before then but, like Killigrew, he had developed a fine troupe of actors – and, more importantly, actresses as well.

It would, in fact, be another two years before the employment of actresses to play women's parts was made an explicit requirement in another document, known as Killigrew's Patent: 'and we do likewise permit and give leave,' ordered the king, 'that all the women's parts to be acted in either of the said two companies for the time to come may be performed by women.'[2] Before the Restoration, all female parts in public theatre performances were played by men, often good-looking boys who specialized in such roles, of whom the best known was Edward Kynaston. However, although it was not the custom in England for women to act in public, aristocratic ladies had been performing in masques and other similar entertainments at court and in private houses since at least the beginning of the seventeenth century. Charles II's grandmother, Anne of Denmark, had featured prominently in a number of Inigo Jones's splendid creations for the court of James I, and his mother, Henrietta Maria, had acted in a court masque in 1626 as part of the celebrations for her sixteenth birthday, in the first year of her marriage to Charles I. The French had embraced the role of the actress much sooner than the English, who were characteristically outraged by the arrival of a troupe made up entirely of female performers in 1628. Charles II had, while in exile in France and Germany, attended a number of theatrical entertainments where women took female roles, and was clearly a supporter of the concept. He was determined that the style of the Restoration stage would reflect European practice. More than that, his patent to Killigrew was actually couched in moralistic terms to justify the change, claiming that the representation of women by men offended public morality and encouraged vice. Given that Restoration actresses would immediately find themselves viewed as sex objects and fair game by their male admirers, managers and playwrights, this seems more than a little disingenuous. 'In practical terms, the freedom women gained to play themselves on the stage was to a large extent the freedom to play the whore.'[3]

The king's enthusiasm for female performers would find its outlet in his bed as well as on the London stage but the identity of the first lady to tread the boards in a public capacity remains shrouded in mystery. Davenant had used a female singer, Mrs Coleman, in his opera *The Siege of Rhodes* in the late 1650s but though this was a non-speaking part in a private production, there were a considerable number of such entertainments throughout the republican period. The Protector himself, hardly a matinee idol, had participated in the revelries for the marriage of his daughter, Mary, to Viscount Fauconberg in November 1657, in a masque written by Andrew Marvell, in which he had appeared as Jove. Cromwell, who loved music, had certainly tolerated Davenant and his operas during the republican period and many of the Cromwellian elite were patrons of the arts. Nevertheless, there were no public performances for eighteen years, since the start of the Civil Wars, when Parliament closed the theatres. Reopening them would prove problematic; there were only three or four left in London, in a state of disrepair, and neither Killigrew nor Davenant saw trying to refurbish them as a viable option. In fact, it was not clear whether they could initially draw audiences at all from among the wider London population, unaccustomed as it was to the entire idea of public performance, and both men concentrated their first business ventures in more modest venues, using tennis courts with roofs, a common solution in Europe. These were quite confined spaces, seating no more than 450 people, and it was hoped that their very intimacy would appeal to the aristocratic audiences who had been deprived of theatre for so long. The demographic of Restoration theatre would change gradually as confidence and interest grew, with audiences encompassing a wide range of occupations. Pepys himself was a great lover of theatre, and though well connected, he was certainly no aristocrat.

The great diarist recorded that the first time he had seen a woman in a female role on the stage was at Killigrew's temporary theatre in Vere Street. It had formerly been Gibbon's tennis court and was poorly lit, with uncomfortable seating, no heating, no scenery and no refreshments, except the fruit offered for sale between acts by the orange girls who plied their wares in front of the stage. Despite the lack of creature comforts and the less-than-impressive performances of the ladies of the company, small though their parts were, Pepys was entranced. It was 3 January 1661 and he wrote in his diary that mid-afternoon performance in the gathering gloom of a midwinter's day that it was 'the first time that ever I saw women come upon the stage.' The first time for him, but there had been other performances with women taking important roles, towards the end of 1660. Davenant had recruited six actresses almost immediately, and Killigrew four. Although we know their names, we do not know which of these ladies took the part of Desdemona in Killigrew's production of *Othello*. Scholars of Restoration theatre favour Anne Marshall, who would soon specialize in tragic roles, as the most probable. The production was first performed on 8 December 1660. Though there are no surviving reviews, Killigrew may have sacrificed sophistication for speed, since it was apparent to Pepys a few weeks later that not all of the actresses had complete command of their lines. As the two theatre companies grew more confident in their productions, such teething troubles disappeared, so that by the summer of 1661 the actress was no longer a phenomenon, but an established and recognized part of the English stage.

To be accepted is one thing. To be respected is quite another. The first English actresses may have been considered ladies of easy virtue by many in their audiences but it was not an easy career to follow. The companies offered a number of plays in repertory so there were constantly lines to be learned, rehearsals attended and rivalries managed. Remuneration was far from generous and women earned less than men. Elizabeth Barry, one of the most successful Restoration actresses, earned fifty shillings a week while her leading man, Thomas Betterton, earned five pounds. Actresses who were married, very often to male performers in their company, were less subject to criticism of their morals and the unwanted attentions of admirers than their single colleagues. Most were not fallen women, in the Victorian sense. In order to carry off the demands of the various roles they were required to play and learn, Restoration actresses needed to be literate and have good memories. Their backgrounds varied; some, like Moll Davis, were bastards of aristocrats, others were from families who had fallen on hard times. They were always a minority in the theatre companies and had limited input to the management of their profession. Those who tried to take a more active role, such as Elizabeth Barry, found themselves the targets of satire and ridicule, as did female playwrights such as Aphra Behn. Restoration actresses struggled with the contradiction that women's voices had become louder as a result of the changes of the mid-seventeenth century – even to be allowed to appear on the stage itself and to be thought of as a functioning individual, distinct from a man, was an achievement – but that society was still largely patriarchal and, while men may have liked the idea of a degree of sexual liberation for women, they were not so keen on expressions of independence. Given these challenges, it is remarkable that one of the most popular comedy actresses of the period, the illiterate daughter of a brothel owner, should have overcome the difficulties of her past to become perhaps the best known of all the mistresses of Charles II.

*

THERE IS NO hard and fast evidence for the date or place of birth of Eleanor (Nell) Gwyn. The city of Hereford claims her, and her most recent biographer, a descendant, believes she was born in Oxford.[4] Nor can her father be identified with any certainty. A satirical poem of 1681 asserted that her father died in Oxford in a debtors' prison. At the time of the Glorious Revolution, in 1688, it was said that he was a certain Captain Thomas Gwyn, of Welsh descent, an officer in the royalist army. These two titbits of information are not, of course, necessarily contradictory. Nell's sister, Rose Gwyn, claimed in an application for bail, made from prison in 1663, that her father had 'lost all in the service of the late King.' The girls' mother, Helena Smith, a Londoner, may never have actually married Thomas Gwyn, even if he was their father. Nell's origins are therefore obscure and the various colourful stories about her upbringing in the Drury Lane area of London cannot themselves be substantiated. She may have found it useful and entertaining to tell people, as she apparently did Samuel Pepys, that she was 'brought up in a bawdy-house to fill strong water to the guests'.[5] The notion that her mother, who does seem to have had problems with alcohol, was also a brothel keeper has gained a great deal of credence. Given the high incidence of prostitution in London at the time, it is not improbable. By 1663, perhaps because of the proximity of her home to Thomas Killigrew's Theatre Royal, Nell had become an orange girl there, selling fruit to theatregoers. The girls needed to be voluble, pert and confident if they were to do their job well. The date most often given for Nell's birth is 1651, which would have made her about twelve or thirteen at the most when she first stood in front of the stage, peddling her wares. Within two years, she would be treading the boards themselves, exhibiting a natural gift as a comedienne which transformed her life.

The wit and vivacity which captivated the king are not immediately obvious in Nell's portraits. Like her past, there is no agreement about her colouring. She has been described as having auburn hair by some writers and being fair by others. In the Lely portrait of 1675, she appears to have been a brunette. As the Restoration court favoured dark-haired women, she could, by then, have dyed it for fashion's sake, as Frances Teresa Stuart did. Her face, with its bulbous eyes and overly rouged cheeks, is interesting but not beautiful. The secrets of her undoubted attraction must have lain in her animation and wicked sense of humour, her capacity for sending herself up as well as others. The little orange girl swiftly became a clever, exhilarating woman, at ease with her sexuality and keen to develop the acting skills that had been discovered by chance. For Nell Gwyn, the stage offered an irresistible chance to escape the grime of London life, to be admired and feted and enjoy the financial security that had eluded her family. That she could follow this path at all was made much easier by her relationship, both on and off the stage, with one of the leading actors of the day, Charles Hart.

Hart had served briefly as a cavalry lieutenant under Prince Rupert at the start of the Civil Wars but had subsequently spent most of his time with a company of exiled English actors on the continent. The theatre was in his blood (his father was an actor) and was a more natural environment for him than the battlefield. He had performed for Charles II during the first year of his exile, in Paris, in 1646. Hart had a financial share in the newly formed King's Company after the Restoration and also helped his fellow actors manage their finances, so his abilities were not confined to pretending to be someone else. Nevertheless, by the time Nell Gwyn came into his life, he was an acknowledged star, well known for playing leading roles in serious drama. He brought such dignity to his performances in tragedy that the company's prompter wrote of his acting 'with such grandeur and agreeable majesty that one of the court was pleased to honour him with this commendation; that Hart might teach any king on earth how to comport himself.'[6] The identity of this admiring courtier is not revealed but it is an interesting comment by a member of a court not noted for its dignity. Hart did not, however, teach Nell Gwyn how to play tragic roles. That was never her forte. Instead, he helped her develop quickly into an outstanding comedienne. Together, they created the so-called 'gay couple' (a term that nowadays would have very different connotations), 'the most distinctive new contribution to comedy of the 1660s, the first new change in the comic form in the Restoration'.[7]

Charles Hart was more than twenty-five years older than Nell Gwyn and may well have been something of a father figure as well as a mentor and lover. Their professional collaboration began in May 1665, shortly before the Great Plague overwhelmed London. The play was James Howard's *All Mistaken*. Hart and the King's Company realized at once that they had found in Nell a leading lady of distinction and flair in comic roles. Pepys, with his characteristic weakness for hyperbole, enthused over their performances: 'Nell's and Hart's mad parts are most excellently done, but especially hers', he would later write.[8] The commercial implications were obvious, especially when the duke of Buckingham offered the company an adaptation of Fletcher's *The Chances* in 1667. Buckingham's version enlarged a non-speaking part originally assigned to a drunken whore and invented a witty, worldly-wise heroine with a gift for repartee. This was precisely the sort of part that Nell Gwyn, who was barely literate when she joined the King's Company, was born to play.[9] How she learned her lines for this and the many other roles required for repertory is something of a mystery. Her fellow actors may have helped her learn to read or simply read her lines off to her so that she could memorize them.

The most successful of all the collaborations of Hart and Gwyn was John Dryden's *Secret Love*, a runaway success for the company, in which the two leads played the 'gay couple', Celadon and

Florimell. It is probable that Dryden wrote the part of Florimell especially for Nell, based on her character and acting skills. Already much admired, her performance in it made her a star. Pepys said that he believed it to be the greatest comical performance the world had ever seen. *Secret Love* became the model for future Restoration comedies with its assertive heroine and the couple's reluctance to surrender to the constrictions of a conventional married relationship. In another play written by Dryden in 1668, *An Evening's Love*, Nell's character, Donna Jacintha, is asked by the hero, Wildblood (played again by Hart), what a gentleman might hope from her. The answer is highly revealing: 'To be admitted to pass my time with, while a better comes: to be the lowest step in my staircase, for a Knight to mount upon him, and a Lord upon him, and a Marquess upon him, and a Duke upon him, till I get as high as I can climb.'[10] Among the spectators were the duke of York and Charles II himself.

*

NELL WAS ALREADY mixing in elevated company, since some of the King's Company's performances were performed privately at court, with costumes paid for out of the royal purse. She knew Buckingham, Sir Charles Sedley, the pudgy-faced, amiable drinking companion of the king and the rakish earl of Rochester. Sedley was noted as a wit and conversationalist, whose fondness for the bottle sometimes involved him in antisocial behaviour. He had written the comedy, *The Mulberry Garden*, in which Nell and Hart had acted. Yet if she harboured the intention of becoming the king's mistress – and, given her fame and popularity, as well as Charles II's love of theatre, why not? – Nell would also have known that there was already an actress in the king's bed, in these years of the declining influence of Lady Castlemaine. This was Mary (Moll) Davis, rumoured to be the illegitimate daughter of Thomas Howard, earl of Berkshire, though later, near-contemporary accounts of her life gave her more prosaic origins as the daughter of a Wiltshire blacksmith. Moll was about the same age as Nell

Gwyn but had appeared on stage earlier, as a singer and dancer. Her skill as a dancer was greatly admired, not least by Pepys, who wrote about her in a similar vein to his panegyrics about Nell. Moll was considerably less admired for her acting skills, however, though she does seem to have been promoted by the Duke's Company, of which she was a member by 1662, as a rival for Nell Gwyn. But it was her singing that really made her stand out; in a revival of one of the plays of Sir William Davenant, the company's founder, she sang 'My lodging it is in the cold ground' so affectingly that, as John Downes put it, 'it raised her from a bed on the cold ground to a bed royal.'

It would be fair to say that there was no love lost between Nell Gwyn and Moll Davis. Rumour even had it that Nell sent her rival sweetmeats laced with laxatives before one tryst with the king and that the effect brought a hasty end to the royal passion for Moll. Even if Nell, who was certainly capable of such a mischievous, some would say spiteful act, hoped to sabotage the relationship, she was clearly unsuccessful. Bishop Burnet, a source of much gossip about the period, claimed that both actresses were dangled in front of Charles II by the duke of Buckingham as part of his feud with Lady Castlemaine, and that the king was initially put off by Nell's demand for a pension of £500 a year if she was to leave the stage and become his mistress. Instead, he fell for Moll Davis, who was not especially pretty but whose elegant legs and suggestive dancing style he found irresistible. His wife was less impressed. Moll's dancing offended Catherine of Braganza so much that she stormed out of a performance at court. Moll, who made no demands on the king, was, however, rewarded. Pepys was told by another actress friend (there is something of the male groupie about the famous diarist's adoration of actresses) 'how Mis [sic] Davis is for certain going away from the Duke's house, the king being in love with her; and a house is taken for her, and furnishings; and she hath a ring given her already worth £600.' The 'Duke's house' mentioned was the lodging provided by Davenant for female members of his company. This reference to

Moll becoming the king's mistress and being given her own establishment dates from the beginning of 1668. The affair continued, spasmodically, until at least 1673, when Moll Davis gave birth to the last of Charles II's fourteen bastard children, the rather oddly named Lady Mary Tudor. By that time, however, Nell Gwyn was playing a much greater role offstage.

In 1667, Nell found a new lover who was willing to pay her £100 a year – considerably less than she had allegedly suggested as her price to the king – in the charmingly dissolute Restoration wit and writer, Charles Sackville, Lord Buckhurst, later sixth earl of Dorset. Buckhurst's family had a long tradition of service to the Crown. His grandmother, Mary, had been governess to Charles I's children, and his mother's family, the Cranfields, were originally a mercantile family that had come to political prominence through an alliance with the first duke of Buckingham in the reign of James I.[11] Buckhurst is said to have been determined to bed Nell Gwyn after she revealed a great deal of leg while rolling about on the floor of the stage in a performance of *All Mistaken*, the play in which she had first shone. He had, as a contemporary poem not so delicately put it, 'through her drawers the powerful charm descried.'[12]

Buckhurst offered Nell a diversion from Hart as a lover and from the stage itself. His offer must have been attractive enough for her to forgo both, at least for a while. She found herself, probably some time in May 1667, in a fine house in Epsom, Surrey, with not just Buckhurst but Charles Sedley for company. Apart from receiving visits from Buckingham and Rochester, little is known about how the trio passed their time. Sedley's reputation for profanity made a local matron invited to attend a dinner party at which he was present very nervous in anticipation, but she did not mention Nell Gwyn. This pastoral interlude did not last long. Buckhurst apparently grew tired of Nell's acerbic wit and her considerable inroads on his purse. By August, he had had enough. Nell resumed her theatrical roles, to the evident relief of Pepys. Her absence had also damaged takings for the King's Company and this, coupled with her treatment of Charles Hart, caused resentment among her fellow actors when she returned. Piqued, Hart took up with Lady Castlemaine, whose enthusiasm for actors matched that of Pepys for actresses. Their liaison did not last long but it drew a line under Nell's affair with her first lover called Charles. By 1669, Nell was pregnant by the man she would refer to as 'her Charles III'. She had got as high as she could climb.

CHAPTER TWELVE

The Protestant Whore

'Hard by Pall Mall lives a wench call'd Nell.
King Charles II he kept her.
She hath got a trick to handle his prick,
But never lays hands on his sceptre.'

From *Poems on Affairs of State*

IT WAS DISINGENUOUS to claim that Nell Gwyn had no interest in politics. The writer of this poem, one of many scurrilous if not downright pornographic verses inspired by the king's cheerful promiscuity, went on to say that, 'all matters of state from her soul she does hate'. Yet Nell's association with Buckingham and the court wits, her rivalry with Louise de Kéroualle, Charles II's French mistress and, indeed, her own inclinations, at least as far as protecting her children by the king were concerned, made her involvement inevitable.[1] But she did not set out to be a political player, it was a by-product of her situation. Nell gave birth to her first son by Charles at the start of the 1670s, a decade that was to be every bit as turbulent as the first ten years of the Restoration.

As Charles contemplated the arrival of yet another illegitimate child, this time by a woman of a startlingly different social class and background from someone like Lady Castlemaine, who had contemptuously described Nell as 'that pitiful strolling actress',[2] another man might have taken stock of what had been achieved in that first decade of his rule. But who was Charles II in 1670? Even the court wits, whose company Nell Gwyn frequented, did not know. Their attitude towards the king was ambivalent. They were his companions, in drinking, in whoring, yet they could – and did – undermine him in their public utterances and behaviour, just as much as they enjoyed his transitory favour. They, at least, knew his inscrutability. Topical and personal lampoons were widespread in the 1670s, a form of media that predated the vicious artistic caricatures of the eighteenth century. An anonymous writer in 1669 managed to impugn the king's political grasp and his sexual prowess by using the metaphor of sailing, one of Charles II's favourite pastimes:

> Our ruler hath got the vertigo of state,
> The world turns round in his politic pate,
> He steers in a sea where his course cannot last,
> And bears too much sail for the strength of his mast.[3]

Charles II shared his thoughts with almost no one except his sister, Minette, who had herself been powerfully affected by the condescension and sense of displacement they experienced as a result of the Civil Wars. The king disliked mulling over things in ministerial meetings, nor did he wish to revisit his past. It was only later in the reign that he carefully crafted his version of the escape from Worcester and then he put a spin on the experience of defeat which modern communicators would admire. Though much of his attitude – his instinctive dissimulation, his mistrust of political advisers, his liking for display at a safe distance from his subjects – could be ascribed to his experiences as a prince and king in exile, as a monarch he did not like to acknowledge failure. He was still on the throne and that, in itself, was no mean feat. His main preoccupations were not, of course, the string of irresistible ladies who occupied his bed, but the much more serious business of ruling. He had still not worked out, or perhaps did not care, that his lifestyle might leave him open to criticism that struck at the very heart of the concept of monarchy.

During the next ten years, religious tensions, encompassing both Protestant dissenters and Roman Catholics, multiplied to fever point and became entwined with the issue of the succession in a manner that seemed to threaten the throne. The king's brother, James, duke of York, and his eldest son, the duke of Monmouth, were at the centre of this national crisis. Charles II's relationship with Nell Gwyn (always a staunch supporter of young Monmouth) flourished in the year 1670–1 but, even as it did, the king was less concerned with Nell than he was with his continuing lack of funds, his testy relationship with Parliament (where the issue of money was always paramount), and foreign affairs. He had got rid of Clarendon as chief minister but had not replaced the exiled earl with a clear favourite. His advisers at this time may be largely unknown to all but specialists in seventeenth-century British history but they are certainly not without interest, and their perceptions of the influence of the king's mistresses played a part in their personal and political calculations.

The five men who were closest to the king in the running of the country are known as the Cabal because of their initials but the term is misleading. Clifford, Arlington, Buckingham, Ashley Cooper and Lauderdale did not function coherently as a ministry and had varying personal agendas. The first two were allies but Buckingham had consistently ploughed his own furrow and, though still prominent in court circles, was excluded from the exercise of power. Anthony Ashley Cooper (later first earl of Shaftesbury) had started the Civil Wars as a royalist but changed sides and later served as one of Oliver Cromwell's councillors. An ambivalent convert to the idea of restoring the Stuarts and a sympathizer with dissenters, he was chancellor of the exchequer in 1670 but the king still did not trust him sufficiently to give him a role in foreign affairs. He would go on to become a leading critic of the government in the late 1670s and play a crucial part in the early days of party politics in Britain. Lauderdale, the uncouth Scottish aristocrat who had so appalled Charles II's courtiers while they were in exile, was the monarch's formidable fixer, north of the border, able to tell the king triumphantly that no monarch had ever been so powerful there. Of these five, the man closest to Charles II between 1668 and 1674 was Henry Bennet, earl of Arlington, the king's secretary of state, often viewed as a nonentity but an able and cunning politician with a great taste for culture and display, as well as being a crypto-Catholic. By 1671, he certainly had his eye on a lady to replace the duchess of Cleveland as the king's unofficial *maîtresse-en-titre*, and it was not Nell Gwyn.

Nell gave birth to her first son, Charles, in mid-May 1670, at a time when the king was heavily involved in the diplomacy surrounding the mission of his sister, the duchess of Orléans, to England and the resulting Secret Treaty of Dover. Charles II's affection for Minette was far greater than that he had ever felt for his mistresses, and as he already had so many other illegitimate children, he took little initial interest in the birth of yet another son. Nell's child was born in a house in Lincoln's Inn Fields. He was christened on 7 June and both the duke of Buckingham and Lord Buckhurst were his godparents. It is unclear when his father first saw him, and for the first six and a half years of his life he had no surname, not even the customary one of Fitzroy that had been given to other royal bastards. His mother, who was not yet twenty, was offered the lease of a house at the unfashionable end of Pall Mall. The residence was on a par with what the king had provided for Moll Davis. This did not suit Nell, who was by no means as diffident as Moll. She wanted better. It has been said that her return to the stage at the end of 1670 in John Dryden's play, *The Conquest of Granada*, was an attempt to embarrass the king into finding her more appropriate lodgings. If this was a ploy, it succeeded. A finer house, number 79 Pall Mall, was made available to her in February 1671, at which point she retired from the stage for good. Charles

II was dilatory in purchasing the freehold for it, eventually doing so in 1677.

The house, which had three storeys and attic rooms for servants, backed on to St James's Park. Within a month of her taking up residence there, John Evelyn witnessed the king and Nell Gwyn chatting familiarly over the garden wall, 'she looking out of her garden on a terrace at the top of the wall and the king standing on the green walk under it.' The encounter sounds charming and was depicted by the Victorian artist Edward Matthew Ward as such, with a nonchalant king leaning on his cane, his two spaniels at his heels, while he chats with a rather overdressed and implausibly virginal-looking Nell. Evelyn, however, was strongly disapproving. 'I was,' he said, 'heartily sorry at this scene.' He went on to add something that might not have pleased Nell Gwyn, had she known: 'Thence the king walked to the Duchess of Cleveland's, another lady of pleasure and curse of our nation.'[4] Nell did not like Barbara's superior attitude. On one occasion, when she was on the receiving end of the duchess's froideur, Nell was reported to have 'clapped her on the shoulder and said she perceived that persons of one trade loved not one another.'[5] This was, of course, a reference to whoring, not acting. Barbara's response, if she deigned to give one, is not known.

This confrontation, though amusing in the retelling, is indicative of one of Nell's main difficulties as Charles II's mistress. She was never really accepted at court. Despite her personality and wit, her background counted against her. It was not just the swearing or the inability to make friends of her own sex – apart from the playwright, Aphra Behn, Nell does not seem to have had many notable female friends – but the calculated desire to raise eyebrows. This may, of course, have been a defence. The satire 'The Lady of Pleasure' begins with the unforgettable lines:

> And now behold a Common Drab become
> The glorious Mate for th'English Monarch's Bum[6]

Even Ralph Montagu's sister, the inveterate gossip and trouble-maker Lady Elizabeth Harvey, who detested Barbara Palmer throughout her career as royal mistress, eventually deserted Nell Gwyn when she thought the actress's hold on the king was slipping, hoping to replace her with Jenny Middleton, daughter of the court beauty Jane Middleton. This was a miscalculation, for, with the exception of Lucy Walter, Charles II never entirely abandoned the women in his life, retaining the same kind of easy affection for them – and especially their children – that he had by now developed for his own wife. At number 79 Pall Mall, he was able to mingle with guests at Nell's social gatherings, listening to music, playing cards, dancing and chatting and enjoying a generous buffet supper, which, according to Nell's accounts, could have included plover and larks (her favourite), herring, salmon and pike, as well as a vast array of meats. Foreign visitors to England were amazed at the sheer quantity of meat consumed and Nell did not stint on offering guests the staples of beef, pork, veal, lamb, bacon and mutton. She was similarly generous with wine, beer and cider. A party at her house reflected the hedonism and penchant for conspicuous consumption of the times.

Nell also made sure that her furniture and accessories demon-strated her greatly changed status. Everyone knew about her extraordinary silver bedstead, her most prized possession, which she commissioned from master silversmith John Coques. Its design, which Nell worked on herself, was based on the king's bed at Whitehall. Ornately decorated with heads of mythical figures, cherubs and even representations of Jacob Hall, Lady Castlemaine's lover, and Louise de Kéroualle, Nell's rival for the king's attentions, the bed showed Nell's sense of humour (as well as her cheerful vulgarity) and perhaps also hinted at her underlying vulnerability. It was meant to impress, amuse and encourage the king at a time when his virility, of which he had been so proud, was on the wane. The bed was also enormously expensive. The bill which Coques delivered at the end of 1674 came to over £1,000. In all, she spent the equivalent of £130,000 in today's money on her bedchamber, with its blue satin curtains, re-glazed windows, silver-framed looking glass and dressing table covered with damask.

On her wardrobe, Nell Gwyn also spent freely. She loved satin shoes and slippers, silk petticoats and nightgowns, pearl-coloured hose and the scented gloves that were so popular with ladies of the period. There are also bills for expensive hairdressing. Nell was not a great user of the dangerous cosmetics of the day, a number of which contained compounds of mercury and arsenic. Instead, she used scented waters, such as rose and orange water, which were often used as a substitute for washing with water in an age when sanitation left much to be desired and bathing was an infrequent occurrence.

Nell liked jewels as much as any other society lady of the period and seems to have had a particular weakness for pearls. These would have suited her complexion and colouring. Her portraits show her wearing pearl necklaces and, in one by Sir Peter Lely, she has pearls in her hair. In 1682, after the death of Charles II's cousin, Prince Rupert, she paid over £4,000, or £644,000 today, for a pearl necklace that the prince had given his mistress, Peg Hughes, herself an actress. It may have been one of the largest single purchases she ever made, greatly outstripping the cost of her famous bed. Where she got the money from is an interesting question, since she was in debt when the king died three years later. It would have swallowed almost all her annual pension. Charles himself does not seem to have showered her with jewels, though he did give her a beautiful diamond cluster ring and a blue enamel and pearl watch set with rose diamonds, as well as a carnelian heart and a locket with a miniature of his father, Charles I. These were not showy gifts but they speak of his love for this girl half his age, whom Pepys called 'pretty, witty Nell.'[7]

Their second son, James, was born on Christmas Day, 1671. Like his brother, he remained merely a royal bastard without a family name. This irked Nell, though her own financial position was becoming more secure. She was given a pension of £4,000 a year in 1674, increased to £5,000 in 1676. At the end of that year, after a great deal of pestering, her elder son was finally given the surname of Beauclerk and created earl of Burford. Little James had to wait a few weeks longer to be allowed to use the new name. His mother was given Burford House in Windsor in 1680 and leases of lands in Bestwood Park, Nottinghamshire the following year. To her portfolio of property and grants were added £800 a year from Irish revenues and a grant from the customs paid on logwood. But while the earl of Burford and his brother, Lord Beauclerk, were given titles, Nell herself was not. Instead, she had to be content with an appointment, in 1675, as lady of the bedchamber to Catherine of Braganza, a post that the duchess of Cleveland had recently vacated. There is no evidence that Nell actually took up this role but she could at least consider herself a lady, even if not formally titled as one.

Nell's past could not entirely be forgotten, especially when her alcoholic mother died, in July 1679. One newspaper of the time reported that she had been sitting by the riverside at her home in Chelsea, fell into the water and was drowned. Other reports, that she was drunk on brandy and fell into a ditch, were more explicit, if not necessarily accurate. True to character, Nell refused to be embarrassed by the manner of her mother's demise. With Buckingham's help, she organized a splendid funeral, riding in her coach with her sister, Rose, through the streets of London from Covent Garden to St Martin-in-the-Fields, where her mother was to be interred, and receiving the support of crowds of well-wishers along the way.

For in this, Nell was very different from Charles II's other mistresses. She was a popular figure, liked for her humble origins, her successful stage career, her generosity and ability to flout convention even after wealth and fame had come her way. And the most famous saying attributed to her, 'Pray be silent, good people, I am the Protestant whore,' when her coach was surrounded by a hostile crowd in Oxford, in 1681, shows how successfully she had positioned herself as quintessentially English and a good Protestant at a time of virulent anti-Catholicism. Though the saying may itself be apocryphal, Nell was being referred to in satires at this time as 'the Protestant whore'. Her sexual morality mattered much less than her religion to a country enflamed in 1678 by the fantasy woven by the disreputable ex-navy chaplain and sometime Catholic convert, Titus Oates.

*

THE POPISH PLOT, as it was known, was based on a series of revelations by a man with a very murky past, who touched on a raw nerve in both the political class and the general public. No one who really knew anything about Oates's background would have seriously credited a word he said. He was unprepossessing in appearance and character. The historian Tim Harris has written that, 'his pastimes included lying, cheating, blasphemy and sod-omizing young boys.'[8] Oates, the son of a Baptist preacher, was a twenty-nine-year-old who had never settled at anything. He left Cambridge without a degree, was dismissed from Anglican orders and a brief stint as a navy chaplain, before converting to Catholicism. His new religious allegiance took him to the English College at Valladolid in Spain but he had not completed his studies there before he was asked to leave. Not one to be daunted, Oates decided to make mileage out of his time in Spain by awarding himself an imaginary doctorate from the university at Salamanca. In June 1678, he was still trying to join the Jesuits at the college at St Omer in France, but the new English head of the seminary there kicked him out, something that must have been becoming wearyingly familiar to Oates by then. His thor-oughly unpleasant character and vile temper counted against him at every turn and successive rejections merely added to his sense of resentment.

Yet, almost as soon as he returned to England, penniless and desperate, he was able to add to this catalogue of deceits and dishonour by renewing his acquaintance with an older, vehemently anti-Catholic former clergyman, Dr Israel Tonge. As Tonge lent an eager ear, encouraging Oates to write down his revelations, the younger man began to turn his desire for vengeance against Catholics in general, and Jesuits in particular, into a plausible story of Catholic designs against the throne and British liberties. Charles II was to be murdered and there would be rebellions in Ireland and Scotland. The Jesuits, Oates claimed, had recently held a secret meeting in London, in April 1678, at which he himself had been present and where treasonable designs were discussed. His web of fabrications and half-truths stunned an already skittish nation and played into the hands of the king's opponents, notably the earl of Shaftesbury, who saw in them a means of allowing Parliament to thwart any attempts by the Crown to introduce a French-style absolutist government, to force the king to divorce Catherine of Braganza and to prevent Charles being succeeded by his brother, the duke of York, who had acknowledged his conversion to Catholicism five years earlier.

Oates, who had never had any influence or credibility before the summer of 1678, now discovered that his imagination, coupled with a powerful sense of grievance, had brought him a welcome pension of £20 per month and lodgings at Whitehall. The life-long outsider had become a national hero. People listened to him and his confidence grew. Soon he was accusing the duchess of York's former secretary, Edward Coleman, a prominent Catholic who wanted to return Britain to the old religion, of treasonable correspondence with Louis XIV's confessor. For good measure, he threw in accusations against the queen's physician, Sir George Wakeman, and Catherine of Braganza herself, claiming that Wakeman had been offered £10,000 to poison the king's medicine and that Catherine had supported this attempt on her husband's life.

The king was incensed by the accusations levelled at his inno-cent, long-suffering wife, who had been living quietly at Somerset House as public sentiment against her grew. Fearing for her safety, and to demonstrate his commitment to her, he suggested that she move back to her apartments in Whitehall. He cross-examined Oates himself, noting how the man got into difficulties describing an allegedly overheard conversation in which the queen had sanctioned poisoning her husband. By this time, Oates had to contend with a rival informant, William Bedloe, who threatened to steal some of his thunder. Combining their stories, the onslaught on Catherine continued and, at the bar of the House of Commons, both accused her of high treason. The Commons' response in these fevered times was not to defend the queen but to demand that she and her household be removed from Whitehall. In her distress, Catherine wrote to her brother, Dom Pedro, in Portugal, asking for advice and assistance. There was fury in Lisbon, where the ministry insisted that those who spoke such lies against Catherine should be severely punished. In fact, Dom Pedro did very little to help Catherine and the affair led to a misunderstanding which could have caused a serious rift between the siblings. The marquis de Arouches, Portuguese ambassador to The Hague, had been sent across to London to help Catherine but the two had not got on and Arouches mischievously reported to Dom Pedro that his sister was displeased with him. Catherine wrote in sorrow to her brother about her husband's support at this distressing development: 'The king will speak on my behalf, and as many as know me, who know that there is no one on earth whom I value more highly than the Prince of Portugal, my brother.' She went on to lament that her enemies were 'practising to take away my life with pure grief.'[9] Assailed in London, doubted in Lisbon, Catherine was at least confident, at last, that Charles II would not desert her. She rode out the storm.

Titus Oates was responsible, in his perjury and venom, for the execution of more than thirty men whom he had falsely accused. Charles II and the duke of York immediately saw right through him but were unable to persuade other members of the Privy Council and an antagonistic House of Commons to their way of thinking. He was tried for perjury before Judge Jeffries at the beginning of the reign of James II, in 1685, and committed to the King's Bench Prison. After James II fled England, three years later, Oates was released. He married, probably more for her money than love, Rebecca Weld, the daughter of a wealthy London draper and, having soon run through her fortune, died in obscurity in 1705, bringing to an end a career of opportunism and lies that is one of the most unusual in British history.

*

GIVEN THIS POISONOUS climate, it is hardly surprising that Nell Gwyn was happy to be viewed as the Protestant whore. She spent some of her time with the king at Windsor and Newmarket during the Popish Plot and its aftermath. Charles still loved horse racing and his visits to Newmarket were one of the great pleasures of his life. But it was at Windsor, where Nell had joined him, that he fell seriously ill in the summer of 1679 with a high fever and, for a while, it was believed he would die. As she had no official status, Nell was not allowed to see him and had to be content with messages conveyed to and fro by her elder son, Lord Burford. Though her life was quieter and she herself was no longer in the bloom that had characterized her as a teenage actress – as unkind commentators were eager to point out – she remained close to Buckingham and also supported the duke of Monmouth. The Popish Plot had led to a deeper crisis about the succession and Nell became involved when Monmouth returned, without permission, from The Hague, to great popular acclaim but the continued displeasure of his father. She offered him a safe haven in her home in Pall Mall and pleaded with the king to forgive his son. Charles would not give way. After acting as hostess to Monmouth for several months, during which time he was a demanding and difficult guest, Nell was obliged to ask him to leave. Her own health was no longer good and the death of James, her younger son, at the age of eight, in Paris, presumably added to her distress, though she had never made any effort to go over to France to see him and it is not clear why he was being schooled there while his brother remained in England. The location of the child's grave is not known.

Nell's madcap days were over and she had settled into a quieter life that bordered on respectability. The wider English public had become her audience and she was secure in their affection. This was more than could be said for her main rival for the king's affections, the Frenchwoman whom she despised and who, with characteristic wit, she gave the unkind name of 'Squintabella'.

Part Six

Baby Face

LOUISE DE KÉROUALLE

1649–1734

CHAPTER THIRTEEN

La Bretonne

'The famous new French maid of honour, Mademoiselle
Quierovil, now coming to be in great favour with the King'
Diary of John Evelyn, 9 October 1671

SHE WAS BORN in an area once considered so remote that they
called it the ends of the earth. Louise Renée de Penancoët de
Kéroualle was from Finistère, in the far western part of France,
in the region of Brittany. With its coastline of rugged headlands
shaped by the Atlantic waves and wild, remote hinterland of
forests and moorland, it was a place apart, steeped in Celtic
legend and with a proud history as an independent duchy until
the late fifteenth century. Louise, who was born at her father's
country seat, the Manoir de Kéroualle, not far from the seaport
of Brest, in 1649, was the second child of Sebastien de Ploeuc,
a local marquess of the minor Breton nobility and his wife, Marie
de Rieux, whose family were well connected in Brittany. On
both sides, Louise was of aristocratic stock but the family, like
many of the provincial upper classes in France, were not well
off. Louise was not brought up amid the trappings of grandeur,
though she certainly acquired a taste for them later in life. The
family were devout Catholics and although we know little of
her upbringing she was probably educated in a nearby Ursuline
convent. She was certainly literate, though her large, looped

handwriting is more reminiscent of the scrawl of a small child than a grown woman. Louise would have been prepared for the life of a provincial lady and might have stayed as such were it not for the fact that she was considered to have an unusually pretty face and pleasing personality, which might act as her passport to a very different life in the French capital. Her parents, who were proud and ambitious, perhaps the more so because of their financially straitened circumstances, were fortunate enough to be offered a place for Louise as maid of honour to Charles II's sister, the duchess of Orléans. The precise circumstances of how this appointment was achieved are unclear, though it may have owed something to a recommendation from the governor of Brittany and possibly to her father's friendship with the duc de Beaufort, chief admiral of France. Louise left home at the age of nineteen to join the household of the woman known simply as Madame.

Princess Henrietta Stuart (Minette), the youngest child of Charles I and Henrietta Maria, was known in France as Henriette Anne, duchess of Orléans. Her marriage to Louis XIV's brother made her the second lady of France and she was a more influential figure at court than the Sun King's naive and undeniably plain Spanish wife, Queen Marie Thérèse. On the face of it, a position in the queen's bedchamber would have appeared more prestigious but the huge household and wealth of the duke and duchess of Orléans constituted a rival centre of power and cultural influence to that of the king and was very much centred on Paris, where the duke was often more popular with the changeable local populace than his brother. At the refurbished Palais Royal and the Orléans country residence of St Cloud, just across the Seine from the capital, Louise experienced grandeur on a major scale. It could not fail to leave its mark on her. Nor could she escape the recognition that all was not well in this gilded world.

The marriage of the duke and duchess was desperately unhappy and the recriminations and sheer nastiness of it all inevitably cast a pall over life in their service. The duke was bisexual and in thrall to an unscrupulous male lover. His wife, of whom he was very jealous, was a young woman who hid her undoubted intelligence beneath a shallow, flirtatious exterior. Frequently unwell, almost constantly pregnant, Henriette Anne was a kind and considerate mistress, regarded with affection by the ladies who served her, but there was little lasting tranquillity in her life or theirs. Royal households were always on the move, their nomadic existence dictated by the demands of the social calendar and the more prosaic necessities of inadequate sanitation and incessant rebuilding. Adapting to this new life and its demands, even given the stimulation of a life very different from that in which she had been raised, called for a calm head and considerable powers of discretion. Louise appears to have managed both successfully, though there is no documentary evidence of how she reacted to her new situation. She had arrived at court somewhat older than many maids of honour, who, both in France and Britain, were often girls in their early, rather than late teens, and her background meant that she had much to learn about the intrigue and backbiting of court life, in a short time. Earlier writers have speculated on her thoughts while in Madame's service but it is extremely unlikely that Henriette Anne would have shared confidences about her marital troubles with a maid of honour.[1]

In June 1670, Louise accompanied Madame on her visit to England and was at Dover with her during the talks that culminated in the Secret Treaty of Dover. Since the real reason for the meeting between Charles II and his sister was carefully guarded, it is unlikely that Louise viewed it as anything other than the family reunion it was supposed to be. Nor do we know if she first came to the king's attention at that time, though his past history would suggest that he always kept a lascivious eye on female courtiers. Louise was only one of several ladies who supported their mistress on this trip and, once the business was done, she returned to France with Madame; her thoughts, if she had any, on what she had seen of England at that time were left unrecorded.

The summer season would soon be in full swing in France, with trips to Fontainebleau and long evenings at St Cloud in prospect. But Louise had not been three weeks back in France when her world was turned upside down.

Henriette Anne collapsed in the late afternoon of 29 June 1670. Her husband was with her, having called in to take his leave for the evening, as he intended to go into the centre of Paris. Punctilious in observing the elaborate formalities that dictated their daily lives, he came in person to inform his duchess. Startled by Henriette's evident pain, he soon realized that she was in a serious condition. In the course of a long evening, doctors administered all the treatments of the vicious quackery of the day, causing Henriette to weaken further, and by the time Louis XIV himself arrived, it was obvious that she did not have long to live. Louise de Kéroualle is not mentioned among the ladies who witnessed her mistress's death at about three in the morning of 30 June, so we do not know if she was present amid all the lamentation. But as the whole of St Cloud was in uproar, it could not have been long before she realized that, with Henriette gone, she faced an uncertain future.

Rumours that Madame had been poisoned soon began to circulate, but this was often the default explanation in those days for a sudden, unexplained death. In the duchess of Orléans's case, they were given some credence because of the widespread knowledge of the state of her marriage. But Philippe, her husband, though the most difficult of spouses, was innocent of any involvement in her demise. Henriette had been in poor health since childhood and an autopsy showed no signs of poison; the likelihood is, given her symptoms, that she died of peritonitis, caused by a ruptured duodenal ulcer. That she had not actually been murdered was cold comfort to her grief-stricken brother, Charles II, who was even more overwhelmed by her death than he had been when, in the year of his restoration, smallpox claimed the lives of his sister, Mary, and brother, Henry, within three months of each other.

After he had got over the initial agony of loss, he began to entertain ideas of how he could honour his sister's memory by meeting the request she had made on her deathbed: Madame had made a special plea that he protect her servants. The letters from 'a person of quality' to Charles II (apparently Ralph Montagu, who may have wished to distance himself in this convenient anonymity from some of the more colourful accusations flying around after Madame's death) stated that 'she recommended to you to help, as much as you could, all her poor servants'.[2] Charles wasted no time in acting on his sister's wishes. Henriette de Bordes, one of her chief ladies, who had attended her mistress during the last hours of Henriette Anne's life and fainted away at her sufferings, arrived in England within a matter of weeks and was given a post as dresser to Catherine of Braganza. She was followed later in the autumn by Louise de Kéroualle, who joined the queen's maids of honour in a similar role to the one she'd had in Madame's household. Despite claims, unsubstantiated by any evidence, that Charles II was desperate for Louise to come to England and that Louis XIV was equally keen for her to be planted there, she was, in fact, left waiting for transport across the Channel at Dieppe when the duke of Buckingham failed to arrange her passage. In October 1670, Ralph Montagu reported that, 'Mademoiselle Kéroualle hath been at Dieppe these ten days and hears nothing of the yacht that the Duke of Buckingham, Mr Godolphin tells me, was to send for her.'[3] This was a humiliating start to Louise's new life.

In view of her subsequent career, the position of maid of honour seems inappropriate, though Louise probably was a maid in the technical sense of being a virgin at the time. But time was passing, if she was to find a husband. Uncertainty about her long-term future remained. Louise's parents could not afford to give her a dowry that would attract gentlemen in the circles in which she now moved, so her appointment by no means guaranteed a prosperous or settled future. Yet there were encouraging precedents. Frances Teresa Stuart, though considerably younger than Louise when she moved from the French court to England, had managed to bewitch a king and marry a duke. Louise would certainly succeed at the former; as for the latter, she would, just three years later, become a duchess in her own right. It is unlikely, however, that she foresaw such a startling trajectory towards riches and influence when she arrived in London, though it very soon became apparent to those around Charles II that he was attracted to her. From this realization, it was just a short step to contemplating how this brunette from Brittany with an arresting figure could be manipulated for their own ends. The French, however, had other ideas.

*

EVEN GIVEN THE king's wide-ranging tastes in women, it is not hard to understand how Charles II fell so quickly for Louise de Kéroualle. She was a link with the beloved sister that he had so recently lost. Her very Frenchness was a powerful draw. The two women did not particularly resemble one another; Minette was always as thin as a rail, whereas Louise was plump and would grow plumper. Minette was an extrovert, Louise more self-contained, and her defensiveness about her background as a provincial lady of limited means made her a snob with a tendency to claim that she was close to people with whom she was barely acquainted. Louise knew how to charm and be pleasant but not how to endear – except where the besotted king was concerned. She could arrange a fine dinner with an almost ostentatious display of good taste but she was not the life and soul of the party. Once the opportunity came her way, she aspired to play a political role without ever really understanding the complexity of British politics or the wider European ambitions of France, the country she had left behind. A tendency to hold herself in high regard made her easy prey for the mockery and wit of Nell Gwyn, while her greed rivalled that of Lady Castlemaine.

Louise was already attracting attention at court by the end of 1670, though not everyone admired her appearance. A portrait painted at about this time shows a young woman of sensual appearance in *déshabillé*, her left breast exposed, with long, loose, curly dark hair, from which peeps out a pearl earring. She is holding a bird (perhaps a dove), and her gaze, directly at the artist, is a striking mixture of innocence and seductiveness. Evelyn was not impressed by her looks, writing in his diary for 1 November 1670, 'I now also saw that famed beauty (but in my opinion of a childish simple and baby face) Mademoiselle Quirreval.' Given his antipathy to all the king's mistresses, Evelyn's criticism might be easily dismissed but it was not so wide of the mark. Louise did have a baby face and she may well have traded on the superficial vulnerability that it suggested.

Her first public appearance at court was as companion to a much less majestic figure than the king. During the Christmas season, she was escorted to a masquerade by Charles II's nephew, William of Orange, who regularly visited England despite his uncle's propensity to make war on the Dutch. William and Louise made an unlikely couple. He was a year younger, short, very thin, slightly hunchbacked and asthmatic. It is not clear whether this rather gauche young man enjoyed having such a beauty, already the talk of the town, on his arm. Relations between the two would become frosty as Louise's influence grew. Charles II's interest, however, intensified as the months passed. Initially, he was careful to observe the proprieties by merely engaging Louise in conversation in the queen's apartments. Like most educated men of his time, the king spoke several foreign languages and was fluent in French. It is not clear how much English Louise had by this time or when she started to learn. Catherine of Braganza, never a Francophile, would not have been pleased to hear French spoken too often in her apartments. Yet while the French ambassador may have been content to play a longer game and let Louise's relationship with the king follow a natural course, Arlington, Charles's chief minister, was not. He was determined to establish Louise as Charles's mistress, and the sooner the better.

Various stories, based on reports in Evelyn's diary and endlessly embroidered by the biographers, both French and English, who have written a great deal of nonsense about Louise, claim that she finally succumbed to the king's sexual desires in October 1671, at Arlington's splendid country house, Euston Hall, in Suffolk. Euston Hall was conveniently situated close to Newmarket, where the king frequently indulged his passion for horse racing and where he had his own stud. Indeed, it might be said that Charles II's passion for horseflesh was just as great as it was for female flesh. Arlington had shrewdly realized that Euston Hall, an old house that he refurbished and extended, could complement his London residence, Goring House, as his seat of power in the country. It was certainly magnificent enough to be the scene of a royal seduction. 'Arlington,' notes the historian Helen Jacobsen, 'transformed Euston into as much of a working home as any town house and into an unrivalled locus of power, wealth, intrigue, entertainment, and erudition.'[4] The earl had made himself indispensable (or so he hoped) to Charles II through his determination to take on the responsibility for handling foreign affairs himself. In order to underline his pre-eminence in this crucial area of government, he had drawn on his experiences as a diplomat and his knowledge of Europe in the design and furnishing of his London and Suffolk homes. Both revealed an impressive display of conspicuous consumption. They were showcases for his power and taste. The architect for the changes made at Euston Hall is unknown but the French influence was everywhere in the external architecture. Inside the house, Arlington used Italian marble from Carrara and frescoes painted by Antonio Verrio. Through his Dutch wife, Isabella van Beverweerd, Arlington also patronized Dutch painters and sculptors. Together, they entertained most of the diplomats resident in London, who were happy to accept Arlington's hospitality. The earl was at the height of his political success when Louise de Kéroualle arrived there with the queen on a royal visit to Newmarket.

John Evelyn, who was present at Euston Hall for nearly two weeks, recorded the rumour that Louise had finally succumbed to Charles during that time. The precise place and circumstances of her seduction remain, however, unknown. Catherine may well have left Suffolk before her husband but it seems odd that she would have acquiesced in leaving one of her maids of honour behind, especially when it was so obvious that the king was smitten with Louise. Equally puzzling is whether Charles II would really have risked insulting his wife, if she was still in residence, by the very public bedding of Louise, which is described in breathless prose, worthy of any cheap historical novel, by one of Louise's French biographers: 'In spite of the grins of the accomplices and the miserable excitement of the depraved women at the sight of an innocent girl dishonouring herself, Louise may have thought that the play would now stop. Wine and exhaustion drew her eyelids down. Suddenly the room was empty and Charles was irresistible.'[5]

Evelyn was more measured in his diary. He had not heard or witnessed anything himself but he accepted that the rumour going round was probably true, writing, 'It was universally reported that the fair Lady was bedded one of these nights, and the stocking flung, after the manner of a married bride: I acknowledge she was for the most part in her undress all day, and that there was fondness and toying with that young wanton.' (Charles II was apparently given to publicly pawing his mistresses, rather in the manner of the French King Henry II and Diane de Poitiers.) But Evelyn denied having been at this 'ceremony': 'I neither saw, nor heard on any such thing whilst I was there, though I had been in her chamber and all over that apartment late enough . . . however, twas with confidence believed that she was first made a *Misse*, as they called these unhappy creatures, with solemnity at this time.'[6] The French ambassador, Colbert de Croissy, reported in early November to the French foreign minister, Louvois, that Louise de Kéroualle had, indeed, become Charles II's mistress, that she was pleased to learn of Louis XIV's approval and that there was every prospect 'that she would hold long what she had conquered.'[7] This was a proud boast in view of Charles's inability to remain faithful for long to any mistress, yet time would prove that Louise de Kéroualle's hold on the king, though challenged, would remain fast until his death.

*

EVELYN THOUGHT LOUISE an unhappy creature, a fallen woman whose life would be ruined by this apparently public loss of her virginity to a sexually incontinent man old enough to be her father. Louise had other ideas. She was almost immediately pregnant but the restrictions this put on her availability allowed her to demonstrate the other aspects of her personality that had attracted Charles in the first place. Her role was to be calm, charming, always ready to listen, to provide a pleasing, safe haven where the king could relax. She quickly honed social skills, some of which were no doubt innate and others learned in the household of Charles's lost sister. Keenly aware that she could enhance her position by making herself useful to the right people in government, Louise exhibited a talent for what today would be known as networking. There was no point in being ashamed of who she was and what she had become. Now was the time to enjoy it and take advantage of the opportunities her new status offered.

Louise's importance was soon underlined by her new domestic arrangements. She was given apartments in Whitehall and did not leave them during the king's lifetime. Unlike his other mistresses, Louise does not seem to have demanded a large house of her own in London or in the country. Her place was at Charles's side and she could make him feel more secure in her devotion by always being there. Before July 1672, when her son, Charles (later duke of Richmond) was born, she was established in lodgings at the end of the Matted Gallery in Whitehall. She soon set about enlarging and extending her domain, which eventually occupied twenty-four rooms and sixteen garrets. The apartments were considered to be far more luxurious than the queen's but this may reflect a difference in style rather than substance, since Catherine of Braganza had, as noted earlier, brought many fine

things with her to England. There was also a pejorative aspect
to the descriptions of Louise's surroundings and belongings,
emphasizing that she was a spendthrift with pretensions above
her station – she was, after all, merely the plaything of a dissolute
king to her many critics. Even the sedan chair she ordered was
said to be 'the famousest chair that . . . ever was seen, beyond
the king's or queen's by far.'[8] Evelyn's personal attacks on Louise
never faltered. As late as 1683, when she was at the height of her
influence, his disapproval was more marked than ever. In October
of that year, he was present at Louise's levée, the formal rising
and robing of royalty that she had copied from the court of Louis
XIV, proving that she and her lover considered her to be a queen
in all but name:

Following his majesty this morning through the Gallery, I went
(with the few who attended him) into the duchess of
Portsmouth's dressing room, within her bedchamber, where she
was in her morning loose garment, her maids combing her,
newly out of bed: his majesty and the gallants standing about
her: but that which engaged my curiosity, was the rich and
splendid furniture of this woman's apartment, now twice or
thrice pulled down and rebuilt to satisfy her prodigal and
expensive pleasures . . . Here I saw the new fabric of French
tapestry, for design, tenderness of work and incomparable imita-
tion of the best paintings; beyond anything I had ever beheld:
some pieces had Versailles, St Germain and other palaces of
the French king with huntings, figures and landscapes, exotic
fowl and all to the life rarely done: then for Japanese cabinets,
screens, pendulum clocks, huge vases of wrought plate, tables,
stands, chimney furniture, sconces, branches, brasiers etc; they
were all of massive silver and without number, besides of his
majesty's best paintings. Surfeiting of this . . . [I] went contentedly home to my poor but quiet villa. Lord, what contentment
can there be in the riches and splendour of this world, purchased
with vice and dishonour.[9]

A year after her son's birth, Charles II created Louise Baroness Petersfield, countess of Fareham and duchess of Portsmouth, establishing her titles in the county of Hampshire, with which she had no connection and seldom visited. In 1674, she was able to arrange a marriage for her younger sister, Henriette Mauricette de Kéroualle, with Philip Herbert, the seventh earl of Pembroke. The Herberts had been courtiers since early Tudor days, though the seventh earl's grandfather had been a supporter of Parliament during the Civil Wars and was, for a while, the guardian of Princess Elizabeth and Prince Henry, the two younger children of Charles I, who were left behind in London when their parents fled the capital in 1642. The marriage was a sign of Louise's influence and allowed her sister, at least, to acquire the respectability that would always elude the new duchess herself.

Louise did not like confrontation and preferred to stay out of the queen's way. She invented her own milieu and never felt the need to heighten her visibility by prominent participation in court events. In this, she was very much the antithesis of Barbara Palmer. Catherine was accustomed to her husband using her household as a recruiting ground for sexual partners, and though she had accepted that he would never change, she still disliked the new mistress intensely. Much of her determination to forge a separate identity and pointedly eschew all things French was a riposte to the king's latest infatuation. As the years went by, she was even more hurt by the fact that this little maid of honour was not a temporary distraction but the recipient of a love that he could never feel for her.

Catherine of Braganza was not the kind of woman to take pleasure in another's misfortunes, and though Charles never gave a fig for her feelings, at least he spared her one 'gift' that would cause Louise considerable suffering. In 1674, the king contracted a sexually transmitted disease (sometimes described as syphilis, though we cannot be sure exactly what it was) with which he proceeded to infect the duchess of Portsmouth. Always a dabbler in matters scientific, Charles treated himself with mercury and was, at least initially, only slightly discommoded by the effects of years of careless indulgence, though the cure he used may have weakened his system over time. Louise was not so lucky. She became very ill and was plagued thereafter by recurring bouts of ill health. She and Charles had no more children and it is not clear how long the sexual side of their relationship lasted. For her, this would have been no great loss. In her own eyes, she had achieved a great deal. Now she needed to ensure that she held on to it.

CHAPTER FOURTEEN

Mrs Carwell

*'I should do myself wrong if I told you that I love you better
than all the world besides, for that were making a comparison where 'tis impossible to express the true passion and
kindness I have for my dearest, dearest fubs'*

Charles II to Louise de Kéroualle,
duchess of Portsmouth

LOUISE SWIFTLY ATTAINED a status akin to that of a queen
consort. Charles II adored her, finding comfort in her apparent
pliability, her desire to please, her French good taste and even her
increasing girth. 'Fubs' was an old English word for someone who
was plump and the king used it as a term of endearment. He
underlined his devotion by naming a new royal yacht *The Fubs*. If
Louise was less than flattered by this very public reference to her
expanding figure, she knew better than to protest. She had what
amounted to her own court in Whitehall. English politicians
scuttled to find favour while the French ambassadors smiled in
satisfaction at the rising power of one of their countrywomen.
Charles II's financial generosity to Louise made her wealthy,
though it was not until the autumn of 1676, five years after her
arrival in England, that she was given a regular pension, amounting
to £8,600 a year. This sum was later increased and, by the end of
the reign, her overall pension and additional payments came to

£20,000 per annum, or £59 million today. This is an astonishing figure given the permanent difficulties in raising money for the Crown that the king faced. And while it gave Louise security and a great deal of perceived influence, it also made her a target for sustained and vicious criticism. The English people detested her. Their hatred and scorn were made public in satire and scurrilous verse, in mock dialogues with Nell Gwyn and in accusations that the baby-faced Bretonne was nothing more than a very expensive French spy. They insulted her pride by anglicizing her surname. To her many detractors, in raucous hostelries and the coffee houses Charles II would eventually ban as hotbeds of sedition, she was always 'Mrs Carwell'.

Piqued by this torrent of vituperation, Louise strove mightily to be accepted. She reached an early accommodation with her conscience about her role. Nell Gwyn may have been content with the knowledge that she was a royal whore but Louise was far too precious about her status to accept such an appellation. We do not need to accept the ridiculous story that she is alleged to have said, in pantomime English, 'Me no bad woman. If me thought me was one bad woman, me would cut my own throat,' to understand the aggravation caused by lines pinned to the door of her apartments which read, 'Within this place a bed's appointed for a French bitch and God's anointed.'[1] At a court full of jealous, preening ladies, the duchess of Portsmouth had more to contend with than a clever comic actress's scathing wit. Two noblewomen, in particular, frowned on Louise de Kéroualle. Elizabeth, duchess of Ormond, the wife of the leading Irish aristocrat and one of the key supporters of Charles II during his exile in the 1650s, was the most implacable of these ladies. The duchess was now over sixty years old and had consistently made her disapproval of the king's mistresses known. She had pointedly never visited Lady Castlemaine, to Barbara's great annoyance, and when Louise tried to call on this elderly guardian of court morals, she was permitted an interview, though none of the duchess's female relations were allowed to be present.

More dramatic was a confrontation between Louise and Mary, marchioness of Worcester, which took place in Tunbridge Wells in the summer of 1674. This went beyond personal slights in private to a very public and, according to one source, physical altercation. The dispute was over rooms that Lady Worcester had rented from under Louise's nose. The duchess of Portsmouth, pulling rank, told the marchioness that she should give way. By now Louise was accustomed to getting what she wanted but she had met her match in Mary. 'The marchioness told her she had better blood in her veins than e'er a French bitch in the world and that the English nobility would not be affronted by her, calling her tall bitch. There might you have seen their towers [headdresses] and hair flying about the room, as the miserable spoils of so fierce an encounter. The Marchioness beat her upon the face, got her down and kicked her, and finally forced her out of doors.' Her husband had stood by during this fight and threatened anyone who tried to part the struggling women. Lady Worcester, emerging victorious, defiantly 'bid the said Portsmouth go to Windsor and tell the King what she had said and done.'[2] The incident does not seem to have done the Worcesters any harm. The marquis was later created first duke of Beaufort and his wife is remembered as a keen gardener and botanist, though a domestic tyrant to her servants.

*

AMBITIOUS POLITICIANS VIEWED the duchess of Portsmouth very differently, though it took some time for her to establish her credit with them. By the mid-1670s, they accepted that she was a conduit to Charles II and made sure that they frequented her apartments, where they could enjoy exquisite soirées, tasteful musical entertainment and fine dining while socializing with the king in a relaxed atmosphere. The true extent of Louise's political influence on her royal lover may well have been considerably less than his ministers imagined, but that did not matter. Her importance lay in the fact that they believed her to have his ear. Certainly,

Louise saw herself as a political player, entering the fray with a confidence that was far from justified, given her unfamiliarity with English politics. The attentions of Charles II's ministers flattered her sense of self-importance and buoyed up her confidence through bouts of recurring illness and Charles's dalliances with other women. She wanted these men who sought high office to understand that she had her own kind of power. There is no way of knowing whether Louise generally initiated discussions with the king about appointments, or if he ever directly sought her views on such matters, but there was a widespread belief that the duchess of Portsmouth was such an indispensable part of his life that the best route to advancement was to gain her goodwill.

One politician who soon discovered that Louise de Kéroualle's support could be fickle was the man who is credited with having pushed her into Charles II's bed, Arlington himself. She dropped the earl in 1674, when he was the chief victim of a concerted campaign against the king's ministers, prompted by England's failure in the third Anglo-Dutch War. Charles II never seemed to be overly concerned by the abject (and very expensive) foreign-policy mistakes made during his reign, but blood was up in the House of Commons and they wanted a scapegoat. In mid-January 1674, Arlington was impeached after Buckingham laid the blame for the regime's policies squarely at his door. He defended himself successfully in what was acknowledged to be a brilliant piece of oratory, something for which he was not known, but his period in high political office was over. He chose to leave government for the post of lord chamberlain in the king's household, a role which still allowed him considerable influence as well as the opportunity to develop the royal image of power and magnificence along the lines of the French monarchy. He remained close to Charles II and retained the king's friendship but Louise no longer saw him as a useful ally. Her failure to realize the extent of Arlington's power in his new role, or how it might be used to the advantage of the French, is an indication of the brittle nature of her political understanding. Instead, Louise chose to bestow her friendship on the coming man, Thomas Osborne, the recently created earl of Danby.

Like Arlington, Danby is a name largely forgotten to English history, though he played a significant part in the politics of four reigns. He was a hard-headed Yorkshireman who had served a long apprenticeship in local politics as a client of the duke of Buckingham. Proud and ambitious, he had entered the national arena as member of Parliament for York in 1665. He soon became aware that the duke's capacity to stir up trouble was greater than his reliability as a patron and that it would be prudent to develop other links, as well as ensuring that he had areas of his own expertise to offer. Accordingly, he attached himself to the duke of York and the Navy Office, where he learned a great deal about foreign policy, as well as demonstrating a talent for accounting and financial management in the role of joint treasurer to the navy. By 1673, he was in the important government post of Lord Treasurer for the country as a whole and had to make some hard decisions about national finances based on his understanding of the damage caused by the Dutch Wars. A convinced Protestant, he was committed to steadying and improving the country's badly damaged finances and weaning Charles II away from his support of the French. Danby was concerned that the king's own inclinations put him in danger of losing the support of his subjects, at least as these were represented in the House of Commons. He wrote:

> Nothing is more necessary than to let the world see he [Charles
> II] will reward and punish and that no longer time must be
> lost therein, for that people begin already to think he will do
> neither. Nothing can spoil his affairs at home but unsteadiness
> of resolution in those steps he has begun and want of vigour
> to discountenance all such as pretend to others . . . Till he can
> fall into the humour of the people [the king] can never be great
> nor rich and while differences continue prerogative must suffer,
> unless he can live without Parliament.

And he went on to note that, 'the condition of his revenue will not permit that.'³ This advice, some of the soundest Charles II ever received, had uncomfortable overtones of the difficulties that had beset the king's father, Charles I, before the Civil Wars.

Given Danby's support of the Church of England, which he saw as a vital ally in achieving his aims, and his antipathy to the French, it is, on the face of it, somewhat extraordinary that Louise should have shown any interest in working with him. Whatever their personal dissimilarities – Danby, as a faithful, loving husband and devoted father to a large family, must have found more than a little to dislike in the king's simpering French Catholic mistress – they managed to forge a relationship of mutual benefit. There was little real friendship in it, as time would tell, but much of Louise's attitude towards someone that she recognized was set to become a powerful politician was based on her need for money. Despite his concern for the king's finances, Danby did not question Louise's increasingly generous pensions.

They also cooperated in a dispute over the government of Ireland when an attempt was made to remove the earl of Essex as Charles II's lord lieutenant there. Essex, the brother of the belligerent marchioness of Worcester, was a conscientious and moderate man, who found, as many had before him, that trying to govern Ireland was a thankless task. His attempts to improve the rotten state of Irish finances brought him into conflict with leading Irish politicians, who feared Essex would undo the lucrative practice of tax farming that made a few of them very rich. Among those who benefited from Irish monetary grants was Louise herself, so her support of Essex was far from altruistic. Essex realized that the support of someone like the duchess of Portsmouth was a double-edged sword, writing to his secretary, William Harbord, who had remained in England to protect his employer's interests:

> For my own part I cannot desire the friendship of any of that sort. To keep fair with them and all the world I shall be glad to do but to make any such friends so as to be useful, or a

support to me, will necessarily oblige me to be assistant to them in finding out money . . . and if once I should begin there would be no end to it . . . as for what you write concerning the duchess of Portsmouth . . . I conceive the only use to be made [of her] is to learn a little of what is doing, but by no means will I fix my reliance upon little people.[4]

Louise would have been mortified by this scathing dismissal of her true value. Had she known, she would certainly not have spoken up for Essex to the king, telling Charles II that she heard he was a very good man 'and serves you well.' It does not seem to have occurred to the king to wonder what on earth Louise actually knew about Irish affairs but, as neither of them had ever set foot in the country, perhaps he thought her views were as good as anybody's. By 1677, Louise had turned against Essex and was championing the duke of Monmouth as his replacement. If true, her efforts proved fruitless, for it was the time-worn Ormond, ever faithful to the Crown, who returned to his native Ireland and survived in charge of its seething tensions and political rivalries until Charles II's death in 1685.

*

As well as latching on to English politicians, Louise also had to manage her relationship with the country of her birth. Four successive ambassadors from the court of Louis XIV were her major contacts with France. Charles Colbert de Croissy, a younger brother of the Sun King's chief finance minister, was in the post when Louise arrived. It was Colbert de Croissy who reported her seduction by Charles II at Euston Hall and though he thought this gave France an undoubted hold over the English king, his view of Louise herself was not always favourable. He lacked confidence in her staying power, given Charles II's roving eye, and was irritated by Louise's interference in the choice of a second wife for the duke of York after the death of Anne Hyde. Louise tried to interest the heir to the throne in one of the beautiful

Elboeuf sisters, whereas the French court favoured the widowed duchess of Guise. In the end, neither party was successful. James chose the fifteen-year-old Italian noblewoman, Mary Beatrice d'Este, who became known as Mary of Modena. But Louise's matchmaking efforts soured her already uncertain relations with Colbert de Croissy and threatened the respectability she sought in France as well as Britain. Louise had set her heart on a French title and estate and her pretensions offended the French ambassador. His family were renowned for their brusqueness and Colbert did not mince his words in reporting the duchess of Portsmouth's vaulting ambition: 'I own I find her on all occasions so ill-disposed for the service of the king [Louis XIV], and showing such ill-humour against France (whether because she feels herself despised there, or whether from an effect of caprice), that I really think she deserves no favour of his Majesty.' However, he tempered this criticism with a realistic analysis of the lady's hold over Charles II, acknowledging that the king's likely reaction to the acceptance or refusal of Louise's request must be taken into account: 'But as the King of England shows her much love and so visibly likes to please her, his Majesty can judge whether it is best not to treat her according to her merits. An attention paid to her will be taken by the King of England as one paid to himself.'[5]

The estate on which Louise had set her hopes was the manor of Aubigny-sur-Nère, in the Berry region of central France. It was in the heart of the countryside, in what the French today call *la France profonde*, and it had a long association with foreign, rather than French, ownership, having originally been granted to John Stuart, the head of a branch of the Scottish royal family, who had made a career as a soldier and courtier in fifteenth-century France. Today, this pretty town with its half-timbered houses is still known as 'the city of the Scots' and proudly displays its historic associations with the Auld Alliance. In 1673, the dukedom was vacant following the death of Frances Teresa Stuart's husband, the duke of Richmond, and the estate had, in theory, reverted to Charles II himself, as Richmond's nearest male relative. He wanted to gift

it to Louise for the rest of her life, with the additional assurance
from Louis XIV that she could dispose of it freely. This proved
something of a stumbling block. Louis took his cousin's request
to mean that the estate would eventually pass to Louise's son by
the king, but as little Charles was illegitimate and Charles II had
no legally recognized male heirs apart from his brother, Louis's
first thought was that the lands and title should revert to the
French Crown. Encouraged by Colbert de Croissy, and perhaps
by his own lack of inclination towards a woman he viewed as
potentially useful, but still something of an unknown quantity,
with pretensions well above her place in society, Louis was not
minded at first to meet Charles II's request. Eventually a compromise
was reached whereby it was agreed that Louise should have
the estate during her lifetime but would not become a French
duchess in her own right. The final arrangement did include a
provision for Aubigny to pass to the male descendants of Louise's
son and only in default of them would it revert to the French
Crown. Charles II was not actually granted the duchy of Aubigny
by Louis XIV until March 1684, at the end of his reign.[6]

   It seems that Louise was emboldened by the success over
Aubigny to ask for further favours for her relations in France.
Through the new French ambassador, Ruvigny, a Protestant, who
kept his feelings about Louise to himself, she asked Louis XIV
for a position as abbess for her aunt and the office of procurer-
general of the Estates of Brittany for a male relative. Both requests
were refused, though the blow to Louise's self-esteem was somewhat offset by the present of an expensive pair of earrings from
the French king. But while the duchess of Portsmouth's place in
the king's affections was recognized in England soon after her
arrival, it was not until 1675 that Louis, his ministers and ambassadors demonstrated any belief that she might have tangible
political influence in England. They wanted Charles II to dissolve
his strongly anti-French Parliament and hoped that Louise could
encourage him to do so. In fact, Parliament was prorogued for
fifteen months but the impetus – apart from Charles's consistently

fraught relationship with his legislators – is more likely to have come from the grant of 100,000 crowns that he accepted from the French than from any blandishments coming from Louise de Kéroualle. His paymasters insisted that he make formal acknowledgement of such payments in writing and kept his receipts in the records of their Ministry for Foreign Affairs. 'I have received,' he wrote, in his own hand, in September 1676, 'from his most Christian Majesty, by the hands of M. Courtin, the sum of a hundred thousand crowns, French money . . . to be deducted from the four hundred thousand crowns payable at the end of this year.'[7]

The Monsieur Courtin referred to in Charles II's businesslike note was the ambassador who replaced Ruvigny in 1676. Honoré Courtin was a genial and cultured man from a prominent Parisian family. He was an experienced diplomat who had already spent time in England and he knew Louise from her time at the French court. But though Louise had been in England for six years, Courtin was the first French diplomat whose instructions explicitly mentioned Louise and the service that might be expected of her. Distrust of her motives and dislike of her pretensions had made Louis XIV and his foreign ministers, Louvois and Pomponne, slow to realize Louise's potential. Now they considered that she could, in effect, become a spy, passing on information and representing French interests in her day-to-day relations with Charles II.

The belated recognition of Louise's usefulness may seem like an oversight but it should be remembered that Charles II was not the focus of Louis XIV's attention. England could be useful to him but his schemes were on a grand European scale and the situation of his cousin, in a country known for its internal restiveness, did not necessarily inspire confidence. He was happy to send Charles financial sweeteners, since they had little impact on his own exchequer, and to take British military aid in his endless wars, but it was not an alliance of equals. In this respect, the relationship between Charles II and Louis XIV has parallels with that of Henry VIII and the emperor Charles V in the sixteenth

century, and Charles II's disastrous foreign policy is a salutary
reminder that, while Frances Teresa Stuart may have sat for the
portrait of Britannia that graced British coinage, it would be a
long time before Britannia ruled the waves.

Despite her friendship with the strongly anti-French Danby,
there were clearly advantages in encouraging Louise. She had been
shown kindness by Louis XIV and was expected to repay it. It
was time to profit from the English king's known weakness for
women. Yet though Louise evidently did form a working relationship with Courtin, who pointed out to Louis XIV the
advantages of his twice-daily access to Louise's apartments, where
the king was often to be found, their influence over Charles II's
actions was minimal. He listened but then made up his own mind.
And in 1677, Courtin was replaced by Paul Barrillon d'Armoncourt,
marquis de Branges. His instructions, as regards Louise, reiterated
the usefulness of her access to the English king while still refusing
her continued requests for positions for her relatives in France.

Barrillon arrived in London in August 1677 and was immediately
faced with a delicate situation. James, duke of York had given his
permission for his elder daughter, Mary (the second in line to the
British throne), to marry her cousin, William of Orange, the son
of James and Charles II's sister, Princess Mary Stuart. This development dismayed the French, since William himself had a claim
to the throne of Britain via his mother, and the possibility that
the union might upset the balance of power in northern Europe
was something that Louis XIV and his advisers correctly anticipated, though eleven years would pass before their fears were
realized. Charles II appears to have used Louise to convey soothing
words to the French about his nephew's marriage but he was
prepared to risk their displeasure because he was well aware of
William's popularity in England. That popularity did not extend
to the distraught bride herself. Fifteen-year-old Mary was ripening
into a great beauty but her education was patchy; she lacked the
Greek and Latin of Queen Elizabeth I, though her French was
fluent and she was more widely read than some of her biographers

have supposed. But she had lived quietly at Richmond Palace during her girlhood and was now to have her entire existence changed in ways that would have challenged someone of considerably greater maturity. Her chief pastimes were playing cards, gardening and writing impassioned letters to female friends. She had in abundance the looks her much shorter husband obviously lacked (her sister, Princess Anne, called him Caliban, after the monster on Prospero's island in *The Tempest*), and Mary found the idea of marrying him so repellent that she is said to have wept solidly for eighteen hours when told of her forthcoming nuptials.

Louise had known William of Orange since she arrived in England and he was often in her apartments during his visits to his uncle. While this is indicative of the widely accepted realization that anyone who wanted more informal access to Charles II would find him with his French mistress, it should not necessarily be interpreted as demonstrating any warmth between Louise and William themselves. Indeed, if such feeling had ever existed, it was soon to be snuffed out, overtaken by events. The political landscape was changing. In January 1679, the Cavalier Parliament was dissolved after twenty-eight difficult years. The king hoped for a more accommodating House of Commons but he had disastrously miscalculated. The general election the following month returned a House that favoured the opposition by a margin of two to one. The great crisis of Charles II's troubled reign was approaching. In its swirling currents, not just Louise but the restored Stuart dynasty itself would be nearly swept away.

CHAPTER FIFTEEN

The Exclusion Crisis

*'At my return [to London] I found men's minds more
disturbed that ever I remember them to have been'*
Algernon Sidney, September 1679

THE ATTEMPT BY Parliament to change the succession to the
English Crown during the years 1679–81 is known as the Exclusion
Crisis, though some historians have questioned the accuracy of
this description.[1] The attempt to exclude the duke of York as
Charles II's rightful heir and replace him with James, duke of
Monmouth was only one aspect of a much wider crisis of confidence in the Restoration settlement, which encompassed many of
the underlying issues that had led to civil war in 1642. Profoundly
different beliefs on how government should be conducted, the
relationship between the king and Parliament, and the management of religious differences had lain simmering not far below
the surface in the first two decades of Charles II's reign. His
approach to managing these tensions was largely a sleight of hand
– something that he was good at – using ministers to shield him
from popular discontent and Louis XIV to prop up his finances,
since Parliament would never vote him the monies he needed.
The one thing that would not go away, that grew ever more problematic as the years went by, was his lack of a legitimate heir of
his own body. There was no precedent for a bastard ascending the

Eleanor (Nell) Gwyn, painted *c*.1670, with a prim expression, in marked contrast to her half-exposed left breast.

Nell Gwyn with her elder
son, posing very revealingly
as Venus and Cupid.

Mary (Moll) Davis, actress,
singer, dancer and rival of
Nell Gwyn. She was the
mother of Charles II's
youngest illegitimate child,
Lady Mary Tudor.

A romantic nineteenth-century painting showing Nell Gwyn leaning over the wall of her Pall Mall house in conversation with Charles II.

James, duke of Monmouth, as an adult, painted in his Garter robes. Handsome and self-centred, he never repaid his father's love.

The chateau of Aubigny-sur-Nère, Louise de Kéroualle's home after her return to France.

Hortense Mancini. Cardinal Mazarin's niece was one of five beautiful sisters born in Italy. Fleeing an unhappy marriage, she eventually settled in England, where she had a brief affair with Charles II.

Armand Charles de La Porte de La Meilleraye, the husband chosen for Hortense Mancini by her uncle, Cardinal Mazarin. Despite his romantic looks, he was already eccentric when Hortense married him and became increasingly obsessive and controlling.

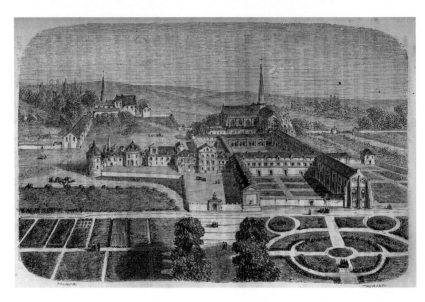

Chelles Abbey outside Paris. Hortense was confined here as a troublesome teenager.

Ralph Montagu. As Charles II's ambassador to France, the ambitious Montagu viewed himself as an indispensable source of information. Not included in his many chatty despatches was the revelation of his affairs with both Barbara Palmer and her eldest daughter, Anne.

Cardinal Jules Mazarin. The wily successor to Richelieu as the most powerful man in France, the Italian-born Mazarin set about ensuring his dynastic legacy through his nieces and nephews.

throne, no matter how personable and loved by his father. Henry VIII had changed the course of English history in his desperate search for a legitimate male heir. Charles II had seven surviving sons by five different mistresses. Was it time to rethink the entire concept of monarchical succession?

The duke of Monmouth was the king's first child and eldest son by the long-dead Lucy Walter. He had much of her looks and many of her weaknesses. Monmouth was now thirty years old, handsome, experienced as a soldier, married, albeit unhappily, to a rich heiress and, most significantly, a Protestant. He also had the ability of courting popularity at a time of political upheaval, when those who either did not know or did not care about his largely dissipated youth, expensive lifestyle and frequently poor judgement could be easily swayed by his public image. He would be whatever they wanted him to be. Before the fall of Danby (deserted by Louise de Kéroualle, who had grown weary of his implacable opposition to a French alliance) in 1678, Monmouth seems not to have considered himself as a political player at all. But others, most notably the earl of Shaftesbury, once a king's man but now the leader of the opposition, were keen to profit from the political vacuum Danby left behind. They wished to encourage in Monmouth the idea that his destiny might be taking a different turn. The young man already knew that his uncle, the duke of York, Charles II's legal heir, had intervened to have his situation spelled out in his latest military commission, when Monmouth was described as the king's 'natural son'. It was an early warning shot in what would become an increasingly vicious battle, as the complex family ties of the Stuarts began to unravel.

The duke of York's conversion to Catholicism was tacitly acknowledged when he was compelled to resign the post of lord high admiral in 1673 because he would not take the Test Act. Publicly, he continued to prevaricate until 1676, despite having married a Catholic second wife. His was a personal journey a long time in the making. Like all his siblings except Henriette Anne, who was raised in the Catholic court of Louis XIV, James had been brought up as a Protestant. He was certainly not close to his mother, Henrietta Maria, but he was well aware of her devotion to the Catholic religion. While in exile, he came to respect the Catholics he knew, and he had served as a soldier of fortune with two Catholic powers, France and Spain, but at the time of the Restoration he was still outwardly conforming to the Church of England. By the late 1660s, both James and his first wife, Anne Hyde, were privately worshipping as Catholics. Charles II, aware of the political fallout that would ensue if his heir and sister-in-law made public their conversion, urged complete silence on the subject. James, though as unfaithful a husband as his brother, was greatly distressed by Anne's painful death in 1671 from breast cancer, her condition apparently exacerbated by an eighth pregnancy. He had been with her in the final hours of her life and felt the disapproval of her brothers and domestic servants. The experience left its mark on him and deepened his faith. James would never be swayed in his commitment to Catholicism from this time. He had found a certainty that would underpin him for the rest of his life. Yet James's very rigidity presented the king with a seemingly intractable problem. Public opinion, as the Popish Plot so clearly demonstrated, was dangerously volatile, and popery was an emotive term. It could readily be exploited by government opponents. Opinions were hardening and the emergence of different political groupings, representing the more conservative Court and the increasingly radical Country interests, would soon transform English politics by the creation of two distinct parties, the Whigs and the Tories.

Between 1679 and 1681 there were three attempts to introduce bills into Parliament that would exclude the Catholic duke of York from the succession. Charles II decided that it would be better if his brother were removed from the scene altogether while he attempted to control the situation, sending the duke and duchess to Brussels. James was unhappy at this new exile but could only wait on events. At home, Danby was forced from office and impeached; Louise de Kéroualle had decided some months previously that he was no longer of any use to her. Determined to stay at the heart of politics, she had already found a new ally in Robert Spencer, earl of Sunderland. Working with the earl of Essex, who had been so dubious about courting Louise's support for his role in Ireland, and with the marquis of Halifax, Sunderland hoped to be able to steady the ship of state and secure the legitimate order of the succession, in defiance of Shaftesbury, who, as president of the Privy Council, had come out for exclusion in April 1679. A serious rebellion in Scotland during the early summer was put down by Monmouth, whose standing rose as a result, alarming Louise's allies in government. The solution to the multiple problems that now beset the chronically underfunded king was hotly debated in council and the decision to recommend the dissolution of Parliament split Charles II's warring advisers. It must also have brought some relief to a worried Louise, who had been criticized in Parliament and her removal demanded.

The duke of York was not the only one watching anxiously from abroad. An alternative to the growing popularity of Monmouth was to balance his presence in England with that of William of Orange, an idea that Sunderland considered for a while, realizing that Louise's attitude towards William, given her influence with Charles II, might be key to the success of this project. Henry Sidney, younger brother of that Algernon Sidney who had once sought Lucy Walter's favours, was the British envoy to The Hague. He was to get William to write to Louise,

and make some application to her, for that she will be of great use to us, particularly against the duke of Monmouth; and I am to let him know how instrumental she hath been in changing the council and in several other things. In short, I am to tell him that she is one Lord Sunderland does make use of and that he must do so too if he intends to do any good with the king. *She hath more power over him than can be imagined.*

Nobody can excuse what she hath done, but I hope well from
her in the future.[2] (My italics.)

This last elliptical reference may be to the suspicion that Louise
had always, in reality, acted in the interests of France. Whether
her influence was as great as Sunderland believed is another matter.
The idea that she could keep abreast of such fast-changing political developments and constantly be discussing and analysing them
with the king, when nobody had a clear picture of what was
happening or the most advantageous course to take, seems far-
fetched. But the mere fact that Louise was considered to have
such influence counted for a great deal in the eyes of the self-
serving men who jockeyed for position in these febrile years. The
calculations of all of them were soon, however, to be thrown up
in the air. At the end of August 1679, Charles fell seriously ill,
causing great alarm on both sides of the North Sea. Had a decisive moment for his kingdoms come so soon?

*

THE KING RECOVERED quickly but his nervous capital did not.
Algernon Sidney, recently elected as member of Parliament for
Amersham in Buckinghamshire, captured the prevailing sense of
unease perfectly in a letter to his friend, Henry Savile: 'there is
no extremity of disorder to be imagined, which we might not
have fallen into if the king had died, or which may not yet reason-
ably be feared if he should relapse.'[3] It is not clear exactly what
form the king's illness had taken – some historians have suggested
that he suffered a stroke – but whatever it was, by the time his
brother, hastily summoned back from Brussels by Sunderland, had
arrived, he was already on the mend. The king seemed relieved by
the duke of York's return but decided that the situation was still
too unpredictable for him to remain in London, so he was sent
instead to Scotland, somewhat to the chagrin of the duke of
Lauderdale, who did not relish James's interference in his quasi-
despotic government of the northern kingdom. Monmouth,

meanwhile, had been exiled to the Netherlands, where William of Orange could keep an eye on him. The Prince and Princess of Orange were extremely sensitive about protecting Mary's position in the English succession and were far from welcoming. Monmouth quickly made up his mind to defy his father's orders and returned unbidden to London in late November 1679, giving heart to the increasingly vocal opposition, now led by Shaftesbury.

In the midst of all this uncertainty, Louise had much to ponder. Her relations with the Yorks had not always been smooth in the 1670s, especially when Mary of Modena snubbed her in favour of one of Louise's rivals, Mary's cousin, Hortense Mancini.[4] But she had been working behind the scenes during and after the king's illness, apparently against Monmouth and in support of the duke of York. But he could not count on her support for any length of time and she herself seems increasingly to have been out of her depth, not knowing which way to turn. In the summer of 1680, as the Exclusion Crisis rumbled on, Louise executed a remarkable volte-face which appeared to destroy any hopes of a reconciliation with the king's brother.

What had brought about this change of heart? There are several possibilities, but the main factors seem to have been fear and a political gamble that went wrong. Her alliance with Sunderland was one of convenience, and his female relatives, especially his wife, detested her. They smelled blood when, at the beginning of January 1680, there appeared in circulation a document with the alarming title, *Articles of High Treason, and other high crimes and misdemeanors, against the Lady Duchess of Portsmouth.* The authorship of these twenty-two charges levelled at Louise remains unknown.[5] They may have been drafted by more than one person, and the involvement of Shaftesbury, or at least his encouragement, is likely, but unproven. It is a document of considerable interest, not just for what it reveals of the furious hatred felt for Louise de Kéroualle by the king's opponents but for their underlying disgust and utter lack of respect for Charles II himself.

The attack on Louise was visceral. It began with the assertion

that she was the cause of Charles II's illness because she was
diseased sexually: 'the said duchess hath, and still doth cohabit
and keep company with the king, having had foul, nauseous and
contagious distempers, which, once possessing her blood, can never
admit of a perfect cure, to the manifest danger and hazard of the
king's person, in whose person is bound up the weal and happiness
of the Protestant religion, our lives, liberties and properties . . .'
Thus was Louise's misfortune in contracting a venereal disease
from Charles II turned into a lurid accusation that she had, in
fact, infected him. The writers knew how to grab attention and,
if what followed was less prurient, it was equally serious. The
duchess of Portsmouth's pernicious influence was ubiquitous. 'She
hath laboured,' the articles went on, 'to alter and subvert the
government of church and state . . . and to introduce popery in
the three kingdoms.' Not only was she a French spy, who 'advised
and still does nourish, foment and maintain that fatal and destruc-
tive corresponding alliance between England and France, being
sent over and pensioned by the French king to the same end and
purpose', but she had meddled and advised 'in matters of the
highest importance in peace and government . . . placed and
displaced great ministers in church and state as she judged might
be most serviceable in promoting the French and popish interest.'
Still greater indignation can be sensed in the hammer blows aimed
at Louise's greed: 'she hath been an unspeakable charge and burden,
having had given her, for many years past, prodigious sums of
money in other people's names . . . as well as out of the public
treasury . . . and such is her ascendancy over the king that, in her
own apartments, she prevailed with the king there to sign and
seal warrants for grants of vast sums of money.' She had, for
example, procured £100,000 for Danby, 'now impeached and in
the Tower.'

Nor was it just money that Louise coveted. She had the throne
itself in her sights, when she encouraged 'her creatures and friends'
to put it about 'that she was married to his majesty and that her
son . . . is his majesty's legitimate son.' Finishing with a flourish

of disdain and barely repressed grief for the damage done to the nation by this foreign Jezebel, the articles against Louise concluded, 'that she hath had the highest honours and rewards conferred on her and her's, to the high dishonour of God, the encouragement of wickedness and vice (which by such examples is overspread the nation and for which God's anger is kindled and enflamed against us) . . . to the eternal reproach of his majesty's reign and government.' The language of the articles against Louise, with their echoes of Bunyan and the Independents of the Civil Wars, conveys not just contempt for a putrid French whore but for the impotent king she dominated.

Louise had considered leaving England for France as the crisis deepened but, though frightened, she stayed, perhaps concerned about leaving her son and the king at this difficult time. The countess of Sunderland, irritated by her lord's accommodation with this creature, wrote that Louise, 'does daily grow so odious that being in any of her affairs were enough to ruin one.'[6] Yet no action was taken as a result of the publication of the articles against Louise. Parliament was prorogued at the time. If it had been in session, the articles would probably have formed the basis of a direct onslaught on the duchess of Portsmouth. Barrillon was worried that she might be formally arraigned for treason and brought before the Court of King's Bench, her case to be considered by Parliament when it sat again. Sunderland looked to his own survival, distancing himself from Louise without formally abandoning her. After a very nervous few months, during which further legal action seemed possible, Louise appeared to be bowing to the inevitable. If she wanted a quiet life and the respectability she had always craved, she would need to distance herself unequivocally from the duke of York. By the late summer of 1680, she had become an exclusionist.

*

'NEWS, NEWS,' BRAYED a newsletter in early November 1680, 'the duchess of Portsmouth is turned to the Protestant religion and, is, 'tis said, one of Shaftesbury's converts and very kind to the duke of Monmouth.'[7] Parliament had met again on 21 October amid a whirlwind of such speculation. The French ambassador, Barrillon, promised Louis XIV that he would try to keep abreast of what was happening and protect his interests, striving always to ensure that 'England does not pass under a form of government which is very close to that of a republic.'[8] This comment is revealing, for it was not merely the succession, but the entire fabric of Restoration government and society that was under threat, and Barrillon, despite being an outsider, clearly recognized this. Whether Louise de Kéroualle fully understood the wider implications of the threat from the king's opponents is open to question. She had always viewed herself as a power broker, but she was closer to being a 'fixer', someone who facilitated meetings and discussions, flitting prettily between the anxious politicians, whose own aims were often couched in the language of the moral high ground, but whose day-to-day concerns were as much about personal ambition as the future health of the nation.

Barrillon, basing his analysis on information he claimed to have received from Ralph Montagu, whose mission to Paris had ended in disgrace and who was now back in England as a member of Parliament, thought he understood Louise's tactics. She had been reconciled to Monmouth, and she and Sunderland had reached an agreement with the duke and Shaftesbury. It gave these two gentlemen the assurance that Charles II would meet Parliament's demands. These covered a range of measures attacking corruption at all levels of government, and greater religious toleration for Protestant Nonconformists, as well as the continued dispute over the succession; in return, Parliament would offer a commitment to provide regular and sufficient financial support for the Crown. There would, of course, be a promise of high office for Shaftesbury and a provision that Charles could name his successor. Given anti-Catholic feeling and the duke of York's unpopularity, that successor was evidently going to be someone else, though the precise identity was left open. Monmouth would naturally expect it to be him, but William of Orange might have other ideas.

That Charles II should have been willing to go along with such fundamental changes to the authority of the Crown seems more unlikely in retrospect than it was to contemporaries. The threat of rebellion and even of civil war was in the air, and feelings were exacerbated by a flurry of political propaganda. But it begs certain questions for which there are no clear answers. One of these is the motivation of Louise herself. Was she genuinely convinced of the viability of this plan, perhaps hoping, as had been suggested in the *Articles of High Treason*, to keep open a door for her own son to succeed his father? Was her support of Shaftesbury merely born of an instinct for self-preservation? They were hardly natural allies. Could she simply not resist intrigue for its own sake? Or was she merely a tool of a king who, although beleaguered, still held important cards and was willing to use her as a stalking horse until she got taken in by his opponents and went too far? Whatever the truth – and perhaps even Louise did not know the answer – when the House of Lords rejected the Exclusion Bill on 15 November, despite its having passed in the Commons, Charles was mightily relieved. He could now show his own disapproval, even if it meant embarrassing his mistress. Louise was still in limbo with regards to her political influence as 1681 dawned. Barrillon reported that she believed she and Sunderland could still persuade Charles to abandon his brother, and James remained highly agitated at the prospect, as well as bitter against Louise. Charles, however, held firm and in 1681 he made a bold move that brought the Exclusion Crisis and its associated furore to an end.

It was an option always open to him and, indeed, he had used it before in his dealings with Parliament. Concerned by the threat of popular unrest, the king determined that the session that was to begin in March 1681 would take place in the traditional royalist stronghold of Oxford, away from the anti-monarchical sentiment of London. Though it had not been unusual for Parliament to meet in various English locations in the Middle Ages, and even later, the Oxford Parliament of 1681 would be the last time the legislature met outside London. It would also be the last of Charles II's reign. When it brought in a third Exclusion Bill, he dissolved it after a week. By that time, he was secure in the knowledge that he had obtained a new financial subsidy from France and had no immediate need for revenue from his own legislature. He was also determined to uphold the rightful succession in the person of his brother and to deal with his Whig opponents, left in disarray by their failure to bring about change, through a concerted effort of propaganda and the crushing of dissent. He began four years of personal rule that, at least in part, reflected his admiration for the absolutist system favoured by his cousin, Louis XIV. He had not merely survived, but was to emerge with a kind of triumph, as 'incontestably the strongest seventeenth century monarch.'⁹ Perhaps, but the Rye House Plot of 1683 showed that there remained opponents among his own aristocracy who were willing to have him and the duke of York assassinated. The implication of Monmouth in this conspiracy distressed his father greatly and sealed the fate of the elderly Algernon Sidney. The man rumoured to have offered money for Lucy Walter's favours thirty-five years earlier was executed on Tower Hill, and the Good Old Cause of republicanism in England, for which he had been such an eloquent and committed apologist, died with him.

Louise was still very much at the king's side in these years, despite having succumbed briefly to the charms of a lover six years her junior, the disreputable Frenchman, Philippe de Vendôme. Charles was jealous, but blamed Vendôme more than Louise. Louis XIV, aware that this distant cousin (Vendôme was an illegitimate grandson of Henry IV) had the potential to cause trouble for the duchess of Portsmouth, ordered him back to France. She was reconciled with the duke of York and dabbled in politics as much as ever. Her stock rose even higher when she made a triumphant visit to France in the spring of 1682. Two years later, she was again very unwell but rallied in time for the Christmas season of 1684. It was reported that 'since her grace's recovery she is greater and more absolute than ever.'

The duchess of Portsmouth's position seemed unassailable then. Yet throughout the 1670s she had good cause to be uneasy. She had other rivals than Nell Gwyn. The most glamorous of these was another woman who had come to Charles II's court from France, but her background was very different from that of the quiet convent girl from Brittany.

Part Seven

The Cardinal's Niece
Hortense Mancini

1646–99

CHAPTER SIXTEEN

An Italian Girl in Paris

'It is necessary to observe all the proprieties in Paris because
everyone is closely watching the conduct of my nieces'
Cardinal Jules Mazarin, January 1660

SEVENTEENTH-CENTURY FRANCE produced an army of
remarkable ladies – letter and memoir writers, courtiers and
courtesans, actresses and novelists, gossips and great beauties,
adventuresses and criminals. Among the most exuberant of these
women was one who, as a little girl of seven, had come to France
with her family to join two older sisters, one of whom had already
married a French duke. The child was Ortensia Mancini, daughter
of Lorenzo Mancini and Hieronyma Mazzarini, both of whom
came from the lower ranks of Roman nobility but were only
distantly connected to the leading Italian aristocratic families.
The child's life, had she remained in Italy, would have been one
of quiet respectability; a convent education and a respectable,
but not brilliant, marriage. The journey she made in the spring
of 1653 would change all that. In Paris, she soon became known
by the French version of her name, Hortense, but her future lay
in the hands of her uncle, Cardinal Jules Mazarin, her mother's
elder brother. As chief minister to the young Louis XIV, he was
not just the leading politician in France, but one of the foremost statesmen in Europe. His wealth and power had opened

up possibilities for his two sisters (Hieronyma's widowed sibling Laura Margherita Martinozzi and her own two daughters travelled with them) and their families. For in these children, seven nieces and two nephews, Cardinal Mazarin was determined that his legacy would live on. They were his flesh and blood and, for Mazarin, as with all seventeenth-century Europeans, family was everything. He would endow them with all the riches, titles and splendour that his position could bring. Yet while they all had outstanding good looks and distinctive personalities, the one thing they would conspicuously lack and that their uncle simply could not arrange for them was the simplest of all: he could not buy them happiness. More than a century would pass before the French revolutionary, St Just, remarked that happiness was a new idea in Europe. Its absence would certainly be keenly felt by the beautiful nieces of Cardinal Mazarin.

His achievement in reaching the height of power in France was, nevertheless, a story of which his relations could be rightly proud. Born Giulio Mazzarini in the Abruzzo in 1602, he had used his great charm, intelligence and gambler's instinct first as a client of the influential Colonna family and then in the diplomatic service of the papacy. Handsome and witty, he had an infinite capacity to please and was a very quick learner. It may well have been the fact that he had risen on his own resources, without the natural advantages of high birth and family connections, that made him so keen to ensure a future for his sisters' offspring. He had been in France since 1634, when he was appointed papal nuncio to the court of Louis XIII. There, he attracted the attention of Cardinal Richelieu, who admired his style and abilities, and took him under his wing. Given such a patron, it seemed only natural for Giulio Mazzarini to become Jules Mazarin. He took French citizenship in 1640 and, two years later, he was made a cardinal. When both Richelieu and Louis XIII died within a few months of each other in 1643, Mazarin's time had come. Although a regency council had been appointed to govern in the name of the five-year-old Louis XIV, in practice it was Mazarin and the child's mother, Anne of Austria, who ruled the country. Theirs was a very close relationship – wagging tongues suggested it was sexual, though it was probably not – based on the fact that they were two outsiders thrust into positions of power unexpectedly. Mazarin had spent time in Spain as a young man and spoke the language well. It was Anne's native tongue (the French called her Anne of Austria because she was a Habsburg, though she was the daughter of Philip III of Spain) and her evening briefings on foreign affairs from Cardinal Mazarin were the highlight of her day. Throughout the 1640s, when France was engulfed in the civil unrest of the Fronde, almost as serious as the Civil War in England, they formed an unbreakable attachment. It was natural that she should support him in his ambitions for his Italian family. They would be received at court, educated as members of the French nobility and would make appropriate marriages. There was only one male among them, Philippe, whose title of duc de Nevers was purchased for him by Mazarin in 1660. The *parlement* of Paris, however, refused to register it, a sign of how unpopular the cardinal remained, well after the disturbances of the Fronde were over. Neither could his nieces, despite their beauty and high spirits, ever quite escape the distaste which many of the old French nobility felt for their upstart uncle. It would have a profound effect on their lives.

*

NONE OF THIS could have been foreseen by the dark, curly-haired child who waited to board a Genoese galley with her mother, aunt, elder sister Marie, brother Philippe and cousins Anne-Marie and Laura Martinozzi, in 1653. Her four-year-old younger sister, the baby of the family, Marianne, was left behind.[1] They were leaving Italy from Rome's port, Civitavecchia, now a busy cruise terminal, but then much more of a fishing harbour. The vessel that they were about to board had been specially commissioned by Mazarin from Genoese boatbuilders. It had been luxuriously fitted out for a relaxed voyage and Hortense's subsequent description makes no mention of the twenty galley slaves who were compelled to row it. Instead, she remembered its elegance: 'I will not stop here,' she later wrote, 'to describe that movable house. It would take up too much time to portray all its beauty, its order, its riches, and its magnificence. Suffice it to say that we were treated like queens there and throughout our voyage, and that the tables of sovereigns are not served with more pomp and brilliance than was ours four times a day.'[2]

After a week's leisurely crossing, the galley reached the French coast, landing in Marseille. The family then spent eight months in the south of France, living in Aix-en-Provence with Hieronyma's eldest daughter, Laure-Victoire, who, at seventeen, was already the duchess of Mercoeur. Married to a husband twenty-four years her senior, Laure-Victoire had been in France for four years and was well placed to coach the new arrivals in the minutiae of French etiquette and what to expect when they arrived at court. Hortense and Marie listened carefully as their sister instructed them on the finer points of inviting and receiving guests, as amused as their mother was shocked to learn that visitors should be greeted with a kiss. They observed the luxurious manner in which Laure-Victoire lived (Hortense later wrote that her brother-in-law entertained her 'in the most magnificent manner conceivable') and a stream of local dignitaries bearing gifts brought home to them just how important their uncle the cardinal was in France.[3]

This impression was reinforced when they arrived in the French capital in February 1654. Their uncle was then living in the Palais Mazarin, a building designed for him by two prominent French architects. What is left of it today forms part of the original site of the Bibliothèque Nationale on Rue de Richelieu in Paris's second arrondissement. Though Mazarin was not much interested in acquiring property, his residence was filled with a collection of gems to rival any of his contemporaries in Europe. His wide-eyed nieces marvelled at objects of great value and breathtaking beauty. There were vases, plates, cups, goblets and small chests, all encrusted with precious stones, as well as exquisite crosses and chandeliers. Some of these pieces can still be seen in the Louvre.

Almost before they had a chance to catch their breath, the Mancini girls were attending the wedding of their sixteen-year-old cousin, Anne-Marie Martinozzi, to the Prince de Conti. Anne-Marie's husband was a member of a family that had been among the most aggressive rebels of the Fronde. They had accepted the need of an alliance with Mazarin's family without enthusiasm. The bride herself, shimmering in 'a dress of brocade enriched with pearls of very great price', had no say in the matter, but her beauty and good nature ensured that her union with a man susceptible to occasional jealousy was largely a success.

Mazarin, ever conscious of the watchful eyes of the French court, had inspected this latest cohort of his family at the Chateau de Villeroy at Corbeil, just to the south of Paris, before permitting them to proceed on the final stage of their journey. He needed to be sure that the children could speak French well enough and had learned sufficient of the elaborate social niceties to hold their own on a stage that was by no means automatically welcoming. The girls seemed to have passed muster initially, but the cardinal soon detected a problem. Hieronyma Mancini (or 'de Mancini', as she became to satisfy the punctilious snobbery of the French aristocracy) did not get on with her daughter Marie. At fifteen, Marie was already something of a rebel. Her own reference to 'my poor eating habits' and the alarm of those around her that she was much too thin suggests anorexia. She claimed that the months of being unsettled, combined with a temperament that was highly strung, 'had reduced me to a pitiful state.'[4]

Alarmed that this awkward and skinny girl would not pass muster in the salons of Paris or the receiving rooms of the Louvre Palace, Mazarin made a decision entirely predictable for the times in which he lived, even if nowadays we might question whether it would make a potentially difficult situation worse. He sent Marie, accompanied by Hortense, who was too young to participate in court life, to a convent, 'to see, as he said,' wrote Marie, 'if it would fatten me up a bit.' It was not clear with what culinary delights the sisters of the Convent of the Visitation, in the Faubourg Saint-Jacques, could cause Marie's figure to bloom, but their credentials in education were much admired by the upper classes and, perhaps to her own surprise, Marie did well studying their curriculum, which was more broadly based than the education she had received in Rome. She and Hortense spent eighteen months in the convent before they were finally deemed acceptable in the rarefied society which awaited them. This period of enforced removal from the rest of their family forged a strong bond between Marie and Hortense, despite the seven-year age gap. They remained devoted to each other through all the vicissitudes of their remarkable lives, until Hortense's death separated them nearly half a century later.

Now much more confident – though no less inclined to stand up for herself – Marie knew that the search to find her a husband would accelerate. This led to further recriminations with her mother, who by now was very ill. As she approached death, Hieronyma shut her daughter out altogether. Lectures from her uncle had no effect on Marie and she and her mother were never reconciled. A couple of months after Hieronyma died, the wedding of Olympe Mancini to Prince Eugene of Savoy, comte de Soissons, was celebrated at Compiègne. The bride, who had been somewhat miffed to be passed over by the Italian d'Este family in favour of her cousin, Laure Martinozzi, had recovered from this snub to dazzle spectacularly at her own wedding, as was becoming the custom with Mazarin's nieces. The *Gazette de France* reported that she was 'dressed in a gown of silver cloth with bouquet of pearls on her head, valued at more than 50,000 livres, and so many jewels that their splendour, joined to the natural *éclat* of her beauty, caused her to be admired by everyone.'[5] Cardinal Mazarin had now arranged superb marriages for both his Martinozzi nieces and two of the Mancini girls. He now turned his attention to the three Mancini girls who remained unwed. Marianne was too young for this to yet be a serious consideration but Marie and Hortense were not. They were both about to discover that the pain brought about by their uncle's ambitions for them was far greater than the wealth and rank his influence could buy.

Hortense had always been her uncle's favourite. She sent him charming little letters, which pleased him, and it was evident that she would be considered the most beautiful of all his nieces. But she soon discovered that he would be relentless in imposing his will on the women of his family. After their mother's death, a governess, Madame de Venelle, was appointed to supervise their daily lives. A rigid, strait-laced lady who stuck firmly to Mazarin's instructions, Madame de Venelle never tried to be a replacement for their mother, and they would not, in any case, have been willing to accept her as such. She was certainly not cruel to Marie and Hortense but they viewed her with growing resentment, chafing under the restrictions she put on them and suspecting, with some justification, that she was as much a spy as a chaperone. Yet despite her dedication to her task, neither she nor the cardinal were able to prevent an episode which was to have repercussions for the rest of Marie's life. It also left a powerful impression of the ephemeral nature of love on Hortense. In the summer of 1658, after surviving a dangerous illness, the twenty-year-old Louis XIV, unmarried and about to assume the reins of power for which Mazarin had so carefully prepared him, fell in love with Marie Mancini.

Despite the lurid speculation of historical novelists and even the misleading title of the most recent biography of the Mancini sisters, there is little evidence to support the view that this was a sexual relationship. Marie was not Louis XIV's mistress, but she was the object of his first serious romance. The realization that the young couple's feelings for each other were deepening dismayed both Anne of Austria, Louis's mother, and Mazarin himself. True, he had sought titles and wealth for his nieces, but even he had not aimed at one of them becoming queen of France. Politically, he had emerged from the Fronde as undisputed first minister of France but he was well aware that he remained unpopular and that the French princes of the blood, of whom there were many, would be happy to take aim at him again. Up till now, he had viewed Marie as headstrong but manageable. Her hold over Louis XIV was a threat that needed to be quashed. Queen Anne had already made clear that her opposition to Marie as a wife for her son would be implacable, telling Mazarin, 'I warn you that all of France would revolt against you and against him; and that I will put myself at the head of the rebels to restrain my son.'[6] She was happy enough for this young Italian woman to encourage an interest in culture and the arts, which Louis had hitherto lacked, but there was no way she could contemplate someone of such comparatively low birth sharing his throne.

Marie hoped otherwise. She spoke to Hortense of her love for Louis XIV but Hortense did not really understand the depths of her sister's feelings. She tried to comfort and support Marie when the king's exasperated mother made it clear to Mazarin that she could not have her son acting love-struck and uninterested in front of the delegation sent from Spain to negotiate a marriage for him with her own niece, Maria Teresa. Marie was, in effect, banished from the court, packed off to accompany Mazarin to the south-west of France. The cardinal himself continued onwards to the border with Spain, to seal the treaty that would end years of hostilities between the two countries. Marie, accompanied by Hortense and Marianne, was left in La Rochelle. There, she continued to correspond with Louis XIV, to the fury of her uncle and the concern of Hortense, who seems, despite the fact that she was barely a teenager herself, to have sensed that all this passion would not end well. Eventually, the king managed to spend a day with Marie and they agreed, with great sadness, that their romance was doomed. Hortense was present at their anguished parting, but she attached no blame to Louis for ending the liaison: 'nothing,' she recalled, 'could equal the passion that the king showed and the tenderness with which he asked Marie's pardon for all that he had made her suffer because of him.'[7] However genuine these sentiments may have been at the time, Louis soon got over Marie. He accepted the inevitability of the Spanish marriage and meanwhile indulged in a little flirtation with Marie's sister, Olympe, an unpleasant young woman only too happy to play the cardinal's game, even if it did hurt her sister.

Having fought and lost, Marie was unwilling to put up with such humiliation for any longer. Submissive and desperate, with only her sisters for support, she wrote to her uncle asking that he arrange a marriage for her without delay. He was pleased with her behaviour, saying that she would find in him, 'a father who loves you with all his heart.' Marie understood the nature of this new-found paternal affection but she still wanted some control over the selection of a husband. She found Charles de Lorraine pleasant enough, until his elderly uncle intervened to pursue her himself, much to Marie's disdain. Lorraine would probably not have been acceptable to Queen Anne and the cardinal in any case, since such a marriage would have kept Marie at the French court. Anne wanted her out of the country altogether, afraid that she still exerted a hold on the emotions of the newly-wed Louis XIV. In February 1661, a marriage contract was signed by which Marie would return to Rome as the wife of an Italian prince, the Grand Constable Lorenzo Onofrio Colonna. Delayed by illness and her own reluctance to be parted from Hortense, Marie finally took up residence in the Roman mansion of her husband four months later. Eight difficult and eventful years passed before the sisters saw one another again, in circumstances neither could have anticipated, but which were perhaps, given their natures, not entirely surprising.

*

CARDINAL MAZARIN'S OWN health was failing at the start of 1661 and he knew that death was not far away. He needed to make sure that Hortense's situation was settled quickly and that a suitable husband might be found for fourteen-year-old Marianne, the youngest of his nieces. To Mazarin, this was a sacred charge and would complete his bequests to the children of his sisters, who had become his dynasty. Hortense had not wanted for admirers. She was one of the most talked-about beauties at the French court and any husband could expect to acquire, through marrying her, an enviable portion of Mazarin's enormous wealth. She was a prize fit for a king and, indeed, one had already come calling. In 1658,

Charles II asked for Hortense's hand but was rebuffed by Mazarin, who reported that he had told her suitor, 'that he was paying me too great an honour.' This withering sarcasm could not have escaped the exiled king of Great Britain, who was a penniless wanderer at the time, living on handouts from Spain in what is now Belgium. Mazarin had made peace with the English republic and was not about to annoy Oliver Cromwell by allying his favourite niece with someone whose prospects of ever regaining the throne seemed impossibly remote. His reservations vanished completely when Charles was unexpectedly restored in 1660, and the king was able to gain some measure of revenge by making it clear that the daughter of minor Italian nobles was not an appropriate choice to be his wife. There would be no Queen Hortense. But Charles II had undoubtedly been smitten by the girl when he first met her in Paris and his ardour was renewed when they met again seventeen years later.

Cardinal Mazarin devoted all his remaining energy to arranging a suitable marriage for Hortense in the weeks leading up to his death. His favoured candidate was Armand-Charles de la Porte de la Meilleraye, a young man from a family with undistinguished origins (not unlike the cardinal's own), whose father held the title of marshal of France. Armand was twenty-nine years old and Hortense not yet fifteen. He had, rather unhealthily, been infatuated with her since she was nine and was still as determined as ever to marry her, though he knew that she had other, more impressive suitors. As Mazarin fought to stay alive, racked by coughing fits and exhausted by insomnia, he decided that Armand would, in effect, fill the role of his only male heir. Philippe, the nephew he detested, had forfeited his right to inherit the cardinal's riches through the kind of hedonism and recklessness that ran like tainted wine through the veins of the younger generation of the Mancini family. Out of consideration for her uncle and perhaps lured by the wealth with which he intended to endow her through this marriage, Hortense agreed to become Armand's wife. The wedding took place at the Palais Mazarin on 1 March 1661. Eight days later, the great cardinal was dead and the new duke and duchess Mazarin, as Armand and Hortense now became, started their life together. That they were almost comically incompatible had not troubled Hortense's late uncle. Yet it was to leave her, in her own words, 'the richest heiress and the unhappiest woman in Christendom.'

Hortense was actually married a month before her sister, Marie. Neither of them, nor, indeed, their siblings, marked the passing of Cardinal Mazarin with an outpouring of grief. 'It is a remarkable thing,' the new duchess Mazarin wrote later, 'that a man of his merit, after having worked all his life to exalt and enrich his family, should have received nothing but expressions of aversion from them, even after his death.' She went on, however, to explain the reasons for this apparently monumental ungratefulness and, in so doing, revealed the root of the unhappiness that would characterize the lives of the Mancini girls, marking them for ever afterwards. 'If you knew with what severity he treated us at all times, you would,' she claimed, 'be less surprised by it. Never has a man had such gentle manners in public and such harsh ones at home; and all our temperaments and inclinations were contrary to his. Add to that incredible subjection under which he held us, our extreme youth, and the insensitivity and carelessness about everything which excessive wealth and privilege ordinarily cause in people of that age, however good a nature they may have.'[8]

The duke and duchess Mazarin (he was denied the 'de' in front of the surname because of his lower social standing) moved into apartments in the Palais Mazarin, surrounded by reminders of the cardinal's wealth. Everything about the place breathed riches and luxury, from the bejewelled vases and plate to the unrivalled collection of statuary and paintings to the opulent furnishings and tapestries. Unhappily for Hortense, it really was to become a gilded cage. Like all women of her age, she was her husband's property, unable to dispose of any item in her uncle's collection without Armand's permission. And the object the duke most jealously guarded was his wife herself.

The extent of what was to become a full-blown obsession, handily spiced with growing religious mania, was not immediately apparent in Duke Mazarin. The couple made at least a minimal effort to get along and to live up to their place in Parisian society, aware that all eyes were upon them. There was certainly nothing obviously disconcerting in Armand's appearance and manner. He was presentable, in the fashion of the times, with the full wig and pencil moustache sported by the king and copied by so many men of fashion. Well dressed and cultured, he could have fitted in perfectly well and perhaps educated his young and frivolous wife to share his interests. Nothing, to those who knew him casually, especially marked him out as the man he was so soon to become. His own father, however, thought differently. Armand's capacity for jealousy and his possessiveness disturbed Charles de la Porte, who had foreseen trouble from the outset.

It was not long coming. Afraid that his wife was at least flirting with Louis XIV in a dangerous manner, Armand brought in a Provençal woman, Madame de Ruz, ostensibly as a friend to replace the ever-present governess, Madame de Venelle. The unsuspecting Hortense did not at first realize that she had swapped the cardinal's dragon for one in her husband's pay. Soon, he was restricting her social life in Paris, dictating who she could and could not receive in their home and banning all theatrical events and concerts at the Palais Mazarin. Viewing Paris as too tempting a place for his much-admired and flighty young wife, he resolved to take her away. He had been given a number of regional governorships and local offices by Louis XIV, and now determined to pursue his responsibilities doggedly, with his wife at his side. Hortense remembered this period of her marriage with indignation:

The deceitful behaviour of Monsieur Mazarin in the choice of this woman, at a time when he could not yet have had any cause to complain of me, is enough to show you his suspicious nature and the frame of mind in which he had married me. As he was fearful of having me stay in Paris, he constantly moved me around among the lands that he possessed and governed. During the first three or four years of our marriage I made three trips to Alsace and as many to Brittany, not to mention several others to Nevers, to Maine, to Bourbon, to Sedan and elsewhere.

Since Armand was always with her on the rare occasions they were at the French court, even the attractions of Paris began to fail. She simply could not get away from him. 'Perhaps,' she went on, 'I never would have tired of that vagabond life if he had not taken excessive advantage of my accommodating nature. Several times he had me travel two hundred leagues while I was with child and even very near to giving birth.'[9]

In the first five years of her marriage, Hortense had done her duty and given birth to four children, often in difficult circumstances, as her memoirs reveal. That the three girls and the long-awaited son (Paul-Jules, born in 1666) were all healthy is a testament to Hortense's robust physique and her determination to cling on. Her husband allowed her no friends, no stability, and moved her on as soon as she showed any sign of settling contentedly in one place. At the same time, his religious devotion, which had always been marked, began to turn into a recognizable mania. This took forms ranging from the disturbing to the hilarious. At the same time that he was holding conversations with the Angel Gabriel in his dreams, the duke Mazarin was becoming an agricultural prude, worrying that milkmaids would be corrupted by the sexual excitement of milking cows, or titillated by milk-churning. He found the earthiness of peasant life disconcerting. This was, though, nothing to the tyranny he was imposing on his unhappy and deeply frustrated wife. For while he was taking a hammer to the genitals of the priceless statuary at the Palais Mazarin, to the horror of his servants, who well understood the value of the collection, he was equally determined to ensure that his wife should hand over all of her jewels and possessions to him. It had dawned on Armand's troubled mind that his wife might rebel and even think of leaving him. He had long suspected her intentions, though without any justification. He could only be sure of her complete subjugation if she was penniless.

This was the last straw for Hortense. On the pretext that he was afraid, because of her natural generosity, that Hortense would give her remaining jewels away, he appropriated them one evening while she was out. Clearly, Hortense was not quite so much of a prisoner at the Palais Mazarin as she made out, but this temporary absence cost her dear. Remonstrations had no effect. Armand did not indulge in shouting matches; it was not his style. Facetiousness and malicious jokes reduced Hortense to tears. She fled through an adjoining door to the wing of the palace in which her brother, Philippe, duke of Nevers, resided. From there, they sent for the youngest Mancini sister, Marianne, who had been married to the duke de Bouillon since 1662 and who had been given the responsibility of bringing up the children of her eldest sister, Laure-Victoire, who died in 1657. Unlike Armand, Marianne's husband adored his wife and admired her literary efforts, while overlooking her love affairs and her increasing girth. This degree of freedom made Marianne confident and forthright. She had little time for Hortense's sufferings. Both Marianne and Philippe counselled an official separation, and as soon as possible, while there was still enough of their uncle's wealth remaining to form the basis of a sensible division of goods between Hortense and Armand. The arcane terms of Hortense's marriage contract made this exceptionally difficult. Only her jewels, despite what Armand might say, were legally hers. Anything else was open to dispute and Hortense knew her husband well enough to anticipate a protracted legal battle.

Her first attempt at leaving her husband saw her temporarily staying with her sister, Olympe, until Colbert, Louis XIV's chief minister, given the unenviable task of mediating the dispute, ordered her to return to Armand, albeit with somewhat greater freedom in the choice of her own household servants. The 'reconciliation' was over as soon as it started. Refusing Armand's commands to accompany him to Alsace, Hortense entered the convent of Notre-Dame-des-Chelles, in the Val de Marne, north of Paris, where one of Armand's aunts was abbess. If she had feared for a severe reception from this relative, she was taken aback; the abbess was gentle, non-judgemental and far from impressed by her nephew. Irritated by the apparently pleasant life his wife was leading at Chelles, Armand had her brought back to the Convent of the Visitation, near the Bastille, where the nuns were stricter.[10] He went to see Hortense there but was as incensed by her refusal to accompany him to Brittany as he was by her adoption of one of the current high-fashion trends – beauty spots of black taffeta applied to the skin, which ladies used to highlight the pallor of their complexions. Armand set off for Brittany in high dudgeon and Hortense was allowed to plead her case personally with Louis XIV, but the opposition of his finance minister, Colbert, threatened to drag things on interminably. Hortense seemed destined to languish at the convent in Paris unless she obeyed her husband. And then she met another detainee, seventeen-year-old Marie-Sidonie, marquise de Courcelles, who fundamentally changed her outlook. Confined at the convent under accusation of adultery, the young marquise had powerful friends at court and she knew how to use them. Together, she and Hortense formed an intense friendship – possibly the first lesbian relationship of Hortense's life – and determined to take on the might of the French legal establishment, so heavily weighted against married women.

Marie-Sidonie provided the impetus and hope that the increasingly depressed duchess Mazarin needed and which her family had failed to provide. Hortense had watched her sister, Marie, wallow in the despair of one of the doomed romantic heroines of the Italian novels that she read to Louis XIV as a love-struck teenager. Now, she was back home in Italy, leading the life of a Roman society lady. Her own troubles would eventually become overwhelming. The other sisters, Olympe and Marianne, dispensed advice and offered occasional physical shelter but were too self-centred to become closely embroiled in Hortense's marital dramas. Laure-Victoire had died shortly after their mother, in 1657, after giving birth to her third child. But Marie-Sidonie was a breath of fresh air. 'As she was very attractive and amusing,' remembered Hortense, 'I obliged her by taking part in some jokes she played on the nuns. People told the king a hundred ridiculous stories about it: that we put ink in the holy water font, so that those good ladies would smudge up their faces; that we went running through the dormitory as they were falling asleep with lots of little dogs, shouting tallyho; and several other things of the sort, which were either completely invented or excessively exaggerated.'[11] Further adventures followed when the young women were sent back to Chelles and panicked when they thought Hortense's husband was coming to remove her by force. They secreted themselves behind a grille in the parlour of their room, only for Hortense to become wedged between two iron bars. Despite her agony and fright, she kept silent and, after a long period of tugging, Marie-Sidonie got her out. But as the lawsuit between the Mazarins dragged on, it became obvious to Hortense and to her brother, Philippe, that she needed a more permanent escape. She would have to flee the country.

*

HORTENSE HAD ENDURED seven years of a disastrous marriage. She had seen her vast fortune dissipated and her life crumble to nothing, dictated by an increasingly unhinged husband whose sole aim, so it seemed, was to control and confine her, to make sure that she never knew happiness or stability. And despite some temporary judgements in her favour in the courts of law, she also knew that Armand could pursue other legal avenues. Her main hope was that the king would keep his promise not to interfere in the Mazarins' quarrels and if she did manage to escape Louis XIV would not try to bring her back. Philippe, standing by his sister, was instrumental in making the arrangements for her flight, though it was thought best that he not accompany her. If all went well, he could join her later. As few people as possible were apprised of her intentions. Hortense left on the night of 13 June 1668, accompanied by her brother's manservant and her own lady's maid. Both women were dressed as men. Later, she would acknowledge that the disguise was far from convincing but it seems to have given her an early taste for cross-dressing that she would indulge during her wanderings. At the Porte Saint-Antoine, the little party of three was joined by Hortense and Philippe's closest ally, the chevalier de Rohan, who provided his own squire as an escort. Hortense's plan was to travel east through Lorraine and Switzerland to join Marie in Milan.

The journey did not go smoothly. Hortense had a fall in the gardens of the palace of the duke of Lorraine, in Nancy, and by the time the travelling party reached Altdorf, near the St Gotthard Pass in Switzerland, her leg was troubling her so much that she feared the onset of gangrene. Forced to remain in Altdorf by the threat of plague in Milan, Hortense received medical attention and recovered. Unwisely, she also added a new tension to the difficult situation of the fugitives by taking Rohan's squire, Courbeville, as her lover. Philippe, who, by now, had set out to join his sister, was exasperated by her behaviour, but he knew that the real threat still lay with Duke Mazarin. A man of Mazarin's disturbed and vindictive character was not going to sit back and accept that his wife had run off and left him. Philippe knew that Mazarin's threat to kidnap Hortense and bring her back to France must be taken seriously. In his fury, Mazarin threw mud at all those he viewed as his enemies, even accusing Philippe of incest with Hortense. Hortense was appalled that 'such odious use could have been made of the exchange of thoughts and feelings between people who are so closely related, finally, that my esteem and friendship for a brother whose merit was as well known as his, and who loved me more than his own life, could have served as a pretext for the most unjust and the cruellest of all defamations.'[12]

Two years later, Hortense left Italy and returned to France. She did not really accept the prospect of a successful outcome to the mediation proposed to end the marital strife between herself and Duke Mazarin but she had not seen her children since 1668. It soon became apparent that her time in France would be brief. Duke Mazarin was implacable and his wife, having tasted freedom, was willing to risk a wandering life for the personal freedom it offered. She wanted lovers and enjoyment, the thrill of not being tied down. In the early 1670s, Marie's marriage also collapsed. She and the Constable Colonna had drifted apart as both pursued love affairs of their own and Marie began to dabble in the kind of necromancy that had attracted her father. The two sisters roamed Europe together, notorious for their beauty and immoral lifestyle. The Mancinis' lives appeared stranger than fiction because they wanted a kind of freedom that was not possible for women of their time. Whether this made them self-indulgent hedonists, able to survive because members of their own social class viewed them as amusing and took pity on them, or early examples of liberated women, struggling for identity and independence in a male-dominated society, is a good question.

Hortense eventually acknowledged that the relentless pursuit of freedom could be wearying. She settled in Savoy and wrote her memoirs in Chambéry, where, she noted, 'I have finally found the peace I had been seeking fruitlessly for so long, and where I have remained ever since, with much more tranquillity than a woman as unfortunate as I should have!'[13] Alas, the peace she had found was fleeting. In 1675, the duke of Savoy, her protector, died. His widow was not inclined to extend any further hospitality to such a notorious fugitive. Hortense was wondering where on earth to go next when she received an unexpected invitation. It was from Ralph Montagu, whom she had known when he was a diplomat in Paris. He suggested that she might like to visit England. Like everything that concerned Ralph, it was not without an ulterior motive.

CHAPTER SEVENTEEN

The Last Mistress

'For since our good king, with all his good parts, hath a weak
side towards women, as great Henry the 4th . . . his grandfather, I think it much more honourable for Great Britain
to have its monarch subdued by a famous Roman dame, than
by an obscure damsel of little Brittain, or by a frisking
comedian'

A coffee-house conversation, in December 1675,
between two Frenchmen and two Englishmen,
reported in the State Papers of Charles II

HORTENSE LEFT CHAMBÉRY regretfully in October 1675. She
had decided that England would be her destination but she was
in no hurry to get there. The length and route of her journey was
partly dictated by the need to avoid France altogether. It would
not be long before word of her departure spread and her husband
would soon have preparations made to detain her if she set foot
in France again. And there was something about Hortense's
personality and the life she had chosen that, full of uncertainty
and danger as it was, had by now made her accept and even
welcome time spent on the road. She knew that every stage of
her circuitous journey through Switzerland, Germany and the
Dutch provinces would be the subject of comment and speculation.
She was a celebrity, a rebellious wife in constant flight from an

unstable, vengeful husband. No wonder she was the talk of the coffee houses in London, famous for being famous, this 'Roman dame', admired so much for her 'great beauty, quality and adroitness, of which there is so great a character in print' that the gossips thought she would have a stronger power over the king, if she became his mistress, than 'the obscure damsel of little Brittain' (it is hard to think of a description more wounding to the snobbish pretensions of Louise de Kéroualle) or the 'frisking comedian' that was Nell Gwyn.[1]

The duchess Mazarin travelled slowly, with a small entourage, calling on old friends who could provide accommodation and company, and she was followed, for part of her travels, by her erstwhile companion Sidonie de Courcelles, who now took a more haughty and dismissive view of Hortense. There was little sisterly support left in Sidonie's references to the woman she had shared high jinks with at the Parisian convent to which they had both been confined years before; hers are the barbs of someone who resented Hortense's fame: 'what is extraordinary,' she wrote peevishly, 'is that this woman triumphs over all her disgraces with an excess of folly that has never been seen. After experiencing this misfortune she thinks only of pleasure. Arriving here she was on horseback, wearing a wig and feathers, with twenty men in her escort, talking only of violins and hunting parties, in short, anything that gives pleasure.'[2]

Hortense and her party were then in Geneva but they knew they had to move on. It was November and winter was fast approaching. She wanted to be in England before the end of the year but when she finally reached the Dutch coast at the port of Brill (a town familiar to Charles II and the exiles of the Civil Wars), the weather was so bad that there was no immediate prospect of setting sail. Reports in the English State Papers are full of ships being delayed or shipwrecked in storms. Then, just a week before Christmas, a correspondent in Harwich noted that a packet boat had arrived at Southwold in Suffolk after a very stormy crossing from Brill in Holland, bearing not just mail but a lady with six or seven servants, 'who, they say, is related to the duchess of York.'[3] The lady was the duchess Mazarin and the country in which she had so shakily set foot on 18 December 1675 was to be her home for the rest of her life.

Opinion in England was divided as to why she had arrived and the motives of the various parties who might have had an interest in persuading Charles II to issue her the invitation to his realm in the first place. Hortense was not your usual type of asylum seeker, even by seventeenth-century standards, when it was not uncommon for members of the nobility or educated classes to fall foul of a particular regime and spend long periods away from their native lands. The king himself certainly knew the reality of being homeless. But Hortense's notoriety as a runaway wife and the colourful life she had led marked her out from the normal run of political exiles. On the face of it, what she needed most was a roof over her head and some degree of financial support while she continued to battle her husband for her share of the wealth that Cardinal Mazarin had endowed them with shortly before his death. But there were suspicions voiced that, while the lady herself might have little knowledge of English politics, she could be very useful to those who did. Perhaps even Louis XIV himself, whose view of Louise de Kéroualle's usefulness had always been rather guarded, might, it was suggested, see Hortense as an alternative. But in the coffee houses, this was considered 'a speculation indeed too poetical.'

One who believed that he personally had something to gain by urging Hortense to accept Charles II's invitation was the man who had played a significant part in its origination, the arch-intriguer, Ralph Montagu, 'that ingenious gentleman . . . so lucky in remote contrivances', as he was pithily described. Ralph had a long-standing grudge against Danby, whom he held responsible for his recall from Paris and subsequent attempts to block the brilliant career that Montagu always believed was his due. If Louise could be replaced then Danby's influence would be reduced, perhaps nullified. Ralph made sure that his sister, the equally interfering Lady Harvey, soon became Hortense's closest female friend in England. Both were convinced that it would not be long before Louise was totally eclipsed and Hortense became the new *maîtresse-en-titre*. They had not counted, however, on the volatility of Hortense herself and whether she really wanted such a role.

Hortense had been drawn to England by more than Ralph Montagu's machinations and the possibility of a fling with a middle-aged royal womanizer. She had a strong family connection in the young duchess of York, whose mother, Laure Martinozzi, was her first cousin. Mary Beatrice lacked the astonishing beauty of her Mancini cousins but she was a handsome young woman, whose appearance had delighted James, duke of York, when he embraced his fifteen-year-old second wife on the beach at Dover two years earlier. Mary's youth and appearance were still not enough to contain the sexual urges of a man who could nearly match his brother for the number of his mistresses but he was, nevertheless, very fond of her and she had considerable influence over him. The duchess of York had taken to her new role with a grace and maturity that might not have been expected when she left Italy with her mother as a nervous and unhappy teenager, whose preference had apparently been to enter a convent. Too much may have been read into her reluctance to leave her home for a country she professed never to have heard of. It was not uncommon for girls her age to find a contemplative life of devotion attractive and it is unlikely that, given her marriage prospects, her family would have ultimately agreed to her taking the veil. Still, she had wept unconsolably when told of the marriage that had been arranged for her, her anguish matching that, a few years later, of the stepdaughter who shared her name. Now, at the age of seventeen, she was pregnant for the second time, having suffered a miscarriage the previous year. The birth was imminent when Hortense arrived, and Mary Beatrice looked forward to the arrival of a relative at such an emotional time. In this respect, the stern Victorian moralizing of Agnes Strickland, the pioneering biographer of England's queens, makes amusing reading, with its criticism of the duke of York having 'the false complaisance to permit his consort to visit this dangerous intriguante . . . [who] openly defied all restraints, both of religion and morality.'⁴ At a court renowned for its open embrace of immorality, Mary Beatrice had by then realized that many so-called ladies, not least the duchess of Portsmouth, were not what they seemed. And, in fact, her cousin Hortense's affair with Charles II would be remarkable for its discretion.

The likelihood is that Hortense became Charles II's mistress in the first months of 1676. Her beauty, vivid personality and the extraordinary life she had led were in strong contrast to the milky charms of Louise de Kéroualle, who was said to be mightily put out by the new arrival. Nobody thought that the king could resist Hortense for long. Yet neither party sought to make a great public display of their relationship. The king had never bothered to conceal his womanizing in the past and Hortense was known for her complete disregard for observing what were considered as the norms of appropriate female behaviour at the time. The truth is that there were awkward implications for both of them if they acknowledged that the frenzy of speculation at court was correct. Charles was genuinely fond of Louise and did not want to increase her distress. Hortense was still trying to get a satisfactory financial settlement out of her husband and realized that it would probably not be wise to incense him still further, neither could she risk the displeasure of Louis XIV, whose support she had always sought, though with little success.

In fact, the king of France and his ambassadors in London were far from sure what to make of this latest episode in Anglo-French relations. When Hortense first arrived in London, the Protestant Ruvigny was ambassador and though he had no personal liking for the duchess of Portsmouth, he had a reasonable working relationship with her. If Charles II was now to be seduced by the volatile Hortense, he was unsure where he stood. Even his rather grudging acknowledgement of the lady's enduring physical charms revealed the uncertainty of his attitude towards her. 'For myself, who have not seen her since the first days of her marriage,' he wrote, 'and who have retained the recollection of what she was like then, I have observed some alteration, which, however, does not prevent her from being more beautiful than anyone in England. I no longer find in her that air of youth, nor that delicacy of features, which perchance she may regain when she has recovered from the fatigues of so difficult a journey.'⁵ In recent years, much of Hortense's life had been a difficult journey and, at twenty-nine (though many thought she looked younger), it is hardly surprising that the air of youth of a fourteen-year-old bride had left the duchess Mazarin. But she still had the power, as Ruvigny so rightly anticipated, to take England and its king by storm.

Ruvigny's first thought was that Hortense should be encouraged to return to France with all possible speed. He did not like the involvement of Ralph Montagu in all this. But he did not have to deal with Hortense for long. In April 1676, he was recalled and replaced by Courtin. The new ambassador carried instructions from his monarch that show how well apprised Louis XIV was of the situation regarding Hortense and reveal an underlying concern that she could cause mischief. Louis had declined a recent request from Charles II and the duke of York that he should 'compel the duc Mazarin to increase to twenty thousand crowns the pension of eight thousand crowns which his majesty desired should be given her, and to restore to her the jewels she left in Paris.' He had told the Stuart brothers that he considered Hortense's pension to be sufficient, 'until such time as she is willing to return to her husband.' By now, everyone involved, with the exception of Hortense's husband himself, knew that such a rapprochement was never going to happen. Piqued by his French cousin's refusal to help such a lovely damsel in distress, Charles II had given Hortense a pension himself. Since Louis XIV was well aware that a substantial part of Charles's finances came from French coffers, he might have reasoned that he was, in any case, paying for the duchess Mazarin to bewitch the English king. He noted that 'the affair has been conducted so far with some secrecy', but believed that 'this growing passion will take the first place in the heart of that prince.' Louis feared that, in refusing Hortense's requests for more pecuniary assistance, she might try to turn Charles II against him. He comforted himself with the belief that she knew that 'her greatest interests are in France and that she has a very real interest in procuring herself the honour of the King's favour.' And he concluded with just the kind of warm but vague assurances he had always given Louise de Kéroualle, 'of His Majesty's good will towards her', instructing Courtin to 'let her hope, though in general terms, that later on she may expect the benefit by his protection and kindness.'[6]

Louis and his advisers displayed a shrewd understanding of the effect that Hortense had on men, but in one crucial respect they were mistaken. Hortense's affair with Charles II lasted no more than a year. She was too tempted by other men and he had not really deserted either his little brown-haired Bretonne or his forth-right and vulgar actress. The duchess Mazarin, meanwhile, had found both a home in England and an unlikely admirer. She was content to remain and to enjoy life in London.

*

FOR THE REST of her life, Hortense was dependent on the support and admiration of a much older man. Charles Marguetel de Saint-Denis, seigneur de Saint-Évremond, was born in 1616 near the cathedral town of Coutances in Normandy. His family on both sides were well connected locally and though he was a younger son their income enabled them to give him a good education, intended to prepare him for a career as a lawyer. He studied philosophy at the University of Caen and at the College of Harcourt in Paris. He was well read, intelligent and clearly highly suitable for the life his parents anticipated for him, but to everyone's surprise, he decided to deviate from what looked like a comfortable and predictable future. Perhaps it was his passion for fencing that made him forsake the robe for the sword. In his mid-teens, he abandoned his studies and entered the army. By

1637, he was in command of a company, as the Thirty Years War dragged on, apparently without any impending resolution. His promotion was a sign of his ability and also his capacity to impress. But already he was known for his exceptional manners and his wit, rather than physical bravery on the field. Neither was it uncommon for younger sons to become soldiers. The army gave them an opportunity to make contacts that would be useful later in life and, during the winters, when campaigning ceased, Saint-Évremond, who by then had become fluent in Italian and Spanish, slipped effortlessly into the salon life of Paris. It was in this milieu of intellectual stimulation and heady romance that the early convictions of his Jesuit teachers during his schooldays were replaced by a more open attitude to philosophy. He began to write essays and satirical pieces, none of them intended for publication, but mostly to amuse the many friends with whom he corresponded frequently.

We know little of Saint-Évremond's private life at this time. There were rumours that the female philosopher, Ninon de Lanclos, as well as the countess d'Olonne were his mistresses, but firm evidence of the reality of such relationships is lacking. It may be that Saint-Évremond was one of those men for whom the company of strong and beautiful women is a vital aspect of their lives, but who need their minds and society rather than their bodies. And while his support of the court during the period of the Fronde was noted, so was his cutting wit and propensity for satire that offended. He lost the support of the Prince de Condé by unwisely ridiculing a man who was known for ridiculing others. The French court, with Anne of Austria and Mazarin in control, viewed Saint-Évremond as entertaining but not entirely reliable, though he was sent on brief diplomatic missions to England and Holland. However, with the fall of Fouquet, Louis XIV's capable but unpopular finance minister, in 1661, Saint-Évremond was to find that his commentary on the Treaty of the Pyrenees, which ended years of conflict between France and Spain, had fallen into the wrong hands. It was discovered among Fouquet's papers.

Perhaps not in itself sufficient to warrant anything other than a reprimand, it seems to have been the final straw for the young king who had so recently assumed the reins of power for himself. The order was given to arrest Saint-Évremond and imprison him in the Bastille. Friends advised a hasty and judicious retreat to his estates in Normandy. He complied, but by the end of 1661, he realized that life anywhere in France had become too dangerous for him. He fled to Holland and thence to England for several years, returning back across the North Sea in 1665. He had good friends and important contacts there, not least William of Orange himself, the English king's nephew. Yet he found life somewhat dull, and when an invitation to reside permanently in London was issued by Charles II in 1670, Saint-Évremond took it eagerly. He amused himself as best he could with parties and bright conversation but, speaking no English, was never entirely at home. He always missed France. Even the arrival of Hortense Mancini could not fully erase his homesickness, though the two soon became inseparable.

It was an intense friendship based on mutual need. Hortense craved admiration and Saint-Évremond needed a focus for his life. At more than sixty years old, disdaining the fashion for wigs beneath a clerical skullcap, and with a huge swelling, or wen, on his neck, Saint-Évremond had no hope and, more probably, no interest in becoming the lover of the beautiful Hortense. She was mistress of his heart rather than his body. Though they met almost daily for many years at the residence in St James's Park that had been provided for Hortense by the duke of York, they also carried on a lively, sometimes intense, correspondence. None of hers survive, which is a pity, as we have no way of knowing if her letters matched the intellectual vigour and range of Saint-Évremond's, though her earlier writings suggest a woman who would have been able to hold her own in discussion. The two exiles, cut adrift from the lands of their upbringing (doubly, in Hortense's case), could relish a debate on Greek and Latin literature while still acknowledging that the refuge they had found in England was far from perfect: 'Tis a great misfortune,' wrote Saint-Évremond in 1676 to Hortense, 'for a man to pass away his life at a distance from his Empire: but then if fortune had not banished me from it, I should not have the happiness to live in yours. You inspire passion in everything that is capable of it; and Reason yields to you even those that are past any sense of passion.'[7] By which, presumably, he meant himself.

There were men – and, indeed, women – besides the elderly man of letters who were by no means past such passion and with whom the duchess Mazarin indulged her sensuality to the full. Saint-Évremond, who saw the advantages of security offered by his muse's affair with Charles II, was disquieted by her liaison with the young and handsome Prince of Monaco, whom she had known in Savoy, within a year of her arrival. Hortense may have been unusually circumspect in her meetings with Charles II, but she abandoned such caution with this new lover. The king was not amused and temporarily halted her pension. The prince's denials – 'Upon my sword, M. Saint-Évremond, I looked another way' – were not believed by anyone who knew the couple. Sidonie de Courcelles, who was making a habit of following Hortense around Europe, had not lost any of her vituperation when she described Charles II's vexation with Hortense: 'The king was yesterday making loud jokes about it, saying that the service of Madame Mazarin was too difficult . . . it was killing her husband as well as all of her noble lovers; Monaco is having dizzy spells like Mazarin did.'[8]

Ambassador Courtin, who was finding it increasingly difficult to keep up with the king's love life and trying to balance the conflicting possibilities of the two duchesses, Portsmouth and Mazarin, from a French perspective, was even more disgusted by the arrival of the marquise de Courcelles, acidly observing that England was becoming a refuge for any woman who had fallen out with her husband. He was relieved to be passing the baton to Paul de Barrillon.

And then there was Hortense's scandalous friendship with the king's elder daughter by Lady Castlemaine, Anne Fitzroy, countess of Sussex. Even before she was seduced by Ralph Montagu in Paris, Anne's reputation had suffered seriously from accusations that she was conducting a lesbian affair with Duchess Mazarin. Anne had been married to Thomas Lennard, baron Dacre, at the age of thirteen at Hampton Court, and her husband was promptly made an earl. The couple were, however, unsuited, he being basically a country squire and she preferring the pleasures of the court. Despite her youth and her mother's desire to curb her behaviour – something that Barbara herself was not noted for – Anne was entranced by Hortense. They were never out of one another's company for a while, in the summer of 1676, and having taken fencing lessons together, raised eyebrows when they went out one night, clad only in their nightdresses and carrying their swords, to practise. The king might have allowed them some leeway initially, but he intervened when Anne refused to live with her husband on his country estates. She was forcibly removed and sent to the convent in Paris where Montagu's blandishments would soon make her forget Hortense.

The duchess survived Titus Oates's spewing of hatred against all Catholics and foreigners amid the maelstrom of the Popish Plot, but though her salon was famous for its literary, musical and political prestige, as well as its gaming tables, Hortense was never as financially secure as she would have liked and her fondness for the bottle (spirits as well as wine) increased with the passing years. It is tempting to view her as 'empowered', to use an overworked and anachronistic phrase much beloved by women writers commentating on the past, but was she really happy? The answer is that she had made the best of a difficult situation but in refusing to bow down to male authority she had, of course, implicitly acknowledged its potency. Cut off from her children and the inheritance that was rightfully hers, removed at a young age from her home and familiar surroundings to satisfy the ego of a powerful uncle, Hortense was as much a victim as a heroine. She fought against her situation for all of her adult life, taking refuge in her beauty and a hedonism that served her well but did not, ultimately, change the fact that she had been cruelly used.

In January 1685, the diarist John Evelyn found her at court, gambling away the evening with the king and two of his other mistresses, the duchesses of Portsmouth and Cleveland. He found the spectacle of the king with Louise, Barbara and Hortense (his concubines, as Evelyn called them) profoundly distasteful. Presumably he was either not near enough or too decorous to report any conversation which passed between these ladies, which is a shame. The king seemed much as he had always been, a self-indulgent monarch who had modelled his court, his private life and, in the four years since he had sent his eternally obstructive Parliament packing at Oxford, even his government on that of his absolutist cousin, Louis XIV. But the sands of time were running out for the great Stuart survivor.

*

CHARLES II HAD survived serious illness in 1678 but there was always going to be a price to pay for his overindulgence in sex, food and wine. His supporters gave him the nickname of 'Old Rowley' after one of his favourite stallions but even the most lively of horses cannot run forever. The king was not quite a glutton but he liked his food and was particularly fond of meat and game. He found the inability of his nephew, William of Orange, to hold his drink amusing, partly because he could consume large quantities of wine himself with little apparent ill effect. Yet increasingly gout troubled him and difficulties with walking reduced the mobility of a man who had always enjoyed walks in St James's Park with his spaniels. To keep syphilis and other sexually trans-mitted diseases at bay, he had self-dosed with mercury, unaware of its pernicious long-term effects on his constitution. He was still a tall and imposing figure but anyone who examined his face closely could not fail to remark the ravages of time. It is evident in some of his later portraits.

Still, his final illness came suddenly and shocked those closest to him. The attendants who always slept in the king's bedchamber were aware of his restlessness on the night of 1–2 February but they and the suite of servants who came to dress him in the morning were unprepared for his ghastly pallor and apparent loss of speech. He looked gravely ill and when he collapsed in convulsions while being prepared for his shave, their fears were confirmed. Contemporaries described him as having had an apoplectic fit, but though this sounds like the effects of a stroke, modern interpretations of his symptoms incline towards severe kidney failure and its associated effects on his system as a whole.

Charles II's physical bravery had never been in doubt and he certainly needed every ounce of it in the last, tortured days of his life. It is ironic that, unless they died suddenly, royal personages were subject to a medical cruelty in their final hours from which the majority of their ordinary subjects were mercifully spared. The king was subjected to the full panoply of medical barbarism – of bleeding, enemas, quack (and often poisonous) lotions and herbal remedies, as well as the gruesome habit of 'cupping' with scalding plasters – that was at the disposal of his increasingly desperate doctors. It says much for Charles's fortitude that he withstood all this without complaint and even rallied briefly. It took him four days to die.

In such circumstances, protocol was strictly observed. Louise de Kéroualle, whose ascendancy in the last years of his reign was unchallenged, could not be allowed to see him. She had to lurk in nearby rooms and corridors, suddenly aware that his death would turn her own life upside down. The queen, Catherine of Braganza, at last accorded the respect that had so long been denied her, was the only woman allowed to enter his bedchamber. Catherine had always been an emotional woman and now, as she knelt in tears, rubbing the king's feet to try to alleviate his sufferings, she swooned. It was a far more understandable reaction than her nosebleed on inadvertently acknowledging the smugly triumphant Barbara Palmer more than twenty years earlier. Steeling herself, Catherine returned but her distress was so great that her attendants removed her. She sent a message to the king asking his forgiveness for her weakness, to which Charles II, with a long overdue display of contrition, is said to have replied, 'Alas! Poor woman! She begs my pardon. I beg hers, with all my heart.'[9] At last, on the morning of 6 February, having asked for the curtains in his chamber to be pulled back so that he could see the sunrise one last time, the king fell into a coma and expired at midday. The previous evening, in circumstances of the utmost secrecy, he had been received into the Roman Catholic Church by Father Huddlestone, the priest who was one of many Catholics who helped him during his flight after the Battle of Worcester. Perhaps more than any other consummation, it was, after all, the one he most devoutly wished.

Charles II remains the most enigmatic sovereign of the British Isles. The hardships of his early life undoubtedly left their mark, while a natural disposition to pleasure and a weakness for women speak to both the French and Scottish sides of his ancestry. The blood of Henry IV of France, his maternal grandfather, and of James IV of Scotland, a more distant predecessor on his father's side, ran strongly in his veins. Both were inveterate womanizers. Yet they were remembered as great rulers. Charles II is immortalized in the scabrous verses of the earl of Rochester, a boon companion who came to despise him:

> Restless he rolls from whore to whore
> A merry monarch, scandalous and poor.

It is for this and for Nell Gwyn, in truth, hardly the most important of his mistresses, that Charles II is remembered today, rather than for the deep divisions in his country that the restoration of the monarchy could not heal. It was a miserable time to be a religious dissenter, whether Catholic or Protestant. Scotland suffered greatly under the iron rule of the venal duke of Lauderdale, and the legacy of the Civil Wars festered in Ireland. Britain's international standing could hardly have been lower, the result of ill-judged wars and a fawning attempt to stay on the right side of Louis XIV. The men who served Charles, often able politicians completely forgotten today, admitted that they could not read the king at all. 'One great objection made to him was the concealing himself and disguising his thoughts,' wrote George Savile, marquis of Halifax, who went on to add that, 'he lived with his ministers as he did with his mistresses; he used them but he did not love them.' The great Whig minister, Charles James Fox, would, a century later, say that Charles II was a disgrace to the history of our country. This judgement may strike the modern reader, accustomed to celebrity gossip and a relaxation in sexual mores, as harsh. Historical reputations come and go and the largely indulgent view of Charles II has proved surprisingly enduring in the popular mind. Perhaps the last word should go to Savile: 'If he dissembled, let us remember first that he was a king and that dissimulation is a jewel of the crown.'[10] No one knew that better than the amorous king.

Epilogue

PARIS, NOVEMBER 1735

Louis XV had been king of France for twenty years when the chatelaine of Aubigny left her estates to journey to Paris that autumn. The French monarch was still a young man, having succeeded to the throne when he was just five years old, on the death of his great-grandfather, the Sun King. His personal life mirrored that of Louis XIV and his more distant cousin, Charles II of England, though a predilection for very young girls as he got older was an unhealthy amusement that neither of his relatives shared. There is no evidence that he ever met the eighty-five-year-old lady who set off from the small town in the rural heart of France, though his officials were well aware of her existence. She had often complained about the dilatory payment of her pension and applied to the French Crown for monies to cover essential repairs to the roof and chapel of the chateau at Aubigny. She could not throw off the habits of her earlier, lavish lifestyle and was constantly in debt.

Louise de Kéroualle, duchess of Portsmouth, returned to France in August 1685, having secured a generous pension for herself and her son, the duke of Richmond, from James II. Aware of her unpopularity in England, she knew as soon as Charles II was dead that she would not be able to stay, but it was typical of Louise that she did not leave until she was financially secure.

This allowed her to pay off most of her major debts, though some of her servants, to whom she had been a difficult employer, were left out of pocket. Once back in France, she got into deep water with Louis XIV by unwisely indulging in tittle-tattle about the woman he had secretly married, Madame Françoise de Maintenon. Only the fortuitous intervention of her old ally, Honoré de Courtin, prevented the issue of an order banishing her from Paris and the court. After this narrow escape, Louise learned to hold her tongue. She had been absent from the French court for many years and was unfamiliar with its dangers. Her importance in England had given her an unwarranted confidence. In France, she was just a dead king's mistress, not the de facto first lady of the land.

Though she did return to England several times, Louise was not really welcome there. In 1688, she attended her niece's wedding and was still in London to witness the furore surrounding the birth of a long-awaited heir to James II. More than a quarter of a century later, she returned following the accession of George I. A new dynasty had come to Britain in the final year of Louis XIV's reign and Louise's sense of time passing would not have been helped by a chance meeting with two other royal mistresses, Catherine Sedley and Elizabeth Villiers, at which the irrepressible Mrs Sedley exclaimed, 'Fancy we three whores meeting like this!'

Constant financial difficulties and an ability to make enemies confined Louise more and more to her lands in Aubigny. During the long years left to her, the duchess's main comfort was in her extended family. Her son, the duke of Richmond, turned out to be a major disappointment; although his loyal wife defended him to her mother-in-law, he frittered away his life in gambling and drink. Still, Louise was naturally grieved by Richmond's early death in 1723. She did, however, have an affectionate relationship with her grandson, the new duke. They exchanged frequent letters in French, and Louise's were full of concern for his welfare and that of his duchess and children. They visited

her on several occasions and she was especially fond of her
great-granddaughter, Caroline.

She took great care with her own health. The frequent illnesses
of the 1670s were long behind her. Louise became a surprisingly
robust old lady, her looks at the age of seventy still striking enough
to attract compliments from the philosopher, Voltaire. He described
her as having 'a face still noble and pleasing, that the years had
never withered.'[1] The journey to Paris in the autumn of 1735 was,
however, her last. She died in the French capital on 14 November,
unremarked on both sides of the English Channel.

Louise outlived her most irritating rival, Nell Gwyn, by nearly
fifty years. Nell was the first of the women who had shared Charles
II's bed to die after the king's passing. She only survived him by
two years, felled by a stroke in her house on Pall Mall in November
1687. She was buried in St Martin-in-the-Fields. Tradition has it
that the king had, on his deathbed, implored his brother, 'Let not
poor Nelly starve.' James II did indeed pay Nell Gwyn's debts and
kept up her pension. She did not live to see him deposed, but in
her will, in a characteristic gesture of generosity and tolerance,
she left money for poor Catholics.

Hortense Mancini died in London in the summer of 1699. Her
accounts show the excessive quantities of alcohol she was
consuming. One bill alone was for hundreds of pounds on gin.[2]
Moderation was never in Hortense's nature. Saint-Évremond, who
tried to counsel restraint, was deeply affected by her death. She
asked him to write her funeral oration and he, of course, obliged
with a lengthy, literary account of the life of this woman whom
he called 'the marvel of the world'. The unbalanced and obsessive
duke Mazarin, whose wife had escaped him in life, was determined
to keep her body with him, now she was dead, moving her coffin
around France, as he had compelled her to accompany him to his
various postings when they were first married. Not until after his
own death, in 1714, was Hortense finally laid to rest in the Collège
des Quatre-Nations in Paris, where her uncle, Cardinal Mazarin,
was also buried.

The colourful life of Barbara Palmer, countess of Castlemaine and duchess of Cleveland, continued with all the drama of a modern soap opera. She returned from France in 1682 but was only occasionally at court in the last three years of Charles II's life. In 1684, she began an affair with the actor Cardell Goodman, her junior by thirteen years. It was rumoured that she had a son by him to add to her remarkable tally of illegitimate offspring, but nothing is known of the child, if it ever existed. This relationship appalled her sons and took a sinister turn when Goodman was convicted of a plot to poison the dukes of Grafton and Northumberland. Undaunted, Barbara continued to see him, and their affair may not have finally ended until Goodman was forced to go into exile in 1696, when he was exposed as a Jacobite conspirator. And still Barbara was not done with scandal.

In 1705, just four months after her husband, Roger Palmer, died, Barbara married again. Or, at least, she thought she had. It transpired that her new spouse, Robert 'Beau' Feilding, was nothing more than an adventurer and conman who was already married; the union was bigamous. To cap it all, Barbara's granddaughter, Charlotte, who had taken refuge with her to escape her own marriage, began an affair with the apparently irresistible Feilding, causing further havoc in Barbara's chaotic household on Bond Street. When the real Mrs Feilding (who had, ironically, deceived Beau into thinking that she was a rich widow) revealed all to Barbara in June 1706, the infuriated duchess of Cleveland confronted her 'husband'. Producing a gun, he threatened to shoot her and she was obliged to call for help through an open window. The marriage was annulled the following year, after a sordid legal battle at the Old Bailey. This debacle was enough to keep even Barbara quiet for the remaining two years of her life. She died in Chiswick in the summer of 1707, leaving her grandson, the duke of Grafton, as her heir.

Queen Catherine, who had forged her own identity in England within the constraints of an unenviable position during her time as Charles II's wife, found it far harder to go home to Portugal than she could ever have anticipated. James II tried to use her Catholicism to support him, both as king and in exile. She was more useful to him in England than back in her native land. Catherine's brother, King Pedro, never more than lukewarm in his support, found endless excuses to delay her departure. Her discomfiture after the Glorious Revolution of 1688 was considerable. William of Orange and his wife Mary, now joint monarchs of Great Britain, were Protestants with little sympathy for her plight. Mary, in particular, was cold and hostile towards the aunt who had shown her much affection when she was a girl.

It was not until 1692 that Catherine was finally given permission by her brother to make the journey home. She chose to go overland, through France, travelling at a leisurely pace. In a country that she had always regarded as inimical to her interests, she was pleasantly surprised to discover that Louis XIV's gracious attitude towards her far exceeded the kind of consideration she might have expected. A number of her English servants, including Lady Tuke, whose furnishings had so impressed John Evelyn, accompanied her and witnessed the joyful response of the citizens of Lisbon when she was welcomed home, in January 1693.

Catherine lived quietly in Portugal for twelve years, until her brother's increasing ill health meant that he could no longer rule. She became regent in 1705. Although she only held the office for a year before her death, at the age of sixty-seven, she proved a popular and able ruler, negotiating an important trade treaty with England which ensured that French influence in the Iberian peninsula, which had greatly increased when Louis XIV's grandson became King Philip V of Spain, was balanced by the renewal of ties with Portugal's long-standing ally. In her will, she named Philip, earl of Chesterfield, lord chamberlain of her English household, as executor for her remaining financial interests in England. Barbara Palmer's first lover was then too infirm and gout-ridden to accept such a responsibility. He begged to decline. He did, however, wish to put on record that, in his eyes, Catherine of Braganza was 'one of the greatest and most illustrious princesses in the world.' Age had not diminished Chesterfield's way with words and he was ever the ladies' man. Yet no contemporary offered such an unqualified tribute to Charles II, the husband Catherine had loved, not wisely, but too well.

Notes

Abbreviations

BL   British Library
ODNB *Oxford Dictionary of National Biography*
TNA   The National Archives, Kew

Chapter One

1 It is now a luxury hotel and wedding venue, the website of which makes no mention of its association with Lucy Walter.
2 J. Clarke, *The Life of James II*, vol. 1, p.492, quoted in Jonathan Scott, *Algernon Sidney and the English Republic, 1623–1677* (1988), p. 118

Chapter Two

1 Anna Keay, *The Last Royal Rebel: The Life and Death of James, Duke of Monmouth* (2016), p. 14
2 For a fuller description of this episode, *see An Historical Account of the Heroick Life and Magnanimous Actions of the Most Illustrious Protestant Prince, James, Duke of Monmouth* (1683), pp. 9–12, and Keay, *The Last Royal Rebel*, pp. 17–19
3 *See* p. 26 and also Chapter Fifteen *passim*
4 Quoted in Mark R. F. Williams, *The King's Irishmen: The Irish in the Exiled Court of Charles II, 1649–1660* (2014), p. 220
5 Thomas Birch (ed.), *A Collection of the State Papers of John Thurloe, Esq.*, vol. 1, no. 684 (1742)

6 Keay, *The Last Royal Rebel*, pp. 24–5
7 *An Historical Account of the Heroick Life and Magnanimous Actions of the Most Illustrious Protestant Prince, James, Duke of Monmouth*, p. 9
8 M. A. E. Green (ed.), *Calendar of State Papers Domestic, Interregnum*, vol. 5 (1656–7), p. 4
9 Quoted in A. I. Dasent, *The Private Life of Charles II* (1927), p. 53
10 *Mercurius Politicus*, 10–17 July 1656, p. 318
11 Clarendon State Papers, vol. 56, f.280 (Bodleian Library)
12 Quoted in Keay, *The Last Royal Rebel*, p. 32

Chapter Three

1 This first daughter born to Charles II is easily confused with the other Charlotte Fitzroy, born in 1664. She was one of the king's six children with Barbara Palmer, Lady Castlemaine, and was adored by her father.
2 I have been unable to find the original source for the date of Catherine Pegge's death and it seems to have become received wisdom by others who have written about Charles II's mistresses. Thomas Pegge's will can be found in TNA, ref. PROB 11/363/469.
3 Quoted in Timothy Crist (ed.), *Charles II to Lord Taaffe: Letters in Exile* (1974), p. 6
4 *See* Antonia Fraser, *King Charles II* (1979), pp. 155–6. Other historians remain unconvinced of the infanta's identity.
5 Crist, *Charles II to Lord Taaffe*, p. 29
6 A. Bryant (ed.), *The Letters, Speeches and Declarations of King Charles II* (1935), p. 84
7 *See* Tim Harris, *Restoration: Charles II and His Kingdoms 1660–1685* (2005), pp. 48–50

Chapter Four

1 Quoted, without source, in G. Steinman, *A Memoir of Barbara, Duchess of Cleveland* (1871), p. 4
2 Abel Boyer, *Annals of the Reign of Queen Anne* (1722), p. 388
3 *Letters of Philip, second earl of Chesterfield* (1835), pp. 77–81
4 Ibid., p. 76
5 The republican government was strict about the observance of Sunday worship and any flirting would have been frowned upon, with potentially awkward repercussions for Barbara's mother and stepfather.

6   *Letters of Philip, second earl of Chesterfield*, pp. 88–9
7   Ibid., pp. 102–3
8   Surrey History Centre, Brodrick (Midleton) Papers, MS 1248/1

Chapter Five

1   Quoted in Tim Harris, *Restoration: Charles II and His Kingdoms 1660–1685* (2005), p. 44
2   Ibid., p. 49
3   *See* Kevin Sharpe, '"Thy Longing Country's Darling and Desire": Aesthetics, Sex and Politics in the England of Charles II', in Julia Marciari Alexander and Catharine MacLeod (eds), *Politics, Transgression and Representation at the Court of Charles II* (2007), pp. 1–32
4   'On the Duchess of Cleveland', attributed to Buckingham, though sometimes to John Wilmot, earl of Rochester. Printed in Christine Phipps (ed.), *Buckingham, Public and Private Man: The Prose, Poems and Commonplace Book of George Villiers, second duke of Buckingham (1628–1687)* (1985), p. 154
5   Gilbert Burnet, *History of His Own Time* (1753), vol.1, p. 129
6   BL Add MS 21,505, f.32
7   *See* Chapter Eight: 'Full of sweetness and goodness', p. 103
8   Pepys, *Diary*, vol. III (1985), p. 147
9   Ibid., pp. 300–1
10 *The Diary of John Evelyn* (2006), p. 471
11 BL Add MS 36916, f.119, quoted in Sonya M. Wynne, *The Mistresses of Charles II and Restoration Court Politics, 1660–1685* (Cambridge University PhD thesis, 1998), p. 37
12 Pepys, *Diary*, vol. III, p. 87
13 The surviving portraits in the Windsor Beauties series hang in the Communications Gallery at Hampton Court Palace. They are remarkable for their facial similarity (and the fact that many of them are clearly wearing the same pearl necklace) and the richness of the sitters' clothing. Whether the entire series was commissioned by Anne Hyde or whether she decided to collect them once they were being painted is unclear. The idea of a series of paintings of great ladies originated in the courts of Europe.
14 Steven N. Zwicker, 'Sites of Instruction: Andrew Marvell and the Tropes of Restoration Portraiture', in Alexander and MacLeod, *Politics, Transgression and Representation at the Court of Charles II* (2008), pp. 126–8
15 The painting was acquired by the National Portrait Gallery in London in 2005, following a nationwide appeal for funds.

16 Bodleian Library, Carte MSS 32, ff.35v and 40, cited in Wynne, *The Mistresses of Charles II*, p. 105

17 *See* Chapter Seven: A Wealthy Wife, p. 87

18 TNA, ref. PRO 31/3/113, 5 June 1664, quoted in Wynne, *The Mistresses of Charles II*, p. 106

19 Pepys, *Diary*, vol. VIII, p. 404

20 Clarendon, *Life*, vol. II, p. 451

21 'Memoirs of Nathaniel, Lord Crew', *Camden Miscellany*, vol. IX (1895), p. 9

22 From the memoirs of Sir John Reresby, quoted in Christine Phipps (ed.), *Buckingham, Public and Private Man: The Prose, Poems and Commonplace Book of George Villiers, second duke of Buckingham (1628–1687)* (1985), p. 6

23 Ibid., p. 3

24 Anthony Hamilton, *Memoirs of the Comte de Gramont*, Allan Fea (ed.) (1906), p. 138

25 Wynne, *The Mistresses of Charles II*, p. 109

26 *See* Part Five: The Stage and the Throne, p. 141

27 Pepys, *Diary*, vol. VIII, p. 17

28 Elizabeth Hamilton, *The Illustrious Lady: A Biography of Barbara Villiers, Countess of Castlemaine* (1980), p. 79

29 *See* Part Four: 'His Coy Mistress', p. 119

30 Pepys, *Diary*, vol. IX, p. 132

31 The Poor Whores Petition (1668)

32 The gracious answer of the most illustrious lady of pleasure the Countess of Castel (1668)

Chapter Six

1 BL Harleian (Harley) MS 7006, f.176, cited in G. Steinman, *A Memoir of Barbara, Duchess of Cleveland* (1871), pp. 163–4. This reference is repeated by Elizabeth Hamilton in *The Illustrious Lady: A Biography of Barbara Villiers, Countess of Castlemaine* (1980), p. 223, but it does not exist in this source. There is also reference to the letter in the *Annual Register 1766*, p. 205, but the original seems to be lost. Barbara herself refers to it in her letter of 16 May 1678 to the king (Steinman, p. 163).

2 Jenny Uglow, *A Gambling Man: Charles II and the Restoration* (2009)

3 James had not yet openly declared his conversion to Catholicism, but his wife, Anne, Clarendon's daughter, did so in 1670.

4 *See* Part Six: Baby Face, p. 169

5 Quoted in Richard Holmes, *Marlborough: England's Fragile Genius* (2008), p. 64

6 BL Harley MS 5277, ff.22–3

7 There is no evidence to support Elizabeth Hamilton's assertion that Charles
   II might have been using Barbara as a conduit to the French king, as some
   sort of replacement for his sister. *See* Hamilton, *The Illustrious Lady*, p. 166.
   Madame had been dead for six years before the duchess of Cleveland
   arrived in Paris.

8 Steinman, *A Memoir of Barbara, Duchess of Cleveland*, pp. 156–64

9 Dorney Court Archives, T15/226, 2 April 1674

Chapter Seven

1 'House of Lords Journal, vol. II: 1660–1666' (His Majesty's Stationery Office,
   London, 1767–1830), p. 241

2 A. R. Disney, *A History of Portugal and the Portuguese Empire: Volume One*
   (2009), p. 224

3 V. Rau (ed.), 'Letters from Catherine of Bragança, Queen-Consort of
   Charles II to her brother, Dom Pedro II, King of Portugal (1679–1691)', in
   The Historical Association: Lisbon Branch, *Annual Report and Review*, 9
   (1945), p. 56

4 E. Rosenthal, 'Notes on Catherine of Bragança, Queen of Charles II of
   England, and her Life in Portugal', in The Historical Association: Lisbon
   Branch, *Annual Report and Review*, 2 (1938), p. 70

5 A. Bryant (ed.), *The Letters, Speeches and Declarations of King Charles II*
   (1935), p. 115

6 Pepys, *Diary*, vol. II, p. 197 and note on p. 198

7 R. C. Anderson (ed.), *The Journal of Edward Montagu, first earl of Sandwich,
   admiral and general at sea, 1659–1665* (Publications of the Navy Records
   Society, vol. 64, 1929), pp. 126–7

8 Ibid.

9 Ibid., p. 132

10 Quoted in Lorraine Madway, 'Rites of Deliverance and Disenchantment:
   The Marriage Celebrations for Charles II and Catherine of Braganza,
   1661–62', in *The Seventeenth Century*, vol. 27:1 (Spring 2012), p. 91

11 BL Bagford Ballads, vol. 3, unfoliated

12 Bryant, *The Letters, Speeches and Declarations of King Charles II*, p. 126

13 Ibid., p. 127

14 Ibid.

15 Ibid., pp. 126–7

16 *The Diary of John Evelyn* (2006), p. 398

17 Madway, 'Rites of Deliverance and Disenchantment', p. 97

18 *The Diary of John Evelyn* (2006), p. 403
19 Bodleian Library Carte MS 31, quoted in Madway, 'Rites of Deliverance and Disenchantment', p. 95

Chapter Eight

1 *Letters of Philip, second earl of Chesterfield* (1835), p. 123
2 Clarendon, *Life*, vol. II, pp. 168–9
3 M. Exwood and H. L. Lehmann (eds), *Journal of William Schellinks' Travels in England, 1661–63*, Camden 5th Series, vol. 1 (Royal Historical Society, 1993), p. 91
4 Clarendon, *Life*, vol. II, pp. 187–91, quoted in Sonya M. Wynne, *The Mistresses of Charles II and Restoration Court Politics, 1660–1685* (Cambridge University PhD thesis, 1998), p. 17
5 Bodleian Library Carte MS 31, f.602
6 *ODNB* entry for Catherine of Braganza (2004)
7 Anna Keay, *The Last Royal Rebel: The Life and Death of James, Duke of Monmouth* (2016), p. 56
8 Lillias Campbell Davidson, *Catherine of Bragança: Infanta of Portugal & Queen Consort of England* (1908), p. 201
9 Ruth Norrington, *My Dearest Minette: Letters Between Charles II and His Sister, the Duchesse d'Orléans* (1996), p. 71
10 Ibid., p. 72
11 Gertrude Z. Thomas, *Richer than Spices* (1965), p. 95
12 *The Diary of John Evelyn* (2006), p. 528
13 Peter Leech, 'Musicians in the Catholic Chapel of Catherine of Braganza, 1662–92', *Early Music*, vol. 29, no. 4 (November 2001), pp. 571–87
14 Ibid., pp. 575–7
15 *See* Edward Corp, 'Catherine of Braganza and Cultural Politics', in Clarissa Campbell Orr (ed.), *Queenship in Britain 1660–1837* (2002), pp. 53–73

Chapter Nine

1 Ruth Norrington, *My Dearest Minette: Letters Between Charles II and His Sister, the Duchesse d'Orléans* (1996), pp. 53–4
2 C. H. Hartmann, *La Belle Stuart* (1924), pp. 27 and 29
3 Pepys, *Diary*, vol. IV, p. 230
4 Ibid., pp. 37–8

Chapter Ten

1 Ronald Hutton, *Charles II: King of England, Scotland, and Ireland* (1991), p. 249

2 Pepys, *Diary*, vol. VIII, p. 83

3 Quoted in Katharine Eustace, 'Britannia: some high points in the iconography of British coinage', *British Numismatic Society Journal*, vol. 76 (2006), p. 328

4 The *ODNB* entry for Katherine Howard states that she remarried Viscount Newburgh some time towards the end of 1648 and that she offered shelter to Charles II during his escape from Hampton Court to the Isle of Wight at that time. As the date of the king's escape was actually in November 1647, the date of her remarriage must be wrong.

5 Anthony Hamilton, *Memoirs of the Comte de Gramont*, Allan Fea (ed.) (1906), pp. 336–8

6 Pepys, *Diary*, vol. VIII, p. 145

7 *ODNB* entry for Lady Mary Sidney (2004)

8 C. H. Hartmann, *La Belle Stuart* (1924), p. 154

9 West Sussex Record Office, Goodwood MSS 1071

10 BL Add MS 21948, f.281

11 BL Stowe MS 200, f.330

12 *ODNB* entry for Charles Stuart, sixth duke of Lennox and third duke of Richmond (2004)

13 West Sussex Record Office, Goodwood MSS 1071

Chapter Eleven

1 Deborah P. Fisk (ed.), *The Cambridge Companion to English Restoration Theatre* (2000), p. 1

2 Ibid., p. 31

3 Harold Weber, quoted in Elizabeth Howe, *The First English Actresses: Women and Drama, 1660–1700* (1992), p. 37

4 Charles Beauclerk, *Nell Gwyn* (2005), pp. 9–12

5 Pepys, *Diary*, vol. VIII, p. 503

6 John Downes, *Roscius Anglicanus: or, An historical review of the stage from 1660 to 1706* (1708), quoted in *ODNB* entry for Charles Hart (2004)

7 Peter Holland, *The Ornament of Action: Text and Performance in Restoration Comedy* (1979), p. 82

8 Pepys, *Diary*, vol. VIII, p. 594

9 *The Cambridge Companion to English Restoration Theatre* states that

Buckingham's adaptation dates from 1664 and that it was performed that year (p. 284). Elizabeth Howe, in *The First English Actresses*, believes that it was not performed by the King's Company until 1667, after Hart and Gwyn had started acting opposite one another. She acknowledges that there is no absolute proof that Nell Gwyn played the female lead, Constancia, but I find her arguments persuasive (p. 67).

10 Quoted in Elizabeth Howe, *The First English Actresses: Women and Drama, 1660–1700* (1992), p. 72

11 The *ODNB* entry for Charles Sackville has his mother, Lady Frances Cranfield, as governess to Charles I's children, but this is an error. Lady Frances was only eight years old when the future Charles II was born. It is Buckhurst's grandmother, born Mary Curzon and later wife of Thomas Sackville, first earl of Dorset, who was the royal governess. She died in 1645.

12 Quoted in Charles Beauclerk, *Nell Gwyn* (2005), p. 105, from a contemporary satirical poem called 'The Lady of Pleasure'. This should not be confused with James Shirley's 1635 play of the same name.

Chapter Twelve

1 For Louise de KérouaIle, *see* Part Six: Baby Face, p. 169
2 Quoted in Ronald Hutton, *Charles II: King of England, Scotland, and Ireland* (1989), p. 279
3 Verse from the New Academy of Compliments, quoted in Matthew Jenkinson, *Culture and Politics at the Court of Charles II, 1660–1685* (2010), p. 170
4 *The Diary of John Evelyn* (2006), p. 498
5 Quoted in the *ODNB* entry for Eleanor Gwyn, by Sonya Wynne
6 Quoted in Charles Beauclerk, *Nell Gwyn* (2005), p.165
7 For more details on Nell's possessions and lifestyle as Charles II's mistress, *see* Charles Beauclerk, *Nell Gwyn* (2005), Chapter 11.
8 Tim Harris, *Restoration: Charles II and His Kingdoms 1660–1685* (2005), p. 136
9 Lillias Campbell Davidson, *Catherine of Bragança: Infanta of Portugal & Queen Consort of England* (1908), pp. 331–2

Chapter Thirteen

1 Bryan Bevan, in his biography of Louise de Kérouaille, *Charles II's French Mistress* (1972), speculates, without any evidence, on Louise's relationship with Henriette Anne. *See* pp. 16–17.

2   T. Bebington (ed.), *The Right Honourable the Earl of Arlington's Letters to Sir William Temple . . . July 1665 to September 1670* (1701), vol. I, p. 445

3   Quoted in Steven Hicks, *Ralph, First Duke of Montagu (1638–1709): Power and Patronage in Late Stuart England* (2015), p. 73

4   Helen Jacobsen, 'Luxury consumption, cultural politics and the career of the earl of Arlington, 1660–1685', *The Historical Journal* 52(2) (2009), p. 307

5   Jeanine Delpech, *The Life and Times of the Duchess of Portsmouth*, translated by A. Lindsay (1953), p. 62, quoted in Sonya M. Wynne, *The Mistresses of Charles II and Restoration Court Politics, 1660–1685* (Cambridge University PhD thesis, 1998)

6   *The Diary of John Evelyn* (2006), pp. 505–6

7   Quoted in Bryan Bevan, *Charles II's French Mistress* (1972), p. 43

8   W. D. Christie (ed.), *Letters addressed from London to Sir Joseph Williamson*, Camden Society, ns, vol. viii (1874), p. 74, quoted in Wynne, *Mistresses of Charles II and Restoration Court Politics*, p. 42

9   *The Diary of John Evelyn* (2006), pp. 678–9

Chapter Fourteen

1   Bryan Bevan, *Charles II's French Mistress* (1972), pp. 43 and 72 (both quotations without source, though the one in pidgin English is reported in H. Forneron, *Louise de Kéroualle, Duchess of Portsmouth*, p. 72)

2   Quoted from a report in the Dutch Royal Archives, in K. H. D. Haley, *William of Orange and the English Opposition, 1672–4* (1953), p. 200. Sonya M. Wynne refers to this incident in *The Mistresses of Charles II and Restoration Court Politics, 1660–1685* (Cambridge University PhD thesis, 1998), p. 45, but gives Lady Worcester's first name as Margaret.

3   Andrew Browning, *Thomas Osborne, Earl of Danby and Duke of Leeds, 1632–1712, vol. 2, Letters* (1944), pp. 69–70

4   *Essex Papers*, p. 265, quoted in Wynne, *The Mistresses of Charles II and Restoration Court Politics*, p. 120

5   Quoted in H. Forneron, *Louise de Kéroualle, Duchess of Portsmouth*, p. 95

6   West Sussex Record Office, Goodwood MSS 1903

7   Quoted in H. Forneron, *Louise de Kéroualle, Duchess of Portsmouth*, p. 171. Most authorities, including Wynne and Hutton, refer to this sum of money as £100,000 rather than the French crowns that Charles II refers to. There is not, however, a direct equivalence.

Chapter Fifteen

1   Notably Jonathan Scott in *Algernon Sidney and the Restoration Crisis, 1677–1683* (1991), p. xiii and *passim*

2   Sidney, *Diary*, p. 15, quoted in Sonya M. Wynne, *The Mistresses of Charles II and Restoration Court Politics, 1660–1685* (Cambridge University PhD thesis, 1998), p. 127

3   Scott, *Algernon Sidney and the Restoration Crisis*, p. 161

4   *See* Part Seven: The Cardinal's Niece, p. 209

5   The text is printed in *The Harleian Miscellany*, vol. 8, pp. 377–91, where a footnote added later suggests that supporters of the duke of York may have been responsible for the production and dissemination of this attack on Louise because of her support for exclusion. As the articles were published in January 1680 and Louise did not come out for exclusion until August that year, this explanation does not fit the timing of events.

6   Sidney, *Diary*, vol. I, p. 232, quoted in Wynne, *The Mistresses of Charles II and Restoration Court Politics*, p. 130

7   Quoted in Wynne, *The Mistresses of Charles II and Restoration Court Politics*, p. 138

8   TNA, ref. PRO 31/3/147, f.367

9   J. R. Jones, *Country and Court: England 1658–1714* (1978), p. 216. A case could be made for William III as a stronger monarch, though his reign ended in 1702.

Chapter Sixteen

1   Two elder sisters, Laure-Victoire and Olympe, were already in Paris.

2   Sarah Nelson (ed. and trans.), *Hortense and Marie Mancini, Memoirs* (2008), p. 85

3   Noel Williams, *Five Fair Sisters* (1906), p. 38

4   Quoted in Elizabeth C. Goldsmith, *The Kings' Mistresses: The Liberated Lives of Marie Mancini, Princess Colonna, and Her Sister Hortense, Duchess Mazarin* (2012), p. 6

5   Williams, *Five Fair Sisters*, p. 61

6   Quoted in Goldsmith, *The Kings' Mistresses*, p. 10

7   Ibid., p. 18

8   Nelson, *Hortense and Marie Mancini, Memoirs*, p. 37

9   Ibid., p. 39

10   This convent was not the same as the one where Hortense and Marie Mancini had earlier lived, on the Rue Saint-Jacques.

11 Mazarin, *Memoirs*, p. 51
12 Quoted in Goldsmith, *The Kings' Mistresses*, p. 72
13 Mazarin, *Memoirs*, p. 81

Chapter Seventeen

1   *Calendar of State Papers Domestic, Charles II* (1675–6), pp. 473–4
2   Quoted in Elizabeth C. Goldsmith, *The Kings' Mistresses: The Liberated Lives of Marie Mancini, Princess Colonna, and Her Sister Hortense, Duchess Mazarin* (2012), p. 140
3   Ibid., p. 452
4   Agnes Strickland, *Lives of the Queens of England*, vol. 9, p. 63
5   *Archives des Affaires Étrangères*, Correspondance Politique Angleterre 117, f.117, quoted in C. H. Hartmann, *The Vagabond Duchess: The Life of Hortense Mancini Duchesse Mazarin* (1926), p. 159
6   Ibid., pp. 168–9
7   John Hayward (ed.), *The Letters of Saint Evremond* (1930), p. 167
8   Quoted in Goldsmith, *The Kings' Mistresses*, p. 156
9   Quoted in Charles Spencer, *To Catch a King: Charles II's Great Escape* (2017), p. 275
10 Mark N. Brown (ed.), *The Works of George Savile, Marquis of Halifax*, vol. 2 (1989), pp. 492 and 504

Epilogue

1   Quoted in Bryan Bevan, *Charles II's French Mistress* (1972), p. 188
2   Montagu Papers at Boughton Court. I am grateful to Crispin Powell, the duke of Buccleuch's archivist at Boughton, for bringing this to my attention.

Select Bibliography

Manuscript Sources

BODLEIAN LIBRARY

Clarendon State Papers, vol. 56
MS Carte, 31–33, 47

BOUGHTON HOUSE, NORTHAMPTONSHIRE

Montagu Papers

BRITISH LIBRARY

Additional MS 28044
Additional MS 21947–21951
Additional MS 61486
Additional MS 88923
Harley MS 5277

DORNEY COURT ARCHIVES, BERKSHIRE

Papers of the Palmer family, T15

SURREY HISTORY CENTRE

Brodrick (Midleton) Papers, MS 1248/1

THE NATIONAL ARCHIVES

Baschet Transcripts, PRO 31/3/105–160

C 104/46
C 212/7/1
E 315/377
E156/20
PRO 30/50/32
PROB 1/56
PROB 11/363/469
PROB 11/466/369
PROB 32/53/38SP 78/115–148
SP 84/165/133
SP 89/15/25

WEST SUSSEX RECORD OFFICE

Goodwood MSS, 1–5, 7, 103, 391, 1071, 1427, 1889, 1990, 1903, 1965, 2245

Primary Sources

(Place of publication for all printed works is London, unless otherwise stated)

A Collection of the State Papers of John Thurloe, Esq., T. Birch (ed.), 7 vols, 1742
Andrew Marvell, The Complete Poems, G. de F. Lord (ed.), 1984
An Historical Account of the Heroick Life and Magnanimous Actions of the Most Illustrious Protestant Prince, James, Duke of Monmouth, 1683
Annals of the Reign of Queen Anne, Abel Boyer (ed.), 1722
Buckingham, Public and Private Man, C. Phipps (ed.), 1985
Burnet, Gilbert, *History of His Own Time*, 1753
Calendar of State Papers Domestic, Charles II, M. A. E. Green (ed.), 28 vols, 1860
Calendar of State Papers Domestic, Interregnum, M. A. E. Green (ed.), 13 vols, 1875
Cases of Divorce for Several Causes: Some Memoirs of the Life of Robert Feilding, Esq., 1715
Charles II to Lord Taaffe: Letters in Exile, Timothy Crist (ed.), Cambridge, 1974
Cresswell, M. and Page, D., *The Poor Whores Petition*, 1668
Hamilton, Anthony, *Memoirs of the Comte de Gramont*, 19, Allan Fea (ed.), 1906
Hortense and Marie Mancini, Memoirs, Sarah Nelson (ed.), 2008
Journal of Edward Montagu, Navy Records Society, 1929
Journal of the House of Lords, accessed through British History Online
Journal of William Schellinks, M. Exwood and H. L. Lehmann (eds), Camden 5th Series, vol. 1, Royal Historical Society, 1993
'Letters from Catherine of Bragança, Queen-Consort of Charles II to her

brother, Dom Pedro II', V. Rau (ed.), The Historical Association, Lisbon Branch, *Annual Report and Review*, 2, 1938

Letters of Philip, second earl of Chesterfield, 1835

Mémoires et Correspondance de la Marquise de Courcelles, P. Pougin (ed.), Paris, 1855

Mercurius Politicus, 1654–1660, M. Nedham (ed.)

Sydney Papers, R. W. Blencowe (ed.), 1825

The Diary of John Evelyn, E. S. De Beer (ed.), 2006

The Diary of Samuel Pepys, R. C. Latham and W. Matthews (eds), 1979–85

The Gracious Answer of the Most Illustrious Lady of Pleasure, the Countess of Castlemaine, 1668

The Harleian Miscellany, vol. 8

The Letters of King Charles II, A. Bryant (ed.), 1935

The Letters of Saint Evremond, J. Hayward (ed.), 1930

The Life of Edward, Earl of Clarendon, written by himself, Oxford, 1817

The Right Honourable the Earl of Arlington's Letters to Sir William Temple, T. Bebington (ed.), 1701

The Works of George Savile, Marquis of Halifax, Mark N. Brown (ed.), 1989

Travels of Cosmo the Third, Grand Duke of Tuscany, Through England During the Reign of King Charles II, Lorenzo Magalotti (ed.), 1821

Secondary Works

Alexander, J. M. and MacLeod, C. (eds), *Politics, Transgression and Representation at the Court of Charles II*, 2007

Barbour, Violet, *Henry Bennet, Earl of Arlington*, 1915

Baxter, Stephen, *William III*, 1966

Beauclerk, Charles, *Nell Gwyn*, 2005

Bevan, Bryan, *Charles II's French Mistress*, 1972

——, *The Duchess Hortense*, 1987

Campbell Orr, Clarissa (ed.), *Queenship in Britain 1660–1837, Royal Patronage, Court Culture and Dynastic Politics*, 2002

Claydon, Tony, *William III*, Oxford, 2002

Dasent, A. I., *The Private Life of Charles II*, 1927

Davidson, Lillias Campbell, *Catherine of Bragança*, 1908

Delpech, Jeanine, *The Life and Times of the Duchess of Portsmouth*, 1953

Eustace, Katharine, 'Britannia: Some high points in the iconography of British coinage', *British Numismatic Society Journal*, vol. 76, 2006

Fisk, Deborah P. (ed.), *English Restoration Theatre*, Cambridge, 2000

Forneron, Henri, *Louise de Kéroualle, Duchess of Portsmouth*, 1887

Fraser, Antonia, *King Charles II*, 1979

Goldsmith, Elizabeth C., *The Kings' Mistresses*, New York, 2012

Grant, Colquhoun (Mrs), *Brittany to Whitehall: Life of Louise Renée de Kéroualle*, 1909

Haley, K. H. D., *William of Orange and the English Opposition, 1672–4*, Oxford, 1953

Hamilton, Elizabeth, *The Illustrious Lady*, 1980

Harris, Tim, *Restoration: Charles II and His Kingdoms*, 2005

Hartmann, C. H., *The King's Friend: The Life of Charles Berkeley*, 1951

——, *La Belle Stuart*, 1924

——, *The Vagabond Duchess*, 1927

Hatton, Ragnhild (ed.), *Louis XIV and Europe*, 1976

Hicks, Steven, *Ralph, First Duke of Montagu*, 2015

Holland, Peter, *The Ornament of Action: Text and Performance in Restoration Comedy*, 1979

Holmes, Richard, *Marlborough: England's Fragile Genius*, 2008

Howe, Elizabeth, *The First English Actresses*, Cambridge, 1992

Hutton, Ronald, *Charles II*, Oxford, 1989

Jacobsen, Helen, 'Luxury consumption, cultural politics and the career of the earl of Arlington', *Historical Journal* 52(2), 2009

Jones, J. R., *Country and Court: England 1658–1714*, 1978

Keay, Anna, *The Last Royal Rebel: The Life and Death of James, Duke of Monmouth*, 2016

——, *The Magnificent Monarch: Charles II and the Ceremonies of Power*, 2008

Kenyon, J. F., *Robert Spencer, Earl of Sunderland, 1641–1702*, 1992

Leech, Peter, 'Musicians in the Catholic Chapel of Catherine of Braganza, 1662–92', *Early Music*, vol. 29, 2001

Macqueen-Pope, W., *Ladies First*, 1952

Madway, Lorraine, 'Rites of Deliverance and Disenchantment: The Marriage Celebrations for Charles II and Catherine of Braganza, 1661–62', *The Seventeenth Century*, vol. 27(1), 2012

Norrington, Ruth, *My Dearest Minette*, 1996

Porter, Linda, *Royal Renegades: The Children of Charles I and the English Civil Wars*, 2016

Porter, Stephen, *Pepys's London*, Stroud, 2011

Renée, Amédée, *Les Nièces de Mazarin*, Paris, 1857

Scott, Jonathan, *Algernon Sidney and the English Republic, 1623–1677*, Cambridge, 1988

——, *Algernon Sidney and the Restoration Crisis, 1677–1683*, Cambridge, 1991

Scott, Lord George, *Lucy Walter: Wife or Mistress*, 1947

Smuts, R. M. (ed.), *The Stuart Courts and Europe*, Cambridge, 1996

Spencer, Charles, *To Catch a King*, 2017

Spurr, J. (ed.), *Anthony Ashley Cooper, First Earl of Shaftesbury*, 2016

Steinman, G., *A Memoir of Barbara, Duchess of Cleveland*, 1871

Strickland, Agnes, *Lives of the Queens of England*, vol. 9

Sutherland, James, *The Restoration Newspaper and its Development*, Cambridge, 1986

Thomas, Gertrude Z., *Richer than Spices*, 1965

Uglow, Jenny, *A Gambling Man: Charles II and the Restoration*, 2009

Williams, Mark R. F., *The King's Irishmen*, Woodbridge, 2014

Williams, Noel, *Five Fair Sisters*, 1906

Wilson, Derek, *All the King's Women: Love, Sex and Politics in the Life of Charles II*, 2004

Wilson, J. H., *All the King's Ladies*, Chicago, 1958

Unpublished Dissertations

Clayton, Roderick, *Diplomats and Diplomacy in London, 1667–1672*, University of Oxford, 1995

Marciari-Alexander, Julia M., *Self-Fashioning and Portraits of Women at the Restoration Court: The Case of Peter Lely and Barbara Villiers, Countess of Castlemaine, 1660–1668*, Yale University, 1999

Wynne, Sonya M., *The Mistresses of Charles II and Restoration Court Politics, 1660–1685*, University of Cambridge, 1997

Picture Acknowledgements

1. Charles II in the early years of his reign. (© National Portrait Gallery, London)
2. Charles II, *c.*1680. The elaborate clothes and shoes cannot hide the ravages of time. (© National Portrait Gallery, London)
3. Princess Mary Stuart, Charles II's sister, and her husband, William II of Orange. (Peter Horree / Alamy Stock Photo)
4. A miniature of Lucy Walter, Charles II's first mistress, painted after her death. No contemporary likenesses of Lucy survive. (The Buccleuch Collections)
5. James, duke of Monmouth, Charles II's son by Lucy Walter, as a child. (19th era / Alamy Stock Photo)
6. Eleanor Needham, Lady Byron, one of Charles II's mistresses in exile. (Bridgeman Images)
7. Barbara Palmer, née Villiers, countess of Castlemaine and duchess of Cleveland, painted as Mary Magdalene by Sir Peter Lely. (National Trust Photographic Library / Jane Mucklow / Bridgeman Images)
8. Barbara Palmer as the Madonna with her eldest son. (Art Collection 4 / Alamy Stock Photo)
9. Roger Palmer, earl of Castlemaine, with his secretary. (© National Trust Images / John Hammond)
10. Philip Stanhope, second earl of Chesterfield and one of Barbara Palmer's earliest lovers. (Chronicle / Alamy Stock Photo)
11. Catherine of Braganza, Charles II's Portuguese queen consort. (Peter Lely [public domain])
12. Queen Catherine shortly after her arrival in England, wearing the Portuguese fashions and hairstyle derided by the king and court. (© National Portrait Gallery, London)
13. John IV of Portugal, Catherine of Braganza's father. (Workshop of Peter Paul Rubens [public domain])

14. Luisa de Guzmán, Catherine of Braganza's Spanish mother. (The Picture Art Collection / Alamy Stock Photo)

15. Catherine of Braganza's arrival at Portsmouth and the king and queen leaving Hampton Court by river for Whitehall, in two contemporary German prints. (Photo © Historic Royal Palaces / Bridgeman Images)

16. Frances Teresa Stuart. The daughter of Scottish royalists, she evaded Charles II's advances and secretly married the duke of Richmond. (The Picture Art Collection / Alamy Stock Photo)

17. Charles Stuart, duke of Richmond and Lennox. (Artokoloro Quint Lox Limited / Alamy Stock Photo)

18. Cobham Hall in Kent, one of the homes of Frances and her husband, in a nineteenth-century painting. (Chronicle / Alamy Stock Photo)

19. Eleanor (Nell) Gwyn, painted c.1670, with a prim expression, in marked contrast to her half-exposed left breast. (© National Portrait Gallery, London)

20. Nell Gwyn with her elder son, posing very revealingly as Venus and Cupid. (The Picture Art Collection / Alamy Stock Photo)

21. Mary (Moll) Davis, actress, singer, dancer and rival of Nell Gwyn. She was the mother of Charles II's youngest illegitimate child, Lady Mary Tudor. (Photo © Philip Mould Ltd, London / Bridgeman Images)

22. A romantic nineteenth-century painting showing Nell Gwyn leaning over the wall of her Pall Mall house in conversation with Charles II. (V&A Images / Alamy Stock Photo)

23. Louise de Kéroualle, duchess of Portsmouth, painted towards the end of Charles II's reign, looking more mature but also very regal. (Bridgeman Images)

24. Princess Henrietta Stuart, also known as Henriette Anne, duchess of Orléans. The youngest child of Charles I and Henrietta Maria, she was Charles II's favourite sibling. (ACTIVE MUSEUM / Alamy Stock Photo)

25. Henry Bennet, earl of Arlington. Credited with facilitating Charles II's seduction of Louise de Kéroualle. (© National Portrait Gallery, London)

26. Thomas Osborne, earl of Danby. (Studio of Peter Lely [public domain])

27. James, duke of Monmouth, as an adult, painted in his Garter robes. (National Trust Photographic Library / Bridgeman Images)

28. The chateau of Aubigny-sur-Nère, Louise de Kéroualle's home after her return to France. (Prisma by Dukas Presseagentur GmbH / Alamy Stock Photo)

29. Hortense Mancini, Cardinal Mazarin's niece. (Art Collection 3 / Alamy Stock Photo)

30. Armand Charles de La Porte de La Meilleraye, the husband chosen for

Hortense Mancini by her uncle, Cardinal Mazarin. (Royal Collection [CC BY-SA 4.0 (https://creativecommons.org/licenses/by-sa/4.0)])

31. Chelles Abbey outside Paris. Hortense was confined here as a troublesome teenager. (Bridgeman Images)

32. Ralph Montagu, Charles II's ambassador to France. (Chronicle / Alamy Stock Photo)

33. Cardinal Jules Mazarin, the wily successor to Richelieu. (GL Archive / Alamy Stock Photo)

Index